Welzenbach's Climbs

WELZENBACH'S CLIMBS

A BIOGRAPHICAL STUDY AND THE
COLLECTED WRITINGS OF WILLO WELZENBACH

ERIC ROBERTS

THE MOUNTAINEERS

THE MOUNTAINEERS: Organized in 1906 "...to explore, study, preserve, and enjoy the natural beauty of the Northwest."

Published in Great Britain in 1980 by West Col Productions, Goring, Reading, Berkshire RG8 9AA (SBN 0-906227-14-3)

Published in the United States in 1981 by The Mountaineers, 719 Pike Street, Seattle, Washington 98101

Published simultaneously in Canada by Douglas & McIntyre, Ltd., 1615 Venables St., Vancouver BC V5L 2H1

Printed in the United States of America

Library of Congress Catalog Card No. 81-80502

ISBN 0-89886-018-0

Contents

Illustrations

EDITOR'S NOTE

ERIC ROBERTS delivered the manuscript for this work the day before he set off to join an American expedition attempting to climb Annapurna I in the Nepal Himalaya. A few weeks later news came through that he and two Americans had been struck by the wind blast from an enormous avalanche on 19th September, 1979. So ended the life of a remarkable British mountaineer, like Welzenbach lost in the prime of manhood both at the age of 33.

The author had devoted five years of research to gather material for the biography and writings of the great German mountaineer. Selected writings of Welzenbach have been published previously in Europe but no attempt has been made until now to examine his diaries and papers, to consult other documents and records in private hands, and to interview his surviving companions of the 1920s and 1930s. All this was done with characteristic thoroughness in preparation for writing this book.

In the circumstances of publication, more than a year after the author's death, it is appropriate to devote a few paragraphs to Eric Roberts' own achievements on mountains. First and foremost he was an equally proficient ski-mountaineer; his catalogue of ascents and traverses on ski in the Alps probably surpasses that of any Englishman, past or present. In summer and winter he reached the summits of rather more than 1,100 peaks in the Alps, and had climbed in all but three or four of the two dozen main areas of the range. All this was accomplished in little more than 20 years, having started at the tender age of 9. At times he had enjoyed seasons of two or three months at a stretch and occasionally he managed seasons of this length twice in the same year. Fluency in German and French made it easy for him to take part-time jobs in the Alps, especially in his student days, and so sustain long visits.

His preparation for ski-ing and climbing was always pain-staking - some would say slow, and among his companions he earned the teasing reputation of being last ready for leaving the hut, tent or bivouac. But once the party got moving he went to the front as the natural leader and master of the problems ahead. With a fairly fast but safe pace he crossed complicated and difficult ground without faltering, and always with the reserve of energy necessary for coaxing companions forward and in-stilling a feeling of confidence.

Almost from the start Eric Roberts had ambitions for climb-ing mountains further afield. In his early twenties he made ascents of Ararat, Demavend and all the major peaks in the Elburz mountains. From these he progressed to many higher summits in varied mountain ranges including Norway and Swed-en, the Balkans, Turkey, the Atlas Mountains of Morocco, Mt. Kenya, Kilimanjaro and the Ruwenzori in East Africa. Latterly he had led expeditions to Noshaq in the Hindu Kush and to Nanda Devi in the Himalaya, both of which were climbed by several members of his parties.

Against this wide background of unusual mountaineering ex-perience Eric Roberts is nearly, but not quite, unique in British annals of the pastime in showing little interest for practising on the cliffs and mountains of Britain. It is thought that he did about 50 rock climbs in Britain, mostly in North Wales, and he rarely climbed on outcrops such as the traditional Derby-shire gritstone. His chief pleasure was undertaking long tra-verses of ridge tops. In recent years this had developed into a casual aim to tread all the 2000 ft. tops of Wales, and at the time of his death about six remained unattained among the 168 listed in Bridge's Tables. On these long walks over the Welsh bogs - sometimes in atrocious conditions, sometimes in a heat-wave and shirtsleeves - companions remember him chattering incessantly with boyish enthusiasm about plans for his next campaign abroad.

In the course of two decades Eric Roberts collected a library and archive of books, magazines, journals, maps, postcards and photographs, much of it from abroad and numbering thousands of items, and amassed documents and correspondence concerning international mountaineering of fascinating and inquisitive interest. For field planning and execution of mountaineering activities in the Alps it remains one of the most important private collections ever built up in Britain. With the passing of Eric Roberts at least a dozen guide books and travel manuals for the Alps and the Himalaya will not appear under his familiar name. He leaves four such books that generations to follow will appreciate.

It was the author's intention to publish as an appendix to this book a list with comments of Welzenbach's first ascents and other notable achievements. Records published to date had been found to be incomplete and in some respects erroneous. While it is believed that Eric Roberts had solved all the problems and queries for publishing this data, we have been able to find only a rough draft manuscript among his papers. An appendix could be pieced together but we are not confident enough that it would meet the author's criteria of accuracy. Regretfully, it has been omitted from the book.

A plan for the illustrations had been devised shortly before the author's death. The appropriate prints for reproduction have been made - some of them of rare value and never seen or published before. A rider to these is that only hours before Eric was last seen in Britain he indicated that he wanted to make a few minor changes and/or additions to the list of illustrations which he would specify on his return. His wishes remain unknown and the illustrations reproduced are those he indicated in his original plan for the book.

Details fail as to those scores of persons to whom the author would have wished to extend his thanks and acknowledgement for assistance in collecting information and material. His files on this book bulge with hundreds of letters, reports and copies of documents, mostly in the German language and collected over a long period of time. To all those who helped and contributed towards the task we apologise for the omission of acknowledgement - a task in itself we do not feel qualified to undertake.

Robin G. Collomb

Introduction

MAROONED above 7000 metres on Nanga Parbat by a savage and unrelenting storm Willo Welzenbach - Germany's greatest mountaineer between World Wars I and II - perished of exhaustion, illness and starvation in the night of 12th-13th July, 1934. He was 33 years old. In 15 years of intense mountaineering activity his remarkable achievements had earned him a permanent place among the masters of alpine climbing.

Welzenbach's reputation does not rest solely upon the prolific amount of climbing he carried out or the quality of the new routes he put up - his records reveal that he climbed 949 peaks and made 43 first ascents. Reinforcing this outstanding field record, several additional factors contribute significantly to his long-term importance as an innovator in the uses of equipment for evolving new techniques and trends in mountaineering. Thus he emerges as the precursor of modern ice climbing and his position is secured as one of the greatest climbers of all time.

After rapidly developing into a fine rock climber on his local Northern Limestone Ranges Welzenbach focussed his attention upon big ice faces and mixed routes throughout the Alps. Over the years he systematically built up an unprecedented list of first ascents, during the course of which he and his companions introduced new ice climbing techniques and thereby inspired a revolution in attitudes to the art of ice climbing. An essential prerequisite for Welzenbach's innovations was the amazing technical progress made in climbing methods immediately before World War I and during the 1920s in the Eastern Alps. These were advances far ahead of developments taking place in the Western Alps where the British had earlier influenced so much. Indeed, leading French alpinist Lucien Devies noted - in a backhander for the conservative hierarchy of the Alpine

Club - that the capital of the mountaineering world had been transferred from London to Munich "where youth was ambitious and innovations were encouraged." It is against this historical background that Welzenbach's contribution to alpinism must be measured. His special genius lay in applying and adapting extreme rock climbing techniques to ice. By his efforts and successes he set new standards and gave alpinism a fresh impulse in the 1920s.

Welzenbach's preoccupation with climbing extended beyond mere physical action to associated mental problems. He devised a new scale of technical difficulties in six categories which still forms the basis of today's grading system. It was this ability to make accurate objective judgements of routes uninfluenced by the earlier assessments of others, together with his thoroughness, that also made him an excellent guidebook editor. The guidebook style of writing suited his relatively laconic prose far better than trying to concoct dramatic accounts of his own adventures. A modest man by nature, he had neither desire nor need to exaggerate his own experiences. As a result outsiders sometimes failed to appreciate the difficulties and dangers he overcame in their true intimidating terms. Not surprisingly, the factual narratives he produced of his own new routes often doubled as guidebook descriptions and in several instances still remain the most reliable source reference information available - a considerable compliment to his unbiased powers of observation. Welzenbach also conducted a lengthy scientific investigation into snow structures and this formed the subject matter for the thesis which later won him his doctorate.

Wilhelm Welzenbach - always called Willo by his parents and friends - was born on 10th November 1900 in Munich where he lived throughout his life. He was the son of a senior technical official with the German State Railways. His final years at secondary school were completed under the shadow of the First World War during which period his father was posted to Salzburg. Consequently Willo, an only child, and his mother spent

14

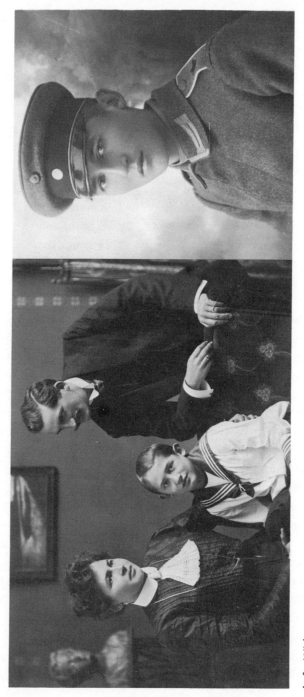

Left: With parents at age about 9. Right: At 14.

their holidays there. It was from Salzburg that he took the opportunity to make his first proper trips into the mountains, exploring the nearby Berchtesgaden Alps. That climbing now figured prominently in his thoughts is illustrated by his subsequent choice of themes such as "The Development of Alpinism" for school talks. Conscription into the Bavarian Infantry Regiment interrupted his education in 1918, but he was spared war action by the November armistice. In 1920 he passed his school-leaving examinations and enrolled at the Technical University in Munich.

The following spring he joined the élite Munich Academic Alpine Club, a move that was to benefit him enormously. Here he found suitable companions of his own age as well as very experienced climbers under whose initial guidance he perfected his own mountain craft. He was soon destined to attain recognition as a master climber. He repeated many of the hardest routes of the time in the Northern Limestone Ranges such as the Fleischbank East Face and the Totenkirchl West Face Direct. Within two years he had become the most accomplished and experienced rock climber in the club. The high technical standard developed during this period laid the foundation for his future achievements when he applied his skills to the greater problems waiting in the Western Alps. Unwittingly he and his companions thereby influenced attitudes to mountaineering in the higher alpine ranges. In German-speaking countries these attitudes were dominated at the beginning of the 1920s by a small group of affluent but mediocre peak baggers - essentially 4000 metre peak collectors - who had been trying to impose their outdated values upon a new and ambitious post-war generation of climbers that in a period of recession had been without the financial means to travel far afield. Sweeping away the traditional concepts, Welzenbach and his contemporaries were later to set new standards in the Swiss Alps.

A thoroughly conscientious student in spite of his passion for mountains, Welzenbach passed his examinations with flying colours in 1924 for a diploma in civil engineering. He worked as a consultant for the German State Railways until he had passed the advanced civil-service examination in 1928 - shortly after recovering from prolonged ill-health which had necessitated convalescence at a Swiss sanatorium. He entered the employment of the Munich City Council as a qualified technical engineer that autumn, and within a year was appointed their surveyor of works. He specialized in drainage systems and his application to the job was unreservedly praised by one of his superiors: "Possessing outstanding general and technical knowledge he carried out his duties in the best possible manner. He worked with absolute reliability and total efficiency ... " Welzenbach earned his doctorate under Professor Wilhelm Paulcke, the initiator of modern scientific research into snow and avalanches as well as the earliest pioneer of ski-mountaineering. Welzenbach's thesis, entitled "Investigations into the stratigraphy of snow deposits and the mechanics of snow movements together with conclusions about processes of accumulation", was issued in 1930 as an illustrated 105 page volume in the "Scientific Publications of the German and Austrian Alpine Club" series. It was of considerable practical significance for the future safeguarding of alpine roads in winter.

Thanks to his secure professional position during an unstable decade and his independence as a bachelor, Welzenbach did not have to worry about the expense involved in visiting the more distant alpine regions. The activities of many of his German and Austrian contemporaries were greatly handicapped by the social and economic problems of the day. Indeed, he often took advantage of his good fortune and boundless energy to make brief trips to relatively far away regions. In this manner some of the great climbs achieved by Welzenbach surpass logical expectations. The quality and quantity of his ascents encourage the assumption that he must have spent half his time climbing (like many youngsters were doing to escape emptiness and disillusionment during this insecure period of poverty and widespread unemployment in Germany), whereas nothing could

17

Recuperating at Leysin in 1927.
With Alfred Drexel (right) at Montenvers in 1933.

be further from the truth. His main annual holiday never exceeded four weeks and many of his climbs were achieved at weekends. One such instance was the first ascent of the Grossglockner North Face in 1926. On that occasion he and Karl Wien, arriving in Austria on a Saturday morning after a tiresome overnight rail journey from Munich, cycled some 20 kilometres up the Fusch Valley and crossed a pass involving 1600 metres of ascent to reach the hut serving as a base for their route. With a 2.30 a.m. start on Sunday, they completed their intricate 1400 metres of ascent, in which the face of 600 metres is now recognized as one of the hardest mixed climbs in the Eastern Alps, and returned to base by dusk. Assisted by a full moon, they re-crossed the pass to the Fusch valley that evening and cycled down to the railway station to catch the night train back to Munich.

Welzenbach's love of climbing did not centre upon big routes to the exclusion of ordinary objectives. He was always prepared to adapt himself according to prevailing circumstances. Action was all important and he detested wasting days in the mountains irrespective of the conditions. Whenever bad weather foiled his plans, he would react flexibly by delighting in the challenge of battling his way up some storm-tossed easy peak. He treated such outings in the mountains as part and parcel of his training. By contrast, he never (not even in his youth) practised on the local rock outcrops outside Munich. Such activity was simply not his concept of true mountaineering and it bore no relevance to him. Even as a city dweller, with the higher ranges so near at hand, he could well afford this attitude.

Little was ever revealed by Welzenbach about his private life. His copious records were almost always concerned with the facts, and personal comments about even his friends, let alone about himself, were conspicuous by their absence. Yet there can be no doubting that he was a popular companion, much liked by his climbing friends as by his colleagues at work. Essentially he was a serious man, yet with his close circle of friends he would indulge in banter or good-natured pranks. To outsiders he was a little restrained but never presumptuous. His undying determination and drive in carrying out plans originating from his own creative mind, whether associated with work or mountaineering, was a constant asset. Everyone respected him for his consideration towards others, his composure and presence of mind under all circumstances, his willingness to help out, and his total unselfishness. A few recollections serve to illustrate these characteristics.

Anderl Heckmair, the great German alpinist who took part in the first ascent of the Eigerwand in 1938, owed much to Welzenbach's help in getting him onto the 1933 mountain guides' training course. Younger companions were not merely initiated into mountaineering; it gave Welzenbach pleasure and satisfaction to introduce anyone displaying aptitude and reliability coupled with enthusiasm and ambition to big climbs. So he led a relatively inexperienced Karl Wien on several Glockner North Faces in 1926; he provided his friend Erich Schulze with his first big opportunity by inviting him to join his Bernese Oberland campaign in 1932. Yet it should not be thought that Welzenbach chose his companions rashly or attempted climbs with disregard for safety and beyond his capabilities. Evidence both of the precaution with which he approached his new routes and of the competence with which he completed them lies in the fact that neither he nor his companions ever sustained even a minor accident in the course of all his trail-blazing alpine career. By contrast consider the hair-raising falls often recounted in the autobiographies of other world-famous climbers.

Welzenbach willingly gave his services in various capacities to several alpine clubs. He was on the committee of the Munich Academic Alpine Club for several years and their president in 1925-6. His experience and practical encouragement were a constant source of strength for its members and he was largely responsible for making the club into a stronghold of extreme mountaineering. A committee member of the German and

20

Austrian Alpine Club's Munich Section from 1925 onwards and their adviser on running their Schwaiger hut in the Glockner region, he also accepted the presidency of the Bayerland Section for 1928. From 1929 to 1933 he served on the central committee of the German and Austrian Alpine Club.

Only once did Welzenbach become seriously involved romantically, appropriately with a girl from Hinterbärenbad in the Kaisergebirge. This attachment foundered in the wake of Welzenbach's all-important Himalayan ambitions. To his close climbing friend and neighbour Heinz Tillmann he confided his own attitude to marriage, namely that serious climbing constituted an irresponsible activity for a family man and that he would finish with extreme climbing before contemplating settling down to married life and its inherent obligations. No doubt he believed that he could not be satisfactorily committed to both!

After Hitler's political take-over in Germany at the beginning of 1933 every healthy government employee was obliged to acknowledge allegiance by joining an army detachment of the so-called storm-troops. Welzenbach's professional position made nominal paid-up membership of the National Socialist Party unavoidable for him. Any objections to registering support for the regime in this manner would have had consequences far more dire than a modern-day employee refusing to join his trade union in a closed shop employment situation. Welzenbach never showed any interest in politics, let alone Nazism. Outside mountaineering he belonged by choice to just one other organization, a students' Catholic association called Aenania which he had joined in 1919.

Welzenbach's sense of duty extended beyond mere moral codes and his ultimate example of self-sacrifice came on Nanga Parbat when, forced to bivouac in the terrible storm that was finally to kill him, he slept on the snow letting the weaker Merkl and Wieland share the climbers' only remaining sleeping bag.

Welzenbach kept a complete outline record of his mountaineering activities in a series of log-books where he entered the

On parade at a National Socialist Party rally in 1933.

bare facts in terse explanations and comments including precise time schedules about all his climbing and ski touring trips. Fortunately either he or one of his companions was persuaded to write accounts of their major new expeditions in the Western Alps but his explorations in the Northern Limestone Ranges - notably in the Wetterstein - are less thoroughly documented and few personal narratives have been published. This explains why his rock climbing successes have gone comparatively unrecognized by subsequent generations of alpinists - not that this would have bothered the man himself. Karl Wien's lucid judgement of Welzenbach's priorities states: "Deeds mean everything, fame and glory nothing. Not only what is achieved counts, but how it is achieved."

The attention of the climbing world at large was first captured through his ascent of the North-West Face of the Grosses Wiesbachhorn in 1924. An event of historical significance because it was the first occasion on which ice pegs - designed by his partner Fritz Rigele - were used. A year later Welzenbach made a further break-through in the development of ice climbing techniques, again applying a manoeuvre previously perfected on rock faces, by performing a tension traverse on the North Face of the Dent d'Hérens. In 1926 he returned to the Glockner region and waged a tenacious campaign on its unclimbed faces. His relentless persistence eventually brought success on three north walls - the Klockerin, Eiskögele and Grossglockner, each one ranking among the most serious mixed climbs in Austria. These routes laid the foundations for similar new climbs on a far larger scale in the Western Alps, though his impetus was checked by the inexplicable arm paralysis that afflicted him that same autumn and obliged him to restrict his mountaineering to less extreme objectives for the next three years. For a while it seemed that Welzenbach's activities might be seriously curtailed were it not for his inexhaustible willpower and prodigious enthusiasm. He soon adapted to relying even more on leg and footwork - a fundamental principle of good climbing technique - to ease the strain

23

on his permanently weakened right arm. Though outwardly of broad build, even prior to this ailment he had not depended upon arm muscle power. The art of balance climbing - the ability to exploit the smallest footholds without pulling up by taking ones weight on hands and arms - had always characterized his deliberate style.

By late 1929 Welzenbach had regained sufficient confidence to start thinking again about the great walls of the Bernese Oberland and in particular about the unsolved problem of the Fiescherwand, a challenge which had been occupying his mind for six years ever since a ski-touring holiday in the region. Although an on-the-spot inspection decided him against going through with the attempt that autumn, he returned the following summer with increased determination and, accompanied by Heinz Tillmann, forced the route in fine style despite unfavourable conditions. This success heralded a systematic assault two years later on the big north walls of the area. Meanwhile his 1931 visit to the Western Alps with Willy Merkl was largely spent on their two-part ascent of the Grands Charmoz North Face which became an epic of endurance in the worst possible weather and afterwards aroused considerable controversy.

In 1932 Welzenbach concentrated with his insatiable fighting spirit on the Bernese Alps. In two sessions $1\frac{1}{2}$ months apart he conquered four of its greatest faces - the Grosshorn, Gspaltenhorn, Gletscherhorn and Lauterbrunnen Breithorn. Although earlier pioneering attempts had been made, Welzenbach was the only real contender for these serious undertakings. Few routes of this nature and difficulty had been done at the time, and his ascents raised climbing standards and concepts almost overnight. In some respects Welzenbach displayed a remarkably similar mentality to the Swiss Hans Lauper. Similarly obsessed with the Bernese Alps during the same era Lauper made a series of important north face climbs that were nonetheless on the whole slightly less demanding and serious except his route on the Eiger by the North-East Face and the North Buttress. Unlike this Swiss contemporary he never employed

24

a guide as a matter of choice, but clearly he could have easily afforded one. Welzenbach's brilliant 1932 campaign in the Oberland undoubtedly marked a high point in inter-war alpine achievements. These outstanding performances during this period invite speculation that had he lived, then the Eigerwand might well have been climbed before 1938. As it was, he returned just once more in 1933 - significantly immediately after unfavourable conditions had dissuaded his party from proceeding with an attempt on the Grandes Jorasses North Face - to add the Nesthorn North Face to his unrivalled list of first ascents in the region.

Welzenbach's climbs were achieved during a period of great social and political turmoil in Germany. In view of the undesirable ulterior motives sometimes attributed by outsiders to the activities of the Germans in the Alps, it is appropriate to examine the validity of international reaction to their radical advances in mountaineering concepts. In the early 1930s German (likewise Italian) climbers increasingly excited envious criticism that their daring exploits were inspired by the upsurge of nationalism. The British had virtually no influence on developments in alpine climbing between the wars, but the ultra-conservative Alpine Club had reacted swiftly against the introduction of new techniques. Pitons were taboo among British mountaineers, supposedly on ethical grounds but also due to ignorance of the safety provided by peg belays on rocks with inadequate natural belay points. Commentary poured forth against the cult of extreme climbing being popularized by the so-called Munich School of which Welzenbach was a leading light. The belief was encouraged that the type of new routes being attempted, involving technical difficulties that would have been considered impossible or irresponsible (if not both) by nearly everyone a decade or so previously, were unjustifiably dangerous if not suicidal. The Germanic style of mountaineering was condemned as a manifestation of an undesirable ideology, climbing - if necessary fighting and dying - for the greater glory of the Fatherland in the aim of enhancing

25

the reputation of National Socialism. Nowadays writers still expound the viewpoint that Germans climbed for nationalistic motivations rather than for the pleasures of mountaineering. They perpetuate the dubious myth built up in no small part by the vast amount of critical and biased reporting in the Alpine Journals of the 1930s, in particular by its editor Colonel E.L. Strutt who incessantly attacked the attitudes and efforts of German mountaineers. Despite just occasionally betraying grudging admiration for certain German mountaineering achievements, unswerving prejudice marked his influential assessments of their activities. In the May 1935 issue of the Alpine Journal he dismissed two of Welzenbach's greatest climbs with retrospectively amazing contempt: "The Fiescherhorn climb was a variation (to the east) of the original, 1926, Swiss route. The North Face of the Dent d'Hérens was equally a direct variant of the original 1923 route. Both the Fiescherhorn and Dent d'Hérens expeditions, as accomplished by Dr. Welzenbach, being on faces completely and continuously raked by ice and stones, as opposed to the ribs and ridges traversed in the original climbs, come under the category of foolish variations." Thus are the seeds of discord sown! Welzenbach's lines were of course the true face climbs and his Dent d'Hérens route has become accepted as a superb ice climb, one of the finest of its genre in the Alps.

In fact the British condemnation of these alleged nationalistic motivations in the activities of the inter-war German climbers appears somewhat suspect if not hypocritical in view of the strong element of national prestige associated with the Everest attempts of the 1920s and the expressed feeling that success would bring credit to England (see Sir Francis Younghusband's "The Epic of Mount Everest", published 1926). For it was in German expeditioneering that nationalism reared its ugly head in that political leaders of the day saw their chance to use such undertakings as a tool for propaganda and could manipulate publicity by means of pumping in financial support. The 1934 Nanga Parbat expedition was probably the first to be so used, but this does not mean that the climbers themselves approved of the political misuse of their aims. It now seems that the sport's governing bodies were obliged to acquiesce with political tactic during the upsurge of the Nazi regime. Again, there is no evidence that Hitler's promise at the 1936 Berlin Olympic Games of a gold medal for the eventual conquerers of the Eigerwand* actually promoted a single attempt. Such thinking ignores the tremendous technical developments achieved by Germans and Austrians in the Eastern Alps and their consequent natural eagerness to apply their methods to the more challenging walls of the Western Alps. It also misinterprets their incredible, admittedly sometimes do-or-die, determination which often inspired them to proceed with an assault where others would have retreated. The much criticized self-glorification of such exploits emanated almost exclusively from the German Press which grew increasingly corrupted by politics.

In truth, most climbers are simply far too individualistic to consider their mountaineering ambitions in the context of nationalistic aims. Welzenbach and most of his contemporaries clearly pursued climbing objectives for their own sakes. Any fanaticism in the methods of their undertakings was related to the mountains and was motivated by personal ambition rather than, as has often been intimated by the British and French, any desire to demonstrate national and ideological supremacy - in this case of the Nazi regime.

That said, it is certainly true that in personal terms Welzenbach did become obsessed with specific major objectives and he readily admitted as much in his accounts. His descriptions of self-examination which introduce accounts of his climbing emphasize how long his mind has been preoccupied with the route in question. Advance preoccupation with a climb worked in effect as a safety valve, for it allowed him time to

---

* Just as Harrer, Heckmair, Kasparek and Vörg were awarded medals, so Hillary and Hunt were awarded knighthoods to celebrate the first ascent of Everest.

consider all potential problems rationally. Certain climbs, such as the Fiescherwand, involved Welzenbach both mentally and physically for several years. Once he had resolved to scale an unclimbed face, then it became an irresistible challenge to which he displayed total commitment. This does not mean he was not prepared to retreat in adverse circumstances; his will to conquer was equalled by a strong sense of responsibility for the rest of the party. As befits the initiator, if the party failed, then Welzenbach simply promised himself to return later and complete the ascent. His writings often refer to successful ascents in terms of triumphs, victories and conquests - again he is thinking in personal terms of the genuine satisfaction and fulfilment that the climbs bestowed upon him and his friends. At times an element of competition heightens the pressure to undertake a climb, as when he and Merkl pipped Heckmair and Kröner for the North Face of the Grands Charmoz. On this occasion an extreme state of commitment (that some might view as fanaticism) and astounding determination were essential prerequisites for bringing the climb to a successful conclusion in appalling conditions.

Any appraisal of Welzenbach's ability and achievements must obviously not ignore the contemporary state of technical developments, in ice climbing especially, which in turn depended partly upon the available equipment during the 1920s and early thirties. Considered in this light, the full impact and significance of his many outstanding exploits are more clearly appreciated. Twelve-point crampons with protruding frontal spikes had not been invented and the heavier old-fashioned 10-point models made tiring sessions of time-consuming step-cutting unavoidable on ice slopes. The use of the ice-axe pick as a hand dagger, another more modern technique that virtually eliminates step-cutting, was unknown. Even the ice peg was an innovation of the period still undergoing experiment. For rock climbing, today's vibram rubber-soled boots had not been conceived. Although special light rock climbing boots (felt or cord soled in the 1920s and 30s) were sometimes taken in anticipation of very hard pitches, the standard footwear on big serious routes was the long since superseded nailed boots which tend to slip on smooth or rounded holds and are only advantageous on greasy rock. Nailed boots restrict versatility especially in dry conditions, being heavier and more cumbersome, and such footwear demands greater skill on the part of the climber.

In addition to these physical restrictions Welzenbach and his companions had to overcome unprogressive mental attitudes in certain influential quarters as to what was sensible, possible or even desirable in mountaineering. Not only their extreme objectives aroused conflicting reactions; criticism was also liable to be levelled at their methods. One such controversy centred upon their unconcealed habit of frequently soloing long sections of faces, climbing together but unroped. On the intimidating Gspaltenhorn North-East Wall, which together with the Eigerwand forms the highest face in the Swiss Alps, his party did not rope up at all. Such tactics brought forth immediate accusations of irresponsibility because the concepts of this era were obviously less advanced. All the same Welzenbach and his companions were behaving quite logically in soloing together and there was a lot of common sense in their methods. To complete long alpine routes safely, reasonable speed is necessary and this often entails simultaneous movement without belaying - tactics that most critics happily accepted. On a pure ice climb there is little point in climbers moving together roped, for their safety in such situations depends upon the individual's personal competence. Of Welzenbach's there can be no doubt; in the course of all his climbs he never suffered the slightest fall and this must surely be unique among mountaineers with comparably prolific records at such high levels of performance.

While Welzenbach faced the inherent hazards of his exploits squarely and with no misconceptions, he never set out to court danger. His actions were always coolly calculated and never reckless. Whenever he forced a new route in adverse circumstances he was always acting rationally in his own mind; even apparently rash climbs had been carefully worked out to minimize the recognized "threatening dangers". Such an instance was the first ascent of the Gletscherhorn North-West Face in 1932. The climb was commenced at midday in rain (an action that aroused a sarcastic rebuke in the Alpine Journal two years later) because it was the last chance for one of his companions to try the route before his holiday ended. Welzenbach knew and noted that "the conditions really did not seem suitable for assailing one of the highest walls in the Western Alps". With this in mind he and his friends bivouacked 400 metres up the face "so that an eventual retreat the next morning would be neither too long nor too dangerous". In the event the weather cleared overnight and the party was able to eagerly secure another opportunist conquest.

Quite intentionally he rarely carried surplus gear, reasoning that taking bivouac equipment made it likely that it would be needed. If he was unsure about completing a climb on account of time or weather and had not passed what he considered the point of no return, usually he preferred to retreat and prepare for another attempt. He also recognized when to withdraw from a dangerous situation, such as he encountered in avalanche prone slopes in an attempt on the Ortler North Face. Yet once he was well embarked upon a climb and totally committed to it, more than once he defied the combined forces of terrible storms, objective dangers and detrimental conditions to win through. His vast physical reserves were proven by emerging unscathed from stormbound bivouacs on several faces; his three-night vigil with Merkl on the storm-tossed Grands Charmoz North Face testifies to exceptional powers of endurance.

Welzenbach loved pitting his strength and wits against the unknown. Indeed this was the principal motivation inspiring his new climbs. In the challenge offered by mountains he found more than simple adventure and discovered a means to personal fulfilment. He declared that through his struggles - physical,

30

mental and moral - with the elements and the resulting successes he "achieved values that make life worth living, that give our existence a lasting meaning". Unpleasant experiences could not diminish his enthusiasm (which he also instilled into his friends): "We had barely escaped the horrors of the Gspaltenhorn Wall, and yet already we yearned for new adventures". Then he valued the complete contrast between taxing himself to the very limits during a climb and subsequently relaxing totally satisfied. After the ascent of the Wiesbachhorn North-West Face in 1924 he wrote: "Continuously strained to breaking-point up to now, we could at long last relax carefree and enjoy our surroundings at leisure. Summit rests such as this are hours of perfect happiness in the life of a mountaineer. Pure enjoyment of the heights is combined with delight at a victorious struggle and in success to produce a feeling of harmony in our hearts. This sense of satisfaction is inseparably bound up with the character of extreme mountaineering, indeed it is what gives this sort of alpinism its aim and purpose".

This physical and emotional satisfaction derived by Welzenback is repeatedly evident in the reactions he recorded after his successes. The ascent of the Grossglockner North Face was another climb providing "total satisfaction" and the "happiness found in achievement" while the Fiescherwand was retrospectively viewed "with the eye of a connoisseur proudly satisfied at having unveiled the problems of this face". It would be wrong to assume that Welzenbach thought in terms of materialistic achievements only, but these were the prerequisites that released his mind to appreciate fully the mountain environment and enabled him to reveal his feelings. He described his impressions on reaching the summit of the Dent d'Hérens: "An almost mysterious tranquillity surrounded us ... Mountain upon mountain stretched out in silent majesty and glory..." After the North Face of the Grossglockner he wrote: "All our tribulations were forgotten thanks to the beauty of the world around us". His fine ascent of the Schüsselkarspitze

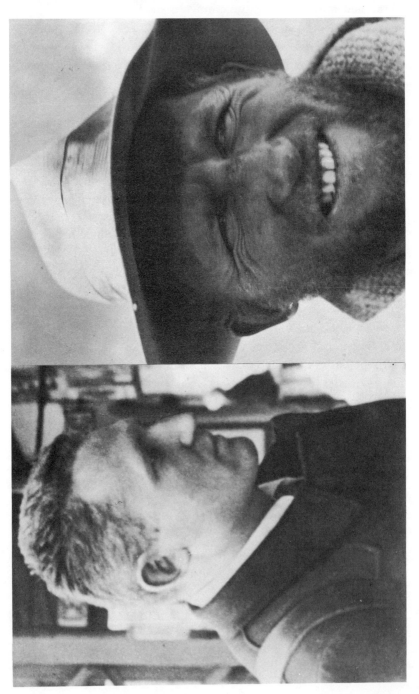

Welzenbach in 1934, in Munich and at Nanga Parbat base camp.

South Face evoked a simple desire "to sit down and do nothing but gaze ... to shout for joy and happiness, for joy at the beauty of the world, for happiness at the fulfilment of a long cherished wish", this almost inevitably bound up with "a feeling of the highest satisfaction after a special achievement, such as is not granted to every climber".

His approach to both individual peaks and whole regions was characterized by systematic involvement. Just as he would return as often as necessary to a specific objective, likewise he would concentrate upon a selected area in his resolve to climb all the worthwhile new routes. This thorough physical and mental preoccupation and advance planning, coupled with on-the-spot decisiveness, efficiency in action, superb judgement of the best line and speed in executing new climbs, were hallmarks of Welzenbach's technique. His outstandingly successful and remarkably comprehensive campaigns in the Wetterstein, the Glockner region and the Bernese Oberland resulted from consistently implementing all these qualities.

Welzenbach's death occurred during a decade of sharp contrast between tumultuous triumph and terrible tragedy for German mountaineering. Two disastrous expeditions to Nanga Parbat wiped out eleven of Germany's finest climbers. These catastrophes were counterbalanced by hard-won victories on the three greatest North Faces in the Alps: the Matterhorn by the Schmid brothers in 1931, the Grandes Jorasses (Croz Spur) by Peters and Meier in 1935, and the Eiger by Heckmair, Vörg, Harrer and Kasparek (the last two being Austrian) in 1938 - magnificent efforts nevertheless exacting a toll of another eight German lives in the course of repeated attempts. Several of these Germans who recorded brilliant performances were also fated to perish in their pursuit of other objectives. Toni Schmid was killed on the Wiesbachhorn North-West Face in 1932, Brendel and Schaller snatched the coveted South Ridge of the Aiguille Noire de Peuterey in 1930 (four years after Welzenbach's attempt with Allwein) only to die the following year on the Predigtstuhl and Kangchenjunga respectively. Willo

Street sign in Munich, 1979. Paul Bauer and Eric Roberts, 1979.

Welzenbach and three of his partners on his most important routes - Drexel, Merkl and Wien - all fell victim to the furies of Nanga Parbat. It was an end not totally unforeseen by Welzenbach in his awareness of the unavoidable hazards of mountaineering. A philosophical note was worked into his Wiesbachhorn account: "For success you need not only ability but luck as well, because the dangers threatening a climber are too diverse and too unpredictable to ever be counteracted by advance deliberation. The destiny of the individual will always remain entrusted to the hands of fate ... sparing the one by happy coincidence but destroying the other". On Nanga Parbat luck deserted Willo Welzenbach and he was delivered into the cruel hands of ill-disposed fate.

Despite dying in his prime, Welzenbach's long list of formidable routes, revolutionary to many of his contemporaries, had already brought international recognition of his stature. Neither his personal reputation nor that of his big mixed routes have been diminished by rising standards over almost half a century. As his friend Erich Schulze remarked of his achievements in the Bernese Alps: "These huge faces demand extraordinary physical performances apart from their considerable technical difficulties ... No comparison can be drawn with pure rock climbs. These routes presuppose nerves of steel, perfect team spirit and absolute reliability on the part of each companion. On these cliffs one slip, one instance of carelessness would spell disaster for all. These climbs could theoretically be made somewhat safer by placing lots of ice and rock pitons. But such tactics would double if not treble the time taken ... greatly increasing the hazard from threatening objective dangers. Such undertakings must therefore be accomplished in the least time possible without using any inessential pegs ... Welzenbach proved that the dangers inherent in his undertakings could to a large extent be counteracted by deliberation and prudent tactics." These comments apply equally to Welzenbach's great climbs in other regions and explain why his routes are still treated with enormous respect.

The high standard of fitness, only acquired by systematic training, and the nervous effort demanded by many of Welzenbach's climbs often frighten off alpinists who admire his lines but do not repeat them. They realize that even a mass of modern equipment aids cannot combat the problems of big wall climbs on mixed terrain, nor serve to offset any deficiencies in skill or speed.

In recent years a resurgence in the cult of ice climbing has attracted much attention to Welzenbach's pure ice routes and has resulted in increasing acknowledgement of his outstanding contribution to alpine climbing. His climbs have secured for him a significant place in mountaineering records as the founder of modern ice techniques and as the greatest ice climbing pioneer of all time.

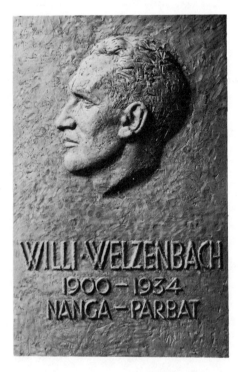

Plaque near Schwaiger hut.

Apprenticeship

ON A CLEAR day the view from any one of Munich's several
church towers extends southwards to the tantalizingly near
yet distant Bavarian Alps. There the Northern Limestone
Ranges of the Eastern Alps run west to east along or near the
frontier with Austria from the Allgäu to the Wetterstein, Karwendel, Kaiser and Berchtesgaden regions. These ranges form
the stamping ground for Munich climbers, and at weekends -
in summer and winter alike - local enthusiasts escape from
city life in response to the call of the mountains. Some sixty
years ago, it was here too that Willo Welzenbach served his
mountaineering apprenticeship, training to perfection with like-
minded extremists prior to launching a series of assaults on
the big walls of the Alps.

In his early teens Welzenbach was introduced to the nearby
alpine foothills by his parents. Their regular wanderings together, ascending easy minor summits on occasion, no doubt
stimulated the passion for mountains which was to influence so
greatly the rest of his life. His parents were nature and mountain lovers, but never mountaineers. By a stroke of luck Willo's
father* was transferred by his employers, the German State
Railways, to Salzburg during the First World War and this
afforded the opportunity for the family to get together there
throughout the school holidays. From Salzburg Welzenbach
undertook exploratory, at times tentative, forays into the nearby Berchtesgaden Alps.

In 1919 he went up the Untersberg several times by various
straightforward routes, traversed both the Hoher Göll and

---

* Willo was so called to distinguish him from his father, likewise christened Wilhelm which in German is often shortened to
Willi (or Willy). The frequent references in mountaineering
literature to Willi Welzenbach are strictly speaking incorrect.
Willo is sometimes found spelt Wilo.

the Watzmann, climbed the Hochkalter by the Blaueis glacier approach - his first snow and ice route, and visited the Steinernes Meer. Late that summer he ventured further afield to the Austrian Stubai, making ascents of the Habicht* and the Lisenser Fernerkogel - his first 3000 metre peaks, always a significant stepping-stone for the German mountaineer. Amongst his other trips a solo but none too difficult descent of the Benediktenwand North Face in the Bavarian Prealps warrants a mention. In winter he spent many of his weekends ski touring locally, often in the Spitzing region. Thus far Welzenbach had undertaken nothing remarkable, fully satisfied with discovering the fascinating pleasures of general mountaineering and steadily acquiring confidence from his rock scrambling experiences.

By 1920 Welzenbach, now equipped with rock climbing boots and rope, felt ready for more adventurous action and sufficiently self-assured to carry out harder climbs. More significantly, he was already turning his mind to the possibility of finding new ways up familiar peaks. The signs of ambition and of the desire to pioneer, albeit as yet on a small scale, were evident. Summer climbs in the Wetterstein and autumn undertakings in the Kaiser boosted his morale further. In fact he rarely spent a weekend away from the mountains. During the summer holidays he seized the chance to join an older and experienced friend, G. Adler from Freilassing, on a lengthier trip to the glaciers of the Glockner region. His terse logbook account of this expedition reveals his intrepid determination: "Thursday, 19.8.20. Via Ferleiten, Pfandlscharte to Franz Josefs Haus with Adler. Friday, 20.8.20. Across Pasterze to Adlersruhe, cloudless early on, towards midday rain and snowstorm. Saturday, 21.8.20. Afternoon Grossglockner, mist and snowstorm all day. Sunday, 22.8.20. Morning descent to Franz Josefs Haus, on to the Oberwalder hut, mist. Monday, 23.8.20. Traverse from the Oberwalder hut by

* Also Eric Roberts' first 3000m. peak, at the age of 9 - publisher.

Bockkarscharte, Keilscharte, Grosser Bärenkopf, Gruber-
scharte, Klockerin, Bratschenkopf, Wielingerscharte, Kaindl
ridge to the Schwaiger hut. From midday onwards rain and
snowstorm." Their programme was completed despite the
weather.

On 9th September Welzenbach tackled his first North Face
problem on the Hochstaufen above Bad Reichenhall in the Bavarian Prealps, and met with failure. Somewhat cryptically he
entered in his logbook: "Start North Face route, home." Next
day he added the comment: "North Face repulsed." One of his
virtues was illustrated by this unsuccessful attempt, namely
that he knew when to retreat and was not afraid to do so. In
his logbooks he recorded faithfully all abandoned climbs and
usually stated the reasons such as rain, snowstorm, mist,
avalanche danger, bad snow conditions, physical indisposition.
This peak also brought out another characteristic reflecting his
unceasing drive and determination, and his preoccupation with
specific objectives. If a route defeated him, he would almost
inevitably return as often as necessary to achieve success. 13
months later he came back with F. Liebler to put up the North
Face Direct on the Hochstaufen, a $2\frac{1}{2}$ hour climb that he described as "very hard and exposed." As with nearly all his first
ascents he produced a precise route description for the annual
journal of the Munich Academic Alpine Club which he had joined
in February 1921. This club had a tremendously beneficial
effect upon his development into a complete mountaineer as
well as supplying him with almost all his future climbing companions. Here he quickly gained invaluable experience under
such men as Hans Pfann, one of the leading guideless climbers
early this century.

Ironically, Welzenbach's first trip with his new club companions - a week's ski touring in the Ötztal Alps - ended in
tragedy. After several energetic days amassing a bag of eleven
3000 metre peaks in the course of high level glacier traverses,
Herbert Kadner, the club's president and leading climber, was
killed on 15th March falling 25 metres unroped into a concealed

crevasse below the Wildspitze. For touring purposes the 13 strong club party, based at the then unwardened Vernagt hut, had divided into two groups throughout their stay and so by chance Welzenbach did not witness the disaster. Despite returning to the scene the following day, it proved impossible to retrieve the body - wedged tight in the depths of the crevasse - with their limited equipment resources and this onerous task was finally carried out by guides from Sölden ten days later. Though Welzenbach did not see the accident happen, it made a deep impact upon him and he treated it as a sadly painful lesson to rope up in future on all glaciers.

Less than ten months later Welzenbach was involved in a second far more shattering ski-touring disaster above the Wattener Lizum, not far south-east of Innsbruck. On 4th January 1922 the three separate parties staying at the Lizumer hut (12 people in all) settled for a short excursion together in view of the poor weather and unusually deep snow. They were approaching the Klammjoch by a slope barely 10 degrees steep when a freshly formed cornice broke off from the summit crest of the Mölser Sonnenspitze. In the freak snow conditions prevailing, this set off a slab avalanche, small at first but rapidly gathering in momentum as it swept downwards, burying five people, the snow piling up several metres high at the foot of the seemingly harmless flank. Of the five caught up in the avalanche, Welzenbach had been carried down some 50 metres, but after ten minutes or so he was extricated uninjured. He escaped badly shocked with the mere loss of his skis and a few items of equipment. One girl had been dragged free immediately, but the other three young victims - Hans Halm, Christoph Körner and Walter Thorey (all from Munich) - could only be dug out dead.

In mitigation it needs to be remembered that immediately after the First World War amongst Germans there was an acute dearth of experience in the high glacier regions of the Alps and especially in winter conditions. The Ötztal trip had been the first major club meet abroad since before the war. In the Wattener Lizum there had not previously been a fatal ski touring

40

accident. Ski touring in any case remained a relatively undeveloped branch of mountaineering and its pioneers had not yet realized that winter - with unconsolidated snow deceptively concealing crevasses and powder snow avalanches treacherously unpredictable - was the least suitable and most hazardous period for their expeditons.

Meanwhile, Welzenbach's summer activities were escalating rapidly. Frequently he spent weekends at the two huts owned by the Munich Academic Alpine Club, the Hermann von Barth hut in the Hornbach chain of the Allgäu and the Erinnerungs hut in the Wetterstein. Even at this early stage he was almost always leading, steadily progressing towards the hardest climbs of the day. In late August 1921 he accomplished three first ascents, all in the Reiteralpe group of the Berchtesgaden Alps: these were the South-West Ridge Direct of the Kleiner Bruder, the North-West Ridge of the Kleines Mühlsturzhorn and the East Face Direct of the Windlochkopf - this last climb with Eugen Röckl impressing Welzenbach on account of its "very hard and exposed cracks".

In 1922 Welzenbach started using rock pegs and karabiners on his now more ambitious climbs. As early as May he completed several enterprising routes around the Erinnerungs hut in the Wetterstein, including a new improved start to the South-West Face of the Scharnitzspitze. At Whitsun during an active club meet at the Hermann von Barth hut he produced three new routes, again with Eugen Röckl: the East Face of the Südlicher Söllerkopf, then on the same day the West and South-East Faces of the Hermannskarturm. In addition they climbed the Wolf-ebnerspitze by four different lines - two of these being second ascents, as well as the Mädelegabel, the Trettachspitze and other lesser summits. In the Kaisergebirge he climbed on the Totenkirchl. Later in the summer he returned to the Reiteralpe group "to examine the feasibility of cliffs near the edge of the area", but on that occasion his ascents in the Berchtesgaden Alps were confined to the Hochkalter group further south-east. Then at the very end of August he travelled to the Karwendel with Willy Merkl and Fritz Bechtold on their first undertaking together, but on 1st September they retreated from the North Face of the Laliderer Wand due to rain.

1923 began like 1922 with a club ski touring meet, but happily this time there were no mishaps despite ominously atrocious conditions in the Stubai Alps. Trapped for several days by snowstorms at the Müller hut on the Italian side of the frontier ridge, on 14th January the foursome (von Ammon, Deitlhauser, Straubel and Welzenbach) finally forced their way over the Wilder Pfaff, with a detour up the Zuckerhütl for good measure, back to the Dresdner hut and the Austrian valleys. Even so, in descent they were met by a panic-stricken club rescue party, urgently organized once it had become known that they were overdue in Munich.

During the university vacation in March Welzenbach and three club friends - Ludwig Böttcher, Walter Hofmeier and Ernst von Siemens* - seized the opportunity of making their first visit to the Western Alps. Due to the then sorry state of the German mark they crammed their rucksacks full of provisions for the rail journey to Switzerland. The first night was spent in the station waiting-room at Basle and not until the third day did they walk up the 23 miles long valley to Zermatt, hiring a mule to carry their baggage. Prior to 1928 the railway line was not kept open beyond Visp during the winter months. Zermatt had no skiing season, an unthinkable development without a train service. All the hotels were closed and they were accommodated by Dr. Hermann Seiler in a vacant outbuilding. In the Monte Rosa group they made ascents of the Dufourspitze and the Signalkuppe, Welzenbach's first 4000 metre peaks. Their overnight stay at the Margherita hut, at 4554 metres the highest in the Alps, on the summit of the latter peak, left a lasting impression magnified in the early morning light by "an overwhelmingly beautiful view of the Monte Rosa East Face with its intimidating rock and ice flanks sweeping down towards

---

* Grandson of the German electrical engineer and inventor, Werner von Siemens.

Macugnaga". Welzenbach had however come to Zermatt with bold climbing aspirations too, but his logbook reveals how he was thwarted on 19th March: "Matterhorn attempt with Böttcher. Retreat due to onset of bad weather." No further details are given and he made no mention of this episode in the account published about the trip. Joined by another club colleague, Günther Grätzer, a highly successful week followed in the Bernese Oberland during which they crisscrossed the glaciers to get at the Mönch, Jungfrau, Finsteraarhorn and Fiescherhörner. In their day the undertakings accomplished by the party rated as important ski ascents and they also reflect the major role played by the university clubs in the development of ski mountaineering.

During 1923 Welzenbach supplied unquestionable evidence of his emergence as an outstanding rock climber by completing the three most significant and possibly hardest pre First World War routes accomplished in the Northern Limestone Ranges. In early summer, with Ludwig Böttcher, he scaled the East Wall of the Fleischbank, first conquered eleven years previously by Dülfer and Schaarschmidt in an exceptional achievement that had startled the climbing world and represents the true beginning of extreme climbing - with its revised ethical concepts regarding the use of artificial aids - in the Kaisergebirge. Now one of the best known classic routes in the Northern Limestone Ranges, almost seventy years later it does not just remain a respected grade V undertaking - in the 1970s it has been raised to V+. Soon after, Welzenbach and Böttcher repeated another superb Dülfer route in the Kaisergebirge (made with von Redwitz in 1913) - the West Wall Direct on the Totenkirchl which is an even more sustained climb today officially rated V+, but considered VI by some. The third of these three big limestone cliffs in question, the South Wall of the Schüsselkarspitze in the Wetterstein, turned into a recurrent problem lasting till late summer. That it had earlier defeated Dülfer testifies to its seriousness and technical difficulty. Eventually forced with artificial aids by Hans Fiechtl and Otto Herzog in 1913, it was among the greatest climbs of its day and represented a further advance in technical concepts. Many young Germans still consider it the acid test for the aspiring extremist, a sort of entrance examination to modern grade VI climbs.

A good measure of the impression made by the Schüsselkarspitze climb upon Welzenbach can be gauged from his account, notably the only detailed personal narrative that he ever published about his pure rock climbs. Also evident is his determination and the extent to which a specific objective preoccupied his mind. Conveniently, the Munich Academic Alpine Club had a few years previously built their Erinnerungs hut on the Scharnitzjoch not far from the foot of the face. Welzenbach's first assault at Whitsun was stifled by atrocious weather and a tentative reconnaissance was literally washed out on the lowest overhangs. Six weeks later he was back, but the conditions had become even worse and frustrating days were wasted waiting vainly for an improvement. In his mind ostensibly withdrawing in permanent renunciation of this objective, no sooner was Welzenbach homeward bound in the train than he retracted his submissive intentions on the grounds that "the momentary moods of mountaineers are never to be taken seriously". After this episode he admitted: "From then onwards the face preyed on my mind. Like a guilty conscience its image pursued me to distant mountains as far away as the Mont Blanc Range and the Pennine Alps." Inevitably Welzenbach returned, this time in late summer with the Möhn brothers (Arwed and Rudolf). Welzenbach's behaviour upon arriving at the key pitch on the lowest overhangs epitomized his intelligent and unflappable approach to climbing problems: "While I was belaying my companions up to this comfortable stance, I had time and leisure to examine the next pitch. Truly it was not inviting, a thin gently rising crack leading round the right-hand edge of the recess, just deep enough to jam my feet in. But what was there for my hands? Smooth bulges on the overhanging wall above. Cautiously I set about the task, slowly inching my way over the smooth rock. Several times I paused during the traverse..."

44

Welzenbach regularly adopted this tactic of weighing up a specific pitch or section of a route to work out the best line. Then he would resolutely tackle the difficulties at hand, climbing without undue haste, calmly making full use of the tiniest holds and in complete control of all his movements. This cool and deliberate approach ensured that he was rarely obliged to retreat.

The next serious problem on this climb came near the top of the Herzog buttress in the form of "a beauty of a groove, clearly a hard nut to crack." Welzenbach described graphically the physical effort required to master this pitch: "I banged in a peg and then set about the task. Pressing one arm deeply into this narrow fissure, I wedged my hand in it and squeezed my body against the crack's retaining walls. Slowly, inch by inch, I squirmed upwards. My hands were grazed till bleeding. It made no difference, I had to get up. Just below the overhang I paused, now bridging as the crack widened. Then I leaned back, levered myself gingerly upwards and felt around for holds above the overhang. Nothing but superficial protuberances on the smooth rock above. Exhaused I backed down for a breather. But resting in such a strenuous position does not aid recovery, it just uses up more strength - So once more I moved upwards, again I reached above the bulge, and this time I found a thin fissure. I jammed my fingers into it and drew upon my last reserves of energy, then I'd done it." Here Welzenbach added a comment underlining his preference for climbing problems dependent upon technical ability rather than pure muscular strength: "I found this pitch hard, damned hard. Overcoming it was a question of brute force. I gave everything I had there. I'm simply neither an athlete nor a bouldering acrobat."

High on the face, Herzog's pendulum traverse held the key to completing the route and it did not fail to impress Welzenbach: "First I attempted to tackle the traverse without aids - Impossible! Twice I was forced back, so I abandoned the idea. No option remained to me but to climb a smooth, wet, slimy crack until I came upon Herzog's pendulum piton below a roof overhang. Now came the most delicate manoeuvre of the entire undertaking - an abseil, almost free, across the smooth cliff. I had barely any contact with the overhanging rock. A few metres to my left I spotted some tiny protrusions. There I expected to find a hold. Slowly I got the rope swinging, gradually further across. Soon I was stretching out for this crucial hold - but in vain. Then swinging across even more forcefully, I finally grabbed it with the extreme tips of two fingers. I pulled myself across and continued by relying on the friction of the rock. Next came a rising tilted slab and a narrow outward-sloping ledge before I reached a peg stance at last and with it the chance to recover from uninterrupted extreme exertion... A leaden feeling of fatigue had come over my body. I tensioned the rope for my companions..."

Above the principal difficulties a fast approaching storm threatened the party. Welzenbach reacted swiftly to a potential crisis: "All haste was now called for. To be caught by a violent storm on this face could be disastrous. Immediately Rudolf had joined me, I hurried on. I moved along a smooth inclined ledge to a short vertical crack leading down to a tiny grassy spot, Herzog's bivouac site. Truly an airy site - a shallow recess surrounded by smooth cliffs... The yells of my friends dismantling the tension traverse rope resounded in my ears. I cursed that they weren't following faster! Even if victory was assured, we still didn't want the success of our expedition to be spoilt at the eleventh hour by a storm-swept forced bivouac ... I carried on. Again the face showed its teeth: a traverse à la Fleischbank East Wall had to be overcome by friction climbing. Then a jubilant shout because I saw a long series of chimneys leading all the way up to the main ridge... It was raining steadily as the three of us moved together up the chimneys. No longer was this climbing according to the principles of mountaineering technique; rather it was a charge upwards, a race against the weather and time... One last difficult pitch checked our rapid progress; we summoned all our strength, then we'd done it..."

Schüsselkarspitze South Face. Fiechtl–Herzog route of 1913 in centre; also shown is a more direct finish made a year later by the Herzog brothers. Climbed with the original finish by Welzenbach in 1923. Further left is the Spindler route of 1927. This popular face is now criss-crossed with routes and variations.

The successful completion of the Schüsselkarspitze South Face ascent immediately produced characteristic reactions from Welzenbach - of "happiness at the fulfilment of a long cherished wish" and "a feeling of the highest satisfaction after a special achievement."

The most important influence upon Welzenbach during 1923 came from joining forces with Hans Pfann, 50 years old and Germany's foremost mountaineer in the Western Alps prior to the First World War. They first climbed together during May and June, mainly in the Kaisergebirge. The combination of Pfann's wealth of experience and Welzenbach's technical skills formed the basis for a fruitful partnership in higher regions too. Pfann quickly recognized Welzenbach's potential and noted that "he had become a first rate climber within the space of a few years due to his numerous undertakings in the Northern Limestone Ranges. Encouraged by his own ability he had trained systematically and was now capable of carrying out the longest and hardest rock routes. As leader or solo he had conquered the most difficult rock ridges and faces in the Kaiser, Wetterstein and Karwendel, thus proving his competence to master the high peaks of the Western Alps." Pfann was in any case on the lookout for an up-and-coming young Munich climber as a companion in the Swiss Alps that summer and accordingly he invited Welzenbach to join him there from 31st July to 28th August.

Welzenbach in turn realized the enormous advantages of being taken to the Western Alps by such an experienced mountaineer, one who had almost always climbed guideless. He accepted gratefully and explained: "I had gained experience of winter climbing off my own bat in the snow and ice of the Eastern and Western Alps, and after the war I had been one of the first German mountaineers to climb a large number of 4000 metre peaks in winter in Switzerland. Nonetheless I still needed to complete my apprenticeship as an ice climber, so I was thrilled and honoured when Pfann requested my company on his 1923 campaign in the Western Alps... Just before our departure

48

we were joined by Frau Eleonore Noll-Hasenclever, the best German lady mountaineer of the day. " Reminiscing about this trip ten years later, Welzenbach acknowledged his debt to Pfann: "I always remember the masterly guidance of this man who introduced me to the great routes of the Western Alps and set me so well on course for my subsequent alpine achievements. I too became a guide for others. Yet Pfann's great merit lies in having re-established traditions forgotten in the misery of the war and the post-war era by bridging the gap between the pre-war school of mountaineers and the rising generation who must win back respect for German climbers in other alpine countries. "

As Pfann's protégé Welzenbach naturally accepted his leader's choice of mountains and routes during this trip. Subsequently he was always the main instigator of his expeditions. On this occasion their time was divided between first the north-east part of the Mont Blanc Range and then the Zermatt district. After limbering up by traversing the Grand and Petit Darrey from the Swiss Saleina hut, they were beaten back by bad weather on the Aiguille d'Argentière. Pfann had also been defeated by the mountain 24 years previously and had no intention of surrendering without a fight. A clear night encouraged another attempt by the steep snow of the Barbey Couloir and this time the ascent was completed without any trouble. The summit view across the Argentière glacier of the Triolet-Courtes-Droites-Verte chain with an awe-inspiring array of formidable faces left Welzenbach visibly impressed. A few days later the party crossed from their Swiss valley base by the Petit Col Ferret to the Italian Triolet hut. Without the then necessary entry visas this escapade required as much caution as any climb. Pfann described how they kept well away from the track and on the Italian side stayed abnormally high up and even crossed the tongue of the Pré de Bar glacier rather than risk encountering a border patrol unit. Writing about their ascent of the Aiguille de Triolet, Pfann recorded how Welzenbach negotiated with the calm assurance of an expert ice climber an eight metres high crevasse wall on the Triolet glacier that had repulsed two guided Italian parties earlier in the same week. And elsewhere it is noted that for this first season in the Western Alps Welzenbach was equipped merely with old-fashioned eight-point crampons! A reminder of the primitive equipment in use. The following night they crossed the Monts Rouges de Triolet ridge to the Pré de Bar glacier by a line reconnoitred and cairned the previous evening. Presumably proceeding at a breakneck pace, they reached the summit of Mont Dolent shortly after sunrise and descended back to the Swiss Val Ferret well in time for lunch.

At this point they travelled to Zermatt. The culmination of their holiday came in the first traverse of the long ridge connecting the Matterhorn with the Dent d'Hérens, a superb but strenuous expedition taking three days from the Schönbiel to the Aosta hut. Though Welzenbach afterwards traversed the Pointe de Zinal and the Zinalrothorn in quick succession with Fritz Rigele - a forty hour round trip from Zermatt with just one night away at the Mountet hut, by far the most vivid and lasting impressions during the first summer season in the Western Alps were stamped on his memory in the course of the classic climb by the Zmutt Ridge to the summit of the Matterhorn and above all on the formidable East Ridge of the Dent d'Hérens.

Matterhorn from north-west. Swiss Hörnli ridge on left, Italian ridge on right, dropping to the Colle and Testa del Leone. Zmutt ridge rising in centre towards summit.

A Long Ridge

WILLO WELZENBACH

THE HIGH peaks of the Pennine Alps are renowned for their ridges, many of which have become coveted mountaineering objectives. One of the most formidable, both on account of length and difficulty, is the tremendously impressive East Ridge of the Dent d'Hérens. Individual sections of the ridge had been traversed now and again, but up to 1923 the only complete ascent had been achieved by the well-known Irishman V.J.E. Ryan with the Lochmatter brothers in 1906. The reason for this may be found in the awkward approach routes to the starting-point at the Colle Tournanche (1) which is only comparatively easy to reach from the south. All the same, I was astonished that nobody had ever even attempted such a worthwhile expedition as the Matterhorn-Dent d'Hérens traverse. (2) I had already made a mental note of it the previous Easter during my first visit to the Pennine Alps, but had hardly dared hope that I should be privileged to undertake the route.

In 1923 Hans Pfann (3) asked me to accompany him on his summer trip to the Western Alps. As a young mountaineer I was highly honoured by this invitation from a doyen of mountaineering, since I could rightly expect to emerge from Pfann's training as an accomplished ice-climber. At the last moment we were joined by Frau Eleonore Noll-Hasenclever whose climbing reputation extended well outside Germany. I was proud to find myself in such élite company.

We successfully undertook several routes in the Mont Blanc Range before switching our attention to the Pennine Alps. That first evening at the Mont Cervin hotel in Zermatt Professor Pfann unfolded his plan. He suggested climbing the Matterhorn by the Zmutt Ridge, descending by the Italian Ridge and subsequently doing the challenging East Ridge of the Dent d'Hérens. After going down the West Ridge the Aosta hut could be reached from the Tiefmattenjoch. We would use the Italian Matterhorn hut (Rifugio Luigi Amedeo di Savoia, 3835m.) as an intermediate base. I was enthusiastic about this proposal and Frau Noll approved the idea immediately, this being a route she had long hankered after.

The following afternoon (11th August) we walked up to the Schönbiel hut. Outside the building we scrutinized our intended ridge thoroughly. From the summit of the Matterhorn the Italian Ridge falls in two steep sections, interrupted by the horizontal shoulder known as the Cresta Tyndall, to the narrow gap at the Colle del Leone (3580m.) which is separated from the snow saddle at the Colle Tournanche by the rock knoll of the Testa del Leone (3715m.). A long snow crest extends as the first section of the East Ridge of the Dent d'Hérens up to Point 3706 metres. (4) The ridge above rises in several huge steps. The next two towers, Punta Maquignaz (3801m.) and Punta Carrel (3841m.), are named after famous guides of the Valtournanche. They are followed by the Punta Bianca (3918m.) and, after another riser, the shoulder (Spalla, 4039m.) which forms the junction with the ridge running south. One final imposing gendarme, the Corno, blocks the crest before the ridge reaches its culminating point.

Sleep did not come easily that evening because I felt so excited about the undoubted challenge that this ridge held in store for us.

At 1.30 a.m. we set off for the Zmutt Ridge. Although I didn't experience any significant technical difficulties, this magnificent classic climb left me with so many breath-taking impressions that I still recall all the details vividly: the nighttime approach across the scree-covered glacier, turning the lower part of the ridge on loose rocks of the west flank; the airy ice arête, the strenuous rock teeth, some exhilerating rock pitches below the Zmutt Nose leading right onto the west face. As we were the sole party on the route we had nothing to fear from stone-falls and we enjoyed a long rest on a small slab at the top of this traverse, viewing the dramatic surroundings at leisure. Continuing the ascent we came to the celebrated Carrel's Gallery from where a rising left-hand movement brought us back onto the Zmutt ridge above the Zmutt Nose overhangs. Nearing the top we scrambled up snowy rocks and reached the Italian summit shortly after midday.

During a prolonged rest luxuriating in the warm sunshine we marvelled at the extensive panorama, highlighted by the gigantic dome of distant Mont Blanc.

At 2 o'clock in the afternoon we set about the descent, sliding down fixed ropes above giddy precipices to the horizontal Cresta Tyndall. Beyond its far end we kept mainly to the south flank, passing below the pinnacled Crête du Coq. Despite missing the best line a few times on complex terrain we reached the Savoia hut below the Grande Tour at 5 p.m.

We were dismayed to find about forty people clustering round the hut that has room for twelve and we resigned ourselves to a restless night. Crammed together like sardines in the over-crowded hut we endured the night half lying, half sitting on our measly bit of floor-space. There was little chance of sleep. In the early morning Herr Pfann was very keen to get going but Frau Noll did not yet feel capable of continuing the traverse. So while she recovered from the hardships of the past night Pfann and I decided to reconnoitre the way round the south side of the Testa del Leone to the Colle Tournanche in preparation for the following night. This task did not tax us unduly, and in order not to waste an involuntary rest day we also climbed the Testa del Leone from the Colle Tournanche side. When we got back to the hut Frau Noll had food and drinks ready. More importantly she had amply replenished our rations, calculated for two days only, with donations of surplus provisions from descending parties. Learning the hard lesson of the previous night we withdrew early to vacant bunks and nothing could have made us budge an inch.

To quit the hut at 1.30 a.m. we had to clamber over a confused mass of bodies on the floor. In pitch darkness with our meagre lantern light it was no easy matter to retrace our steps of the day before, even though the presence of fixed ropes assisted us on the steeper sections. At 3 o'clock we reached the Colle del Leone and stopped 30 minutes to brew tea to compensate for setting off without breakfast. The cairns we had placed the day before for route-finding purposes served us well on the traverse below the Testa del Leone and half an hour later we stood on the flat snow saddle of the Colle Tournanche just as the gigantic form of the Matterhorn began to take shape at the first glimmer of light.

There were no difficulties worth mentioning on the first section of the ridge, but beyond the first hump (Point 3706m.) the character of the route changed dramatically. A narrow rock crest led down to a gap. (5) We descended steep scree-covered slabs on its southern flank, then traversed into the couloir (6) rising from the Chérillon glacier to this gap between Point 3706 metres and the Punta Maquignaz. After some very exposed pitches on the steep yellow wall above the gap we stood on the summit of the Punta Maquignaz at 8.45 a.m.

A sharp snow arête brought us to the foot of the Punta Carrel. The overhangs falling to the col below it are unassailable, likewise the sheer cliff on the left, so we had no choice but to move onto the north flank which sweeps down to the Tiefmatten glacier with hair-raising steepness. There we found a crack that widened into a chimney further up. The sight of this crack really whetted my climbing appetite and I would have just loved to lead it. But there was no way of talking master climber Pfann into relinquishing his guiding responsibilities. (7) Making good use of every chockstone he wriggled up the verglassed fissure. Then I followed. Pfann continued up the chimney while I was belaying Frau Noll up to my stance. Suddenly I was shocked by an almighty jerk; the rope stretched and groaned under the strain. A boulder frozen into the crack had come away as Frau Noll had pulled up on it and she had fallen through no fault of her own. (8) I brought her up to me, tugging the rope

Looking down the East ridge of the Dent d'Hérens to the Zmutt (left) and Italian (centre) ridges of the Matterhorn.

with all my strength, while on the Tiefmatten glacier below the rumbling noise made by rock debris crashing down died away. Soon we exited through a cleft splitting the summit tower and in a few more minutes reached the top of the Punta Carrel by its crest.

Earlier in the morning we thought we had heard voices and now we spotted four climbers on a short ice slope between the Punta Bianca and the shoulder. We were utterly baffled as to where this party had come from because we hadn't seen any steps in the snow.

Difficult rocks along the edge of the ridge brought us to the next gap, bridged by a thin snow crest partly melted away by the sun. We were enormously relieved to get across this fragile structure safely, even though the steep rocks of the Punta Bianca now loomed up forbiddingly ahead. It seemed an appropriate moment to gather forces with a midday siesta in preparation for the exertions to come. 45 minutes later we started cautiously upwards, keeping left of the ridge on the steep face falling spectacularly to the Chérillon glacier. From the top of this tower we inspected the final section of the ridge where two steep steps still barred the way.

Beyond the next gap we climbed ice and steep rock on the right of the crest. In the brittle ice here we at last came across tracks of the party ahead. We found the climbing unusually dangerous and moved gingerly up rock formations of loose boulders frozen together. Topping this step we came to the shoulder at the junction with the south ridge and for the first time we had an unrestricted view of the huge glacier terrace embedded in the North Face of the Dent d'Hérens. A mysterious trail of cut steps curving like a string of pearls rose from this sloping terrace to the ridge. Its origins perplexed us for the time being, but upon our return to Zermatt the puzzle was answered. It was the track of George Ingle Finch (9) who on 2nd August 1923 had opened a bold new route from the uppermost basin of the Tiefmatten glacier by this snow terrace across the North Face of the Dent d'Hérens to the shoulder on the East Ridge.

During the climb we had eyed the step rising to the forepeak with increasing suspicion. All along it had looked down on us threateningly. But now that we stood on the shoulder our lingering doubts evaporated straightaway. We scrambled along rock ledges on the south flank and climbed a shallow gully to rejoin the ridge behind the forepeak. Exuberant at our success we hastened along the rock crest and plonked ourselves down for a well-earned rest by the summit cairn of the Dent d'Hérens at 4 o'clock in the afternoon.

The sun shone down warmly out of a cloudless sky. Not a breath of air stirred. Disbelievingly we gazed peacefully at the endless ridge we had come along, never before linked together in one continuous traverse on the same day.

We descended by the West-North-West Face and West Ridge to the Tiefmattenjoch. Despite slabby rocks and icy slopes Frau Noll set such a brisk pace that we had a hard job keeping up with her. You would hardly have guessed that she had just mastered one of the longest and most strenuous ridges in the Alps. From the saddle we followed the tracks of the party in front southwards down a snow couloir to the Grandes Murailles glacier, and caught them up abseiling in the ice-fall. They were a group of guideless Italians including the well-known alpinist Francesco Ravelli. (10) We learnt that they had climbed from the Chérillon glacier to the gap before the Punta Maquignaz the previous day and had bivouacked there. So now we understood why we had seen no tracks on the first snow section of the East Ridge. Together we continued down to the Aosta hut by 7 p.m. Next morning we returned across the Col de Valpelline to Zermatt, spurred on by the threat of a brewing storm.

Author's notes:

1. The Benedetti bivouac hut was erected about 100 metres from this col in 1950.

2. Unknown to Welzenbach and shortly after Ryan's ascent,
58

Geoffrey Winthrop Young set out accompanied by Rudolf Lochmatter with the aim of "ridging the Matterhorn and Dent d'Hérens in a continuous two days' expedition". In his autobiography, "On High Hills", Young wrote: "The two great peaks are as two crests upon an isolated wave of height; and to traverse them from end to end must be an enterprise worthy of their joint magnificence. The first day I proposed to cross the Matterhorn from east to west ... From the Italian Matterhorn hut, on the second day, the traverse of the Dent d'Hérens would give an opportunity of making friends with its sensational castellated east ridge ... " Young was thwarted by the onset of bad weather overnight at the Italian Matterhorn hut.

3. One of the leading guideless climbers from the turn of the century onwards. His achievements included the first traverse and second ascent of the main summit of Ushba (Caucasus) in 1903, first ascent of Illampu (Andes) in 1928. Pointe Pfann (3983m.), a tower on the south-west side of Mont Blanc, carries his name after his first ascent with H. von Hertling in 1909. On 1st September 1906 he had made the first solo ascent (16th overall) of the Zmutt Ridge. Pfann was described by George Ingle Finch as "the best all-round German mountaineer".

4. An unnamed knoll in 1923, now called Punta Maria Cristina.

5. Col Maquignaz (3637m.).

6. Later I learnt that this couloir has been used several times as an approach to the East Ridge of the Dent d'Hérens - W. W. It is extremely exposed to stone-falls - E. B. R.

7. At this point in his account, published in his first book "Führerlose Gipfelfahrten", Pfann commented: "I led throughout the ascent because on account of the rock frequently being loose I did not want to hand over the responsibility of going first to my youthful companion in spite of his exceptional climbing ability." Less than a year later, Pfann was more than happy to let Welzenbach lead the ice-climbing pitches on their ascent of the Triftji Ridge of the Breithorn.

8. Understandably charitable as Welzenbach contributed this account to Eleonore Noll-Hasenclever's book "Den Bergen Verfallen" after her death in 1925 in an avalanche on the Bis glacier just below the East Ridge of the Weisshorn. Pfann escaped from the same accident with a broken thigh.

9. With Guy Forster and Raymond Peto.

10. The other three Italians were Erasmo Barisone, Guido Rivetti and Carlo Virando who are historically credited as the first party to make an East Ridge-West Ridge traverse of the Dent d'Hérens. It has been overlooked that the Pfann, Noll-Hasenclever, Welzenbach party in fact also achieved the first complete East Ridge-West Ridge traverse of the mountain from the Colle Tournanche to the Tiefmattenjoch.

59

The Ice Man Cometh

BACK AT the Mont Cervin hotel in Zermatt after the Matter-horn-Dent d'Hérens traverse Welzenbach was introduced to Fritz Rigele by Pfann. This fortuitous meeting led to an historically significant partnership between the two men. Rigele - an unusually adventurous representative of the old school of mountaineering despite being blind in one eye, and Welzenbach - the prototype of the new ambitious breed of climbers making up the socalled Munich School, held a common interest in the development of ice climbing techniques. Moreover, Rigele knew of an ice face whose conquest would require the implementation of revolutionary ice climbing techniques. Not unexpectedly, he had little difficulty in arousing Welzenbach's avid enthusiasm for such a project; and so it came about that their 1924 summer plans already revolved round tackling the North-West Face of the Grosses Wiesbachhorn in the Glockner region. For Welzenbach, captivated by the thought of climbing his first proper ice face and implementing new technical methods at the same time, the plan soon developed into a fixed idea.

Meanwhile he enjoyed a very active winter season. In addition to conventional ski touring, he now began to undertake rock climbs for their own sake in winter conditions - mainly in the Bavarian Alps. That Welzenbach climbed or went ski touring almost each weekend throughout the year, come fair weather or foul, illustrates his unquenchable enthusiasm for the mountains. His logbook records show that nearly half his ascents were carried out in winter or spring. There were several years when he chalked up more than 100 routes overall.

While ski touring with Hubert Rüsch in the Albula group of Eastern Switzerland during March 1924, views of the Bernina Alps from Piz d'Err and other summits inspired Welzenbach with the idea of making the first winter ascent of Piz Bernina's

Biancograt (the "white ridge"). He knew that this was a long cherished winter objective of the Pontresina guides. However, the bold plan to attempt this classic ridge climb was shelved due to inclement weather*, and the closing days of their trip were spent in the Bregaglia.

Welzenbach spent a second consecutive Easter vacation, again accompanied by Walter Hofmeier as well as Karl von Ammon, Joachim Leupold and Karl Wien, ski mountaineering in the Bernese Oberland and the Pennine Alps. He repeated the Fiescherhörner tour, traversed the Grünegghorn to the Gross Grünhorn and finally ascended all the 4000 metre ski peaks between Saas Fee and Zermatt - the Alphubel, Allalinhorn, Strahlhorn and Rimpfischhorn.

At Whitsun he returned to the Engadine with Paul Bauer. Rock climbs in the Bregaglia were their first priority. On 3rd June they traversed Piz Bacun by its South and North Ridges, then added the Cima dal Largh for good measure. Erroneously they wrote up the Piz Bacun South Ridge route as a new climb, obviously unaware that this grade IV ridge had already received its first ascent by N. S. Finzi with J. Biner and A. Schaller on 29th August 1921. In German mountaineering literature this mistake recurs uncorrected in a 1960 publication.

This energetic pair next crisscrossed the Bernina Alps on ski - taking in Piz Palü and Piz Zupo amongst other summits - while impatiently awaiting suitable weather for the Biancograt. On 10th June their determination was rewarded, even though they had to contend with all the hallmarks of winter conditions: tiresome snow-plastered rocks, delicate double cornices and unreliable brittle ice. Mostly they revelled in the unusual difficulties, occasionally they cursed, irrespectively they battled on enthusiastically. Welzenbach commented (above the Fuorcla Prievlusa): "Here the climbing was damned unpleasant. We had to dig holds in the snow with our frozen fingers and scrape out steps on the thickly verglassed rock...

* The first winter ascent of the Biancograt was made on 15th March 1929 by C. Colmus with C. and U. Grass.

I recollect that the snow got up the sleeves of my jacket and behind my shirt-collar, and that there was a complete absence of belay points, so I was awfully glad to reach the crest of the ridge at last... A superb bit of ridge climbing led over the second tower, notwithstanding the problems of it being snow-covered and corniced... What a fascinatingly beautiful picture the ridge now presented, soaring as an elegant snow crest high into the clear sky. This wonderful view worked like a stimulant. I could hardly wait to get going. Lord, what a superb route this promised to be... What a joy it was to swing my axe into the brittle ice, spraying fragments like sparks in the blazing sun... We changed the lead a few times at the insistence of the second man and always to the regret of the person in front. With one's ambition and zest for action aroused, just who would choose to have such fine ice climbing work snatched away from him? ... Several steep pitches of ice followed, split by gaping crevasses. With our Eckenstein crampons* we mastered these without cutting hardly a step. Then the ridge suddenly eased off and a 30 degrees snow arête rose to Pizzo Bianco... We had underestimated the bad state of the summit rocks. Damned steep and plastered in snow, with virtually no holds apparent, they took us over another two hours. We had to cross two more gaps and climb two towers before victory was ours. It was a contented summit rest thanks to the edifying feeling of having triumphed by honest hard work. "

In July Welzenbach and Rigele joined forces again for their assault on the Wiesbachhorn face. Thorough preparations had been necessary for this undertaking, for never before had such a steep ice climb been accomplished. Going back to the 1860s and 70s surprisingly daring snow and ice climbs - such as the Pallavicini Couloir on the Grossglockner and the Monte Rosa East Face - had been carried out by the application of step-cutting techniques combined with exceptional physical fitness

* The most modern crampon of the day had been redesigned by Oscar Eckenstein, British but with a German father and a founder member of the Climbers' Club.

at a time when contemporary pioneers were frequently defeated by steep rock. In the intervening years, however, tremendous advances had been made in rock climbing techniques. The introduction and rapid development of rock pegs and other artificial aids such as karabiners between the turn of the century and the beginning of the Great War revolutionized concepts. Direct peg aid made previously impossible pitches feasible. Further, rock pegs increased safety at belay stances and were placed as running belays by the leader for self-protection. By comparison, ice climbing techniques had remained at a standstill. Eckenstein had produced lighter crampons and a shorter ice-axe, but, as Rigele observed, "even with such aids vertical or only 75 degrees steep ice could not be mastered." To this end, ice climbing methods needed re-thinking.

Several years earlier, the idea of hammering a steel peg into ice in the same way and for the same purpose as on rock - for aid and as a belay - had occured to Rigele. This brainwave inspired the birth of the ice peg which Rigele began to develop following a misunderstood conversation with Hermann Angerer in 1922. Benighted on the Schrammacher North-West Face in the Zillertal Alps, Angerer had hung his lantern on a peg driven into a rock crack at the edge of an ice slope, this to continue cutting steps in the ice unimpeded. Rigele originally misinterpreted Angerer's account to mean that he had actually banged the peg into the ice. Encouraged, soon after he tested prototypes with Colonel Georg Bilgeri on the Krimmler glacier ice-fall in the Venediger region. To his delight he discovered that a steel peg driven into ice immediately freezes solidly.

For the Wiesbachhorn climb Rigele had three pegs designed to his specifications by the master locksmith Hilzensauer in his home town of Saalfelden. These were $7\frac{1}{2}$-8 inches long with a rectangular box cross-section and flared head, made of a harder steel than rock pegs. He also brought along a few conventional pitons in reserve. Setting out with these equipment aids, Rigele and Welzenbach were ready to apply the techniques of rock climbing to ice.

GROSSES WIESBACHHORN
3570m

Wielinger
Glacier

Grosses Wiesbachhorn North-West Face. A modern photograph showing the usual rising traverse taken to reach the centre of the face today.

Birth of a Technique

WILLO WELZENBACH

I FIRST met Fritz Rigele in Zermatt. Although he was nearly twice my age (1), I recognized in him one of the few eternally young representatives of the old school of mountaineering, ever ready to speak up for the innovations of the new generation of climbers, also still fired with enthusiasm to undertake the boldest and hardest routes. Similar opinions and interests rapidly forged a close bond between us, and Rigele soon suggested a climb together.

An eventful traverse of the Zinalrothorn lay behind us and we were descending to Zermatt when Rigele entrusted me with a special secret. He told me about an unconquered ice face, about the frightening steepness of its flanks, about its tremendous ice overhangs - an inviolate bastion that defies any attempt at an ascent. In addition he told me about a party of enterprising diehards who, according to rumour, had suffered a dreadful fall on the face and owed their lives to the soft snow of the glacier basin below.

This description aroused my imagination enormously. Throughout the following winter it monopolized my thoughts. In my mind I often pictured myself cutting steps up an endless ice wall and clinging to a bulging ice overhang. These ideas wouldn't go away; the face just had to be conquerable. (2)

The summer of 1924 was upon us. Towards evening on a sultry day in July (3) Fritz Rigele and I were sitting on the rotten summit slabs of the Fochezkopf, staring fixedly at a tremendous ice wall. Forbiddingly steep ice soared heavenwards, formidable bulges blocked its central zone. So that was it, the goal of my dreams, the be-all and end-all of my thoughts: the North-West Face of the Grosses Wiesbachhorn.

65

The mere idea of testing our strength on this face seemed inconceivable and, glancing surreptitiously at Rigele, I observed that the expression on his face betrayed anything but confidence.

However, the longer we gazed at the face, the more accustomed we grew to its perspectives and the less frightening the sight of it became. Gradually our initial reaction of "Impossible" gave way to a dubious feeling of "Perhaps".

The lower part of the face soared upwards as steeply as can be and thinly grooved black ice was evident everywhere. Nonetheless it could surely be climbed with a good pair of crampons, competent step-cutting technique and the necessary perseverance.

Above, the central zone posed the big question mark. Its right half extended in the shape of an overhanging wall of ice into the middle of the face and the left-hand side was dominated by a smoothly arched ice bulge; both were insurmountable obstacles. The sole weakness in the face lay in a slight rut where these two barriers met in the summit fall-line. At this point we should have to force a way through if we were to crack the crux of the problem. It just remained necessary to consider the best line of approach to the foot of the face, then with night coming on we returned pensively to the Schwaiger hut.

Next morning we made an unusually early start from the hut by standards in the Eastern Alps; for one thing we wanted if possible to avoid being seen by tourists ascending the Kaindl ridge; moreover, due to the threat of falling ice we considered it absolutely essential to climb the lower section of the face before it got warm. The moon was sinking behind the hazy horizon in the south-west as we scrambled sleepily up the shale rock flank towards the Fochezkopf. Instead of that cold nip of fresh air associated with fine weather a warm humid wind was wafting across from the Riffltor. Dawn was with us as we set foot on the dome of the Fochezkopf. The summit pyramid of the Wiesbachhorn stood out as a dark black outline against the bright morning sky. Ahead of us the face seemed to soar from bottomless depths, still concealed by the gloom of night, to the

66

shining heights. Gradually the uppermost part of the face began to gleam in the light of day. A glimmer reached the edge of the overhanging ice bulge and only made the flank below appear all the more off-putting. Fading shadows revealed the yawning crevasses of the Wielinger glacier.

The impact of all these impressions was quite disheartening. Talk of retreat was on the tip of our tongues but neither of us dared to express his thoughts.

Hesitantly we started down the ridge to the north. Where the firm snow gave way to loose rock we headed right down steep rotten slopes onto the upper basin of the Wielinger glacier. The terrain was horrible; greasy rock, broken scree-covered slabs, and ready below lurked the jaws of huge crevasses. Squatting on a sloping block, we put on our crampons and in a few steps we were crunching ice under our feet. We descended steeply to the gently inclined glacier cwm which we crossed southwards, finally rising steeply to the bergschrund.

We crossed this gaping chasm by a thin snow bridge and within a few steps our crampon spikes were already biting into hard ice. Our axes swung into action and ice sprayed up as we nicked out step after step, each one just wide enough for our crampon points. Trending left we worked towards the centre of the face. The angle grew steeper and steeper, and soon we banged in our first pegs (4) to belay. Slowly the rope ran through the karabiners, but steadily we gained height.

Shreds of mist were meanwhile creeping up from the Wielinger glacier and originating from nothing they licked their way greedily up the ice face, then dispersed to make room for more. Soon they were gathering rapidly like demonic apparitions and began to settle all around us. We became engulfed in their clammy embrace and were denied any view whatsoever. Our spirits sank to a low ebb amidst such incredibly steep ice flanks which apparently shot down from infinite space and yet had now vanished in the thick mist; something invisible but instinctively perceptible seemed to threaten us from above; an uncanny silence was broken only by the blows of the axe and the chips of ice hailing down. All these impressions created a lot of mounting nervous tension in us.

On top of all this there remained one crucial question: could we actually complete the route? If not, we should be forced to descend the precipitous face in our hastily cut steps. To merely think of such a possibility gave me the creeps.

Parting mists suddenly revealed unusual ice formations outlined against the murky grey above us. We were just below the séracs. A few more pitches and we would reach the crux. In direct relation to the mist blowing away, our gloomy spirits gave way to renewed optimism as we hacked our way upwards towards the shallow depression breaching the main barrier. Here an almost vertical step first rose about ten metres, leaning back but gradually above. Soon we stood at the spot where the angle changed from sloping to vertical, and just to retain our balance we had to press ourselves against the cliff. (5)

The first of several pegs was hammered into the ice. Step after step and hold after hold were carved out on the cliff. Our numb fingers grasped these thin nicks, and slowly we eased our bodies upwards. Metre by metre we were forcing the route and all the details remain clearly imprinted in my mind; directly above me Rigele stood clinging to the ice. Cautiously, so that the swinging action of his ice axe did not unbalance him, he cut one step after another, working his way upwards in the manner of a complete master. I paid the closest attention to every movement of my companion. Uneasily I watched the rope running out, praying above all that it would reach the next stance. But it was not long enough and just a few metres below a ledge promising deliverance Rigele called upon me to follow. (6) Gingerly I moved upwards testing each step deliberately, while it required a supreme effort on Rigele's part to hold out on his tiny stance. Suddenly he yelled frantically: "Hurry, hurry, I can't stand here any longer." One thought only flashed through my mind: "God help us if he falls now." I hastened up to the next peg, grabbed the running belay and relieved the situation by calling out: "Carry on." Immediately he continued

68

upwards and soon disappeared from view behind an ice rib rising at the right-hand edge of the recess in the face. Just a few more metres, then the crux was overcome and he shouted down jubilantly: "Climb when you're ready."

The task awaiting me was anything but pleasant. I had to extract the pegs, all driven in deeply. While my right arm suffered spasmodic cramps under the prolonged strain of wielding my ice axe single-handed, the fingers of my left hand grew numb clutching the chilly ice. At last I had done it and the worst lay below us, even though the face still rose for many rope lengths above.

With the sun's rays beaming out a pleasant warmth and fanned by a mild south wind, nothing would have been nicer than a rest if we could have found a comfortable stance. But the face shot up at a relentlessly steep angle, and immediately below it dropped away like a ski jump into the void.

So once more we cut a staircase of steps up the slope. For pitch after pitch our unceasing movements were entirely motivated by our desire to get up and off the face as quickly as possible so as to give our weary bodies a long needed rest. The face grew narrower, the mountain tops sank around us, the view extended further afield, we were nearing our goal...

A little later two contented adventurers stretched out on the soft summit snow of the Wiesbachhorn. (7) Continuously strained to breaking-point up to now, we could at long last relax carefree and enjoy our surroundings at leisure. Summit rests such as this are hours of perfect happiness in the life of a mountaineer. Pure enjoyment of the heights is combined with delight at a victorious struggle and in success to produce a feeling of harmony in our hearts. This sense of satisfaction is inseparably bound up with the character of extreme mountaineering, indeed it is what gives this sort of alpinism its aim and purpose.

Reluctantly we started downwards. We hadn't quite reached the rocks below the Fochezkopf when we heard a muffled crash, apparently coming from the direction of the Wielinger glacier,

69

followed by a prolonged rumbling noise, then silence again. Strange! ...

On our way to the Oberwalder hut the following morning our route again led up to the Fochezkopf. Upon treading its summit we stopped rooted to the spot, totally bewildered. Was that still our face ahead of us? Had we really climbed this black ice flank, scoured smooth and curiously furrowed? Our tracks had been completely obliterated. The mass of debris in the glacier basin below hadn't been there previously! Slowly the truth dawned on us: the puzzling rumbling crashing noise of the previous day was now explained and we realized just how fortunately we had escaped disaster. An ice avalanche had swept the face barely an hour after we had reached the top...

For success you need not only ability but luck as well, because the dangers threatening a climber are too diverse and too unpredictable to ever be counteracted by advance deliberation. The destiny of the individual will always remain entrusted to the hands of fate, hanging like the sword of Damocles over every climber's head, sparing the one by happy coincidence but destroying the other. (8)

Author's notes:

1. In August 1923 Rigele was just 45, Welzenbach almost 23 years old.

2. Accordingly, Welzenbach wrote to Rigele that the face must be climbed, by them naturally.

3. By chance they timed the climb well (15th July), for the next day Max Hilber, Richard Gerin and Roman Szalay planned to attempt the route.

4. An historical moment marking the introduction of the ice peg to climbing.

5. The angle of this ice bulge, to which the face owed much of its considerable reputation, was estimated by Welzenbach at 75-80 degrees in his report for the annual journal of the Munich Academic Alpine Club 1923/24. It has since virtually melted away and nowadays the angle steepens to 55-60 degrees hereabouts.

6. In his account Rigele contradicts Welzenbach about this key pitch, emphasizing that he stopped only because he had used all his pegs. He describes how Welzenbach followed, removing the first 4 pegs which were then dragged up attached to a spare length of rope and provided the wherewithal to continue.

7. Times noted by Rigele: left hut 4 a.m., foot of face 6.30, well over an hour for the ice bulge, summit 11.00.

8. In view of the resigned philosophy expressed here, it seems appropriate to record that Toni Schmid was killed on this route in May 1932, just 8 months after his dramatic first ascent of the Matterhorn North Face with brother Franz. Nearing the summit he slipped and pulled his companion, Ernst Krebs, off too. Both plunged to the foot of the face. Amazingly Krebs survived despite terrible multiple injuries. He recovered to win a gold medal as a canoeist at the 1936 Berlin Olympics but ironically died after a fall on a building site in 1970.

Improving a Technique

THE Wiesbachhorn ascent marked a significant breakthrough in the development of ice climbing as the first occasion on which ice pegs were used. It had now been proved that rock climbing techniques could be adapted to ice. This success was also an important milestone in Welzenbach's climbing career. As his first extreme ice route it not only signalled the start of a campaign in the Glockner region, it formed a stepping stone to big wall climbs on mixed terrain in the Western Alps. For the first time too his name captured the attention of the climbing world at large. Rather unjustly, insufficient credit was attributed to Rigele's role and the impression has been handed to later generations that Welzenbach invented the ice peg. It would be more accurate to remember that while Rigele (1) designed the ice peg and even led the key pitch, Welzenbach was the driving force behind the undertaking of the Wiesbachhorn climb. Nowadays the route rates as an essential classic for the competent ice climber and ranks as the most fashionable ice face in Austria, though the ice bulge is now far less intimidating. The modern climber arrives with the psychological confidence born of higher standards in mountaineering, these in no small measure due to vastly superior equipment and the benefits of the experiences of his forerunners.

Welzenbach had barely readjusted to everyday life after the Wiesbachhorn triumph before he was preparing for a fortnight's holiday with Eugen Allwein in the Swiss Pennine Alps. At Zermatt they were joined on their first expedition by Hans Pfann and Eleonore Noll-Hasenclever. A bivouac on the Triftji rocks preceded their climb of the Breithorn by its North Spur, one of the most varied snow and ice routes in the district and an ideal introduction for Allwein to the larger scale of mountaineering in the Western Alps. His comments upon the methods applied by Welzenbach to overcome an ice chimney reveal admiration and total confidence in his friend: "Here I learnt about a completely new kind of ice climbing technique. For a long while he stood at the bottom hacking at the ice, carving out steps and enlarging tiny cracks into handholds. Only then did he start up (the chimney). Bridging as on rock he crunched his crampon points into the brittle ice. A few more blows of the axe, then he was sitting on the thin ice crest above and brought me up. While I was belaying Pfann, he carried on straightaway, cut steps up the next short ice wall, traversed right along a narrow ledge and eventually called down with relief: 'We're on top.' Up to this point I had always considered myself a competent ice climber, but after this pitch I realized that my ice routes in the Eastern Alps had merely been a preparatory exercise. I was also aware that in my friend Welzenbach I had certainly found a master craftsman to teach me the skills of ice climbing." In his second volume of memoirs, "Aus meinem Bergerleben", Pfann too acknowledged Welzenbach's lead as "a masterly performance of delicate ice climbing."

On 6th August Welzenbach and Allwein set off early from Zermatt and climbed the Obergabelhorn via the Wellenkuppe. This involved 2500 metres of ascent from the village and in those days parties normally shortened the approach by staying overnight at the Trift hotel. (The Rothorn hut, the present-day higher starting-point for the climb, was not built until 1949). To complete a traverse of the mountain they descended by the splendid rock ridge of the Arbengrat and made such good time that they were back in the village by late afternoon. Two days later they traversed the Nadelgrat from the Lenzspitze to the Hohberghorn. With four 4000 metre peaks pocketed in an exhilerating morning's ridge romp they were entitled to enjoy their early afternoon coffee back at the Seiler tea-garden in Zermatt.

Rigele now arrived and it had been agreed in advance that they would tackle the Monte Rosa East Face by the Marinelli

Couloir. Its first ascent in 1872 had been a remarkable performance well ahead of its time in concept. The reputation and attraction of this famous ice climb hangs upon a combination of difficulty and danger (from avalanches) amidst magnificently wild surroundings. The face is the highest in the Alps, 1600 metres in route terms but in all sweeping down some 2400 metres to the Belvedere glacier. The climb itself starts from the Marinelli hut, conveniently situated near the top of a rock spur one third of the way up the face. To get there Welzenbach's party crossed the Neues Weisstor and dropped down to the head of the Macugnaga valley before toiling up 1100 metres to the hut. Off again at 2 a.m. they climbed almost 1300 metres up steep snow and ice to the Grenzgipfel buttress in merely five hours. Nobody had ever recorded such a fast time to this point. But from then on Rigele suffered from mountain sickness, not altogether surprisingly so. Unlike his younger companions he was not acclimatized and two hours sleep to recuperate from an unusually long and circuitous approach the previous day was hardly the ideal preparation for such a strenuous face climb. It took Welzenbach and Allwein another four hours to coax him between spells of sickness and nausea up the buttress rocks, 300 metres high, to the Grenzgipfel. A short connecting ridge to the Dufourspitze, the highest summit in Switzerland, then the descent supplied the means of relief and recovery. Hampered by deteriorating weather, the holiday ended with a brisk 4000 metre peak bagging outing on the minor tops of the Monte Rosa massif.

Just a fortnight later, on 29th August, Welzenbach and Allwein put up a new route in the Berchtesgaden Alps with their ascent of the Schärtenspitze West Ridge. But on this occasion Welzenbach was not fully satisfied with their line, so the next day they returned to improve the route. This typical reaction characterizes Welzenbach's patient persistence in pursuing specific aims to their completion.

Welzenbach devoted September to the Kaisergebirge. With Adolf Deye he climbed the Piaz Route on the West Wall of the

Totenkirchl, then made the third ascent of the Fiechtl - Wien-
berger Route on the Predigtstuhl with Paul Bauer and Fedor
Möhn. First climbed only the year before and amongst the
finest performances of the day, it still warrants a V+ grading.
The undoubted highlight of the month came on the 18th with his
remarkably fast solo traverse of all twenty peaks surrounding
the Griessnerkar from the Predigtstuhl to the Larcheck. This
feat bore further witness to his amazing overall capacity as
well as to his efficient competence on rock. Just one party had
previously accomplished this testing circuit uninterrupted, yet
Welzenbach even found surplus energy to make a new improved
finish to the West Ridge of the Westliches Törleck in the course
of his expedition. The same evening he jotted down on a scrap
of paper, as was often his practice, a list of the times taken
between each named point on his itinerary. On the reverse
side he summarized the day's events: "Time taken between
the summits 10 hr. 40 min. , rests 3 hr. 40 min. , approach
and return 3 hr. 10 min. , total time for the trip 17 hr. 30 min. "
Such notes illustrate his systematic mind and scrupulous attention to detail. When he entered these details in his logbook,
he merely added: "Weather superb and hot. Very thirsty!
Moonlight at night. "

Even Welzenbach was not immune to the occasional reverse
such as he suffered in the company of Adolf Deye on the Maukspitze South Face in the Kaisergebirge. In mitigation this short
wall was an extreme test, technically tougher than anything he
had so far tried. For the 10th October he noted in his logbook:
"Via Maukalm to the start of the Maukspitze South Face. Abort-
ive attempt! Then by the South Ridge up Maukspitze. Traverse
to Ackerlspitze. Very unpleasant descent in the dark to the
Pflaum hut. " Creditably they made the most of their failure
by completing a respectable outing by normal standards.

Welzenbach's summer extended well into November. On the
8th to the 9th he made a night-time ascent of the Totenkirchl,
then he soloed the Ellmauer Halt by its classic Kopftörlgrat -
one of the finest middle grade climbs in the Northern Limestone

Ranges. With Paul Bauer he traversed the Waxenstein summits in the Wetterstein on the 16th.

In December Welzenbach went ski touring with Hubert Rüsch in the Stubai Alps. Apart from the Ruderhofspitze and the Schrankogel their eight peaks included a first winter ascent of the West Ridge of the Westliche Seespitze. A few weeks later Welzenbach climbed the Zsigmondy Spitze, a noteworthy winter success on the finest rock peak in the Zillertal Alps.

March 1925 found Welzenbach with four Munich Academic Alpine Club friends - Allwein, Berthold, Grätzer and von Siemens - on the Grand Combin. This serious and superb winter expedition is highly prized in ski mountaineering circles due to the combination of height (4314 metres), length (scale and remoteness reminiscent of the Himalaya), danger (the inescapable exposure to the threat of ice avalanches and falling séracs in the socalled Corridor, a glacier band supplying the only line of ascent on ski) and difficulty (the Mur de la Côte ice slope). Only he and Allwein reached the highest summit of this the most dominant mountain between the Matterhorn and Mont Blanc. For good measure they took in its three subsidiary 4000 metre tops. Next day they skied back down to Lourtier in the Val de Bagnes. A traverse to Zermatt was planned for the second part of their trip. In winter or spring they were in fact one of the first post World War I parties to tackle even a modified version of the High Level Route, which on ski remained an exceptional expedition. However, their efforts were foiled by persisting bad weather. The first night they failed to find the Chanrion hut in a snowstorm and were obliged to bivouac thankfully in a dilapidated snow-filled cattle shack nearby. After the monotonous slog up the endless Otemma glacier they waited two days at the Jenkins hut (2), trapped by a blizzard, before skiing down by compass bearings to Arolla and Evolène.

Admiring the splendid view of the Mont Blanc Range from the Grand Combin, the tremendous Peuterey Ridge had captured the attention of Welzenbach and Allwein above all else.

76

They had resolved there and then to attempt it in the summer.
So on 25th July they travelled to Courmayeur and once there
the settled fine weather encouraged them to set out for the
Peuterey Ridge straightaway, virtually treating it as a training
climb for their main programme in the Swiss Pennine Alps!
The Peuterey Ridge, in essence the traverse of the Aiguille
Blanche de Peuterey extended to Mont Blanc, enjoyed a big
reputation as one of the hardest mixed climbs of the day and
was described as "the finest route in the Alps" by Hans Pfann.
A serious undertaking on account of its length at high altitude
combined with the risk of bad weather and stonefall danger, it
had by 1925 received merely five ascents - all parties taking
the original route from the Brenva glacier up the North-East
Flank of the Aiguille Blanche de Peuterey. (3) In the style of
self-confessed irrepressible optimists, Welzenbach and Allwein
hoped by dint of a midnight start from their bivouac at 2700
metres on the east bank of the Brenva glacier (4) to avoid a
second night out. In the event, first they were held up by unforeseen route-finding problems on the chaotically crevassed
glacier, then snow-plastered and verglassed rocks on the
North-East Flank of the Aiguille Blanche upset their schedule
further. The traverse of this remote 4000 metre peak completed, they were obliged to bivouac again on the snowy plateau
of the Col de Peuterey. The next morning as they continued up
the steep ridge to the top of the Eckpfeiler buttress and Mont
Blanc de Courmayeur, they found themselves battling with a
rising storm. Despite obviously poor conditions nothing held
them up until the final steep slope where they had to contend
with "bare ice concealed under a treacherous layer of fresh
snow and then steep verglassed rocks ending one rope's length
below the summit cornice." 10 minutes later they were steer-
ing by compass in a white-out along the connecting ridge to the
top of Mont Blanc. On the way down they were trapped for two
days by a raging storm in the Vallot hut. Their plan of descending from Mont Blanc by Mont Maudit and Mont Blanc du
Tacul to a rendez-vous with friends at the Torino hut on the

Col du Géant had to be scrapped in favour of going straight down to Courmayeur.

By the time Welzenbach and Allwein arrived in Zermatt a lot more fresh snow had fallen. Undaunted they traversed the Täschhorn from the Täschalp to Randa. On its South-East Ridge, better known as the Mischabelgrat, they encountered snow-plastered rocks and enormous cornices. Buffeted by a bitterly cold wind sweeping in evil-looking clouds, they reached the summit as another storm broke upon them. Without stopping they headed down the complex Kin snow face and glacier, not without missing the best line more than once in the mist.

Bad weather persisting, Welzenbach climbed the Riffelhorn, the traditional local training peak, by the Glacier Couloir route rather than hang around inactive in the valley.

When the weather at last improved, Welzenbach decided the time had come to try something more ambitious. In the North-East Face of the Liskamm he chose one of the most impressive ice walls in the Alps. It had been climbed by Ludwig Norman-Neruda with Christian Klucker and Josef Reinstadler in 1890. This party reached the summit of the East Peak by a steep rock rib above the lower ice slopes, but Welzenbach chose a new variation line due to the prevailing conditions and possibly influenced by his innate preference for ice. Accompanied on this expedition by Rudolf Wolter of the Bern University Alpine Club because Allwein felt compelled to tick off the Matterhorn, Welzenbach explained his route decision logically: "In early August the rib was impossible because of ice and deep fresh snow, so we were obliged to climb the ice face on the left of it." He produced a concise guidebook-like report for his club's annual journal: "... We went up the steep snow flank towards the foot of the rib. There we slanted up left, chipping steps, onto the snow and ice to the east of the rib. This section of the face steadily steepens and at the same time tapers off into a narrow ice couloir, bounded on its left by overhanging séracs and on its right by the rock rib. We cut steps up the couloir and at the appropriate spot above the séracs trended left onto the uniformly angled ice flank rising to the summit rocks. These led quickly to the top. In favourable conditions and at an extremely fast pace we recorded the following times: Monte Rosa hut - foot of face 2 hr. 30 min. , rest there 40 min. , foot of face - bergschrund 20 min. , bergschrund - summit 3 hr. 30 min. " In a concluding note Welzenbach added: "This route is undoubtedly to be preferred in a snowy summer. In dry seasons it would however require endless step-cutting, so in such circumstances the Norman-Neruda Route seems more advantageous. "

Welzenbach's rapid ascent of the Liskamm North-East Face prompted accusations of "irresponsible record-breaking" from Christian Klucker, perhaps not an impartial attack by Norman-Neruda's celebrated guide on the first ascent which had taken seven hours from the bergschrund to the summit. Welzenbach's ascent was the third, and first guideless one. His accurate assessment of the conditions and necessary strategy, reinforced by his exceptional fitness, explain his party's speed more dispassionately. His couloir line being a bit more exposed to falling ice than the rock rib, simple common sense in any case called for time-saving tactics.

A week later on 15th August Welzenbach carried out a most unusual traverse, again from the Monte Rosa hut, this time with Alexander Matschunas. It involved descending from the Nordend by its North-East Ridge, the Cresta di Santa Caterina, a difficult rock climb above 4000 metres throughout and in a remote setting. Welzenbach had found nothing published about an ascent of this route and only later learnt that it had been climbed by V. J. E. Ryan with the Lochmatter brothers in 1906. He was however aware that the ridge had previously been descended three times, first by Walter Flender with Heinrich Burgener and Ferdinand Furrer in 1899. But in each of these instances all the key pitches had been abseiled. Welzenbach not only free climbed down the hardest pitches, he also climbed back up them to prove their feasibility in ascent and to help him prepare an accurate description of the climb. (5) An incredible performance on a ridge where two of the previous three descent parties had been forced to bivouac, it spoke volumes for Welzenbach's competence and confidence. His handling of this route testifies to his absolute thoroughness and can surely have few parallels in the history of alpinism. Later he commented that this rock climb was harder than any other he had accomplished in the Swiss Pennine Alps.

Welzenbach wound up his holiday with Hubert Rüsch on the Dent Blanche which they climbed by its classic route, the notoriously variable Viereselsgrat - so named because Ulrich Almer remarked upon completing the first ascent: "We are nothing less than four asses (vier Esel) to have climbed up this way." Surprisingly, Welzenbach was not exactly enthusiastic about this long and serious mixed climb, maintaining afterwards: "It is most aptly named, only in the meantime there have been many more asses than four." He did not bother to record dislocating his shoulder on one of the most exposed pitches. Even though Rüsch complied with his cool request to force the arm back into position, overcoming this handicap can hardly have been conducive to appreciating the superbly airy situations on the upper section of the ridge.

Between his two visits to the Monte Rosa hut Welzenbach made his sensational first ascent of the Dent d'Hérens North Face. For several years it was to remain the hardest ice climb in the Alps. If in Zermatt the local guides' response to this outstanding achievement was of dubious admiration, the printed reaction of the Alpine Journal illustrated short-sighted attitudes in British mountaineering and the antipathy shown during this period to technical advances in mountaineering, especially those made by German climbers. Almost a decade later, its unappreciative editor E. L. Strutt condemned the route as coming under the category of "foolish variations by guideless if misguided amateurs on faces completely and continuously raked by ice and stones." Actually, in good conditions this magnificent ice climb, nowadays rated one of the finest undertakings of its genre in the Alps, is only slightly exposed to objective dangers.

Strutt ignored the fact that in the course of this ascent Welzenbach once again achieved a momentous breakthrough in the development of ice climbing techniques. By carrying out a tension traverse on the crux pitch he succeeded in applying to ice climbing a rope manoeuvre previously only used on rock. In so doing he had introduced a new concept to alpinism, pointing the way to the solution of the ultimate problems on ice and extending the bounds of possibility a little further. This climb was the springboard for a new era of ice climbing in the Alps.

The conquest of the Dent d'Hérens North Face in 1924 by Welzenbach and Allwein extricated the mountain from the shadow of the Matterhorn and pushed it into the limelight accorded to epoch-making innovations.

Author's notes:

1. Rigele, a notary by profession, died tragically on 10th October 1937 as the result of a bizarre accident. Overtaking a mule on the way up to a hut in the Hochkalter group, he fell from the path fracturing his skull fatally. Of political interest, his sister had married Hermann Göring, the German air minister 1933-45 and founder of the Gestapo. Because of this, Rigele had been given a good job in Berlin, but out of disapproval for the government set-up he soon returned to Saalfelden in Austria.

2. The Jenkins hut, built in 1923, was replaced by the Vignettes hut in 1946.

3. First ascent of the Peuterey Ridge: Paul Güssfeldt with Emile Rey, Christian Klucker and César Ollier, 14-17 August 1893. First ascent of the safer modern classic Peuterey Ridge route from the Brèche Nord des Dames Anglaises: L. Obersteiner and K. Schreiner, 30-31 July 1927.

4. Had time permitted, a bivouac on the west bank of the Brenva glacier at the foot of the Aiguille Blanche would have been preferable to crossing its maze by lantern light.

5. Published in the 1924/25 issue of the Munich Academic Alpine Club Journal and probably the most detailed description existing albeit without any grading of the technical difficulties.

Dent d'Hérens North Face. A sideways view. East ridge climbed by Welzenbach in 1923 is seen as the skyline.

Where shall we go tomorrow?

WILLO WELZENBACH

IF ANYONE had suggested to me at Easter 1923 that I would attempt the Dent d'Hérens North Face two years later, I would have been seized with fear. On that occasion at the Schönbiel hut, while my companions were preparing a simple meal, I looked out on a clear winter night: a series of ice avalanches were roaring down the North flank of the Dent d'Hérens. I shuddered. - Was it the coldness of the night or the unrestrained power of nature's forces? Since then this face had often occupied my mind. The fear that I originally experienced in its presence made way for discreet thoughts. To find a practicable route up this wall struck me as one of the highest ranking objectives in the Pennine Alps. At first I did not contemplate the possibility seriously. I was merely playing with the idea. However, the more it occupied my mind the more it became an obsession.

My friend Allwein and I had been completely successful in the Mont Blanc Range by taking advantage of the conditions. But success demands its like. That is human nature. One evening in mid August we were sitting in the Mont Cervin hotel debating the situation. Heavy snow had fallen during the previous few days, so that difficult and large-scale climbs did not come under consideration from a rational point of view. Yet normal routes attracted us little. Allwein was first to raise the disagreeable question: "Where shall we go tomorrow?" I shrugged my shoulders. Then, for the sake of saying something, I suggested: "Dent d'Hérens." - "By which route?" - "North Face," I announced. I expected Allwein either to burst into peals of laughter or to pronounce me crazy. Yet no such thing happened. With total nonchalance he replied: "Fine."

For a few seconds I was dumbfounded by this reaction. However, my companion's down-to-earth response banished all remaining doubts and the matter was settled from that moment.

Next afternoon we walked up to the Schönbiel hut. It was sultry; this suited us admirably, for the snow quickly disappeared from the lower slopes. By contrast, high up around 4000 metres ridges and flanks glistened in deepest winter conditions. As one approaches the hut, all at once the landscape changes. The Matterhorn loses its bold towering shape and becomes an indeterminate mass of rocks, while another mountain peak thrusts itself upon the eye; the Dent d'Hérens. Serrated like a monster's coat of mail, the East ridge rises from the Colle Tournanche. The elongated North flank, forbiddingly steep, consists of a single hanging glacier cut by rock ribs and avalanche gullies. It is as if this wall was created to complete the unparalleled wilderness of the Zmutt glacier basin. The sun was already setting in the west. We hurried onwards as we still wished to inspect the face with the hut warden's binoculars. Soon we were seated in front of the hut door examining the ice slopes of the Dent d'Hérens, bathed in the red evening glow.

The structure of the face is unusual. About three-fifths of the way up, a glacier terrace* cuts across the otherwise intimidatingly steep flank, rising gently from the north-west rib across the face to the east ridge. Below the bottom edge of the terrace the face is marked by a rib which is covered in its upper part by a steep broken hanging glacier. In its lower part the rib divides into two branches stretching down to the Zmutt glacier. We chose this rib, and more precisely its eastern branch, for our line of ascent. Shattered rocks being evident, there could not be any insuperable difficulties in the way here. Moreover it seemed tolerably safe from ice avalanches. Mastering the hanging glacier that rises above the junction of both branches must also be feasible given the necessary time. But

* This terrace was first ascended by Captain George Ingle Finch, Guy Forster and Raymond Peto on 2nd August, 1923.

a big question-mark lay over the point where the hanging glacier joined the snow terrace. If there were a deep cleft and an impassable ice wall there, as we suspected, and from the hut the position could not be judged with certainty, this would jeopardize the success of the whole expedition. In that case, the only remaining possibility lay in attempting to turn the sérac zone by a long curving movement to its left. If we succeeded in overcoming this zone, a second question-mark still awaited: the summit wall. In dry conditions the 55 to 60 degrees angled slabs must be reasonable to climb. That fact I had been able to establish during a traverse of the Dent d'Hérens in the summer of 1923. But under the prevailing conditions, snowed up and iced up, they would present considerable if not insuperable difficulties.

When we went back into the hut at nightfall we were little the wiser. The face still concealed many a problem that could only be resolved by resolute action on our part.

It was 2.30 a.m. The last glimmer of the setting moon dallied on the top of the Matterhorn. We probed our way laboriously by lantern light, stumbling over boulders, treading in pools of water, slithering around on the steep moraines. In short we suffered fully the lot of all guideless mountaineers, namely night-time route-finding on unfamiliar terrain. After a good deal of effort we reached the steep moraine wall round the base of the Stockji at the junction of the Schönbiel and Zmutt glaciers. We followed this moraine up to some broken rock then moved onto the Zmutt glacier. We headed southwards in a shallow basin below the first large icefall towards the foot of the face.

The atmosphere was mild and sultry, the snow was soggy - In a nutshell the conditions seemed positively unfavourable for our plans, above all on account of the increased icefall danger. As we could not however rely upon the weather holding much longer, today might offer the last opportunity of tackling the problem. This consideration was decisive.

In the morning twilight we carefully sought our way amidst

treacherous crevasse systems right up to the face. The day had dawned by the time we reached the foot of the climb.

A steep snow slope, grooved by stone- and ice-fall, marked the start of the ascent. It was split midway by a wide bergschrund. This obstacle caused us a lot of trouble despite our own considerable height. After we had outwitted it in good style at a suitable spot, we climbed as directly as possible towards the foot of the rock rib. At first broad, the moderately difficult though loose rock allowed us to carry on upwards at will. We found the rope merely a hindrance here, so we took it off. As we gained height the rib gradually narrowed into a sharp steep crest composed of broken rocks. The climbing required some care but was exceptionally varied and interesting throughout - I might almost say enjoyable. To the right one looked in a single sweep down steep furrowed snow and ice slopes to the Zmutt glacier; to the left one's eyes gazed upon a wild funnel-shaped avalanche channel fed by the overhanging séracs of the central zone. Climbing quickly we soon reached the top of the rocks. A short steep slope followed before we set foot on the bottom snow dome of the hanging glacier. Here in the last position safe from ice fall we rested a short while in order to examine the route ahead.

Two possibilities now presented themselves: a direct ascent of the hanging glacier or a flanking movement to its left. From the point of view of objective dangers the first solution could be termed relatively safe. But at the same time a serious question came to the fore. Would we be able to continue by this route? Would it be possible to climb from the hanging glacier onto the snow terrace? The second option would mean ascending about 200 metres below overhanging tottering séracs and attempting to get up somewhat broken ice walls onto the glacier terrace. This route appeared at least as problematic and was extremely exposed to ice fall danger besides. After a short discussion we therefore decided to ascend the hanging glacier.

We roped up again and climbed towards the first ice wall.

This dropped from a narrow and slightly overhanging prow to our level on the snow. Only on its left-hand flank did it present a slope; we started our attack there. A minor shoulder above the overhanging wall had to be reached by a steep pitch. One step followed another. All of a sudden my ice-axe pierced the thin surface and a narrow fissure opened up. I cleared the bridge away completely, revealing that the foremost layer of ice had become detached from the massif and was poised threateningly over an abyss. Gingerly, for fear that the blows of the axe might cause the formation to collapse, I cut one nick after the other. Some ten steps more, then this delicate pitch had been overcome and the shoulder above the wall reached. We climbed moderately steep snow to the second step on the hanging glacier.

Once again a steep wall rose in front of us - this time wider. Vertical on the right and at the centre, only on the left did it slope back slightly. We tried our luck there. We overcame the first ten metres of hard ice-climbing by hacking out handholds and steps. Painstaking step-cutting ensued on the 60 to 65 degrees wall. Eventually we found a comfortable stance on a spacious ice bastion. To reach gentler ground we still had to cross a steep bay to the west.

We could already see the outer edge of the glacier terrace glistening in sunlight. A few more rope lengths, then the issue must be decided. For the time being all the answers were hidden from us by a gently arched snow knoll. I rushed up the final slopes in a fever of impatience, in a hurry to know for certain whether our attempt had succeeded or failed. The edge of the glacier terrace rose higher and higher, the terrain ahead sank lower and lower. And when we reached the level of the snow knoll we both stood there dismayed and speechless. A shallow cleft extended in front of us and beyond it an absolutely smooth ice wall, slightly overhanging, rose 30 to 40 metres. We stepped into the bottom of the cleft, followed it to the right, to the left - everywhere the same result. Nowhere was there the slightest possibility of getting through. It was as if the bare glittering ice walls were mocking us pitilessly: "Thus far and no further! "

This was a bitter disappointment. We had wasted valuable hours in vain. Nothing remained but to retreat and attempt the flanking movement to the left.

Belaying carefully we descended the steep ice slopes. Above the final wall we headed eastwards. A hair-raising period then began, traversing for hours below threatening icefalls in the oppressively sultry heat. Smooth polished rocks alternated with bare ice. Belay stances were completely non-existent. Anyhow, what use would any belay have been in the event of ice avalanches thundering down? I cut one step after another in feverish haste, now and again glancing warily upwards at any slight cracking or crashing sound in the séracs. The time lost due to our fruitless attempt upon the hanging glacier now made itself fully felt with thoroughly unpleasant and worrying consequences. Due to longer and longer exposure to the sun, water first began to trickle off the séracs and was soon streaming down. In no time we were soaked through. In addition, a serious objective danger manifested itself and could not be underestimated. Metre long icicles, as thick as one's arm and created by the coldness of the night, started to break off from the edge of the icefall above. Like bolts they fell with substantial force onto the ice slope in front of us, behind us, beside us. I had selected as our immediate goal a rock turret protruding from the ice and itself covered by an overhanging layer of ice. There we were sheltered to some extent and could review the situation.

A corner jutting out near our stance obscured our view of a steep groove in the vertical wall behind. The wall doubled back beyond this groove and stuck out at right angles to its previous direction. I noticed in this protruding flank a round hole which we had first to reach. Only from there did it appear practicable to ascend to the terrace.

While Allwein made himself as comfortable as possible at his belay stance, I set off on this delicate and crucial pitch.

I moved round the corner and could now survey the groove in the wall. In its upper part it was composed of vertical ice, in its lower part of steep powder snow only superficially consolidated. For a few metres it remained possible to work diagonally upwards cutting steps, then one had to step over onto the snow face. The angle was positively alarming; I estimated it at 70 degrees. Standing unaided was out of the question. Accordingly I put into practice a special technique. I thrust my fist through the thin surface of the snow slab and dug my arm into the loose baseless mass in order to establish a firm hold. I repeated this act a dozen times. My fingers had become numb with cold, as in the heat of the struggle I had forgotten to put on my gloves and this was now impossible on the traverse. I was constantly occupied by a frightening question: "Would the snow slab hold? Wouldn't it avalanche into the depths under my weight?"

But it did hold. I reached the ice hole after twenty eternal minutes. As I was massaging my fingers or warming them up alternately in my mouth and in my trouser pockets, there was a loud cracking and rumbling noise. Startled, I looked up and saw an ice wall breaking off barely 100 metres away from our stance. The avalanche roared down the flanks we had just crossed and onto the Zmutt glacier.

Allwein had followed. The two of us were now sitting in the hole with chattering teeth. We were wretchedly cold there in the shade. A steep narrow gangway led out of our hollow. We could examine the first few metres up to where it curved round a corner. I cut some steps cautiously, moved forward and peered round it. The ledge continued a couple of metres further up to a bulge arched out of the ice at chest height. Beyond this bulge I saw a shallow recess from where it appeared possible to proceed with the ascent. It was therefore imperative to reach this recess.

I hammered a long piton into the brittle ice, attached the karabiner, passed the rope through - and then for the job in hand. I first tried to climb the traverse somehow, but I immediately realized the fruitlessness of this task. Even when my foot found adequate support with its crampon, there were still no handholds for my fingers on the ice bulge. An excellent idea then occurred to me: I would attempt to overcome the pitch by a rope traverse. For what purpose had we learnt such technical skills in the rock regions of the Eastern Alps? "Tight rope!" I shouted to Allwein. I pushed my feet firmly against the extreme edge of the gangway and laid my weight on the rope. Upon the further order, "Slacken the rope slowly", my body moved gradually to the left. My hand reached a thin crack. I jammed my fist into it and swung myself across. A short gully followed - then I was standing in the recess.

I drove another piton into the ice to belay Allwein and called him to follow. He was just moving round the corner and at that point I couldn't help laughing at his flabbergasted expression. "How did you get across there?" he asked in amazement. "I just came across," I replied somewhat maliciously without divulging the secret. For all that he made short work of it, grasping the rope and swinging himself across to me in the recess.

Scarcely twelve metres above us the sun was glittering on the rim of the glacier terrace - our salvation beckoned.

A steep narrow ramp with a thin overlying layer of snow supplied the line of ascent on the ice wall above. It ended in a round shallow cave just below the top of the wall. But now it really seemed that no further headway could be made. The roof of the cave jutted out uninvitingly as a snow overhang. It would have taken hours of hard work to cut this roof away with an ice axe. Allwein then had a brainwave; he rammed the long shaft of his old-fashioned ice axe - I had teased him very often because of its length - through the cave's one metre thick roof; I moved carefully up to the lip of the overhang, just managed to grab hold of the spike of the axe sticking out of the snow, a mantelshelf movement and I was up on gentle slopes in the bright warm sunshine.

Allwein followed briskly,* then we ascended the soft snow slopes at a leisurely pace, turning some crevasses on the right. We felt extremely happy. We had escaped from the dark terrible abyss after an arduous and difficult battle; we had regained our freedom.

But my joyful mood quickly evaporated as I eyed the summit wall dubiously. Angled at 55 to 60 degrees, this wall sweeps down in tremendous flights of slabs to the snow terrace. More to the point, these slabs were coated with smooth ice and plastered with powder snow. They were a most disconcerting prospect. After all the day's difficulties and exertions this summit wall might yet present impossible problems.

We chose to make for the bottom of a gully coming down between the top and an easterly forepeak. After crossing the bergschrund we headed up a steep ice slope directly in line with the gully. We soon realized that the gully itself was unclimbable, so we crossed to the rib bounding its west side. Things went quite well there for a few rope lengths until polished rocks forced us further right into the centre of the summit wall - and this gave us plenty of trouble. We toiled upwards for ages. Verglassed slabs alternated with snow, then there were slabs again - continually, endlessly. We had to dig each handhold and each step individually out of the snow. There were no stances at all; each belay was made merely as a matter of course. We both knew that if one of us fell, it would be the end of both.

For the first few rope lengths we led through, but soon I entrusted all the leading to Allwein. He was to work out the route from now on. I felt utterly exhausted by my strenuous efforts in the central zone of the face and preferred to climb mechanically behind my companion. However often I looked up at the ridge or down into the depths, both always seemed equidistant

---

* Allwein's account in the 1926 German and Austrian Alpine Club Yearbook records that they reached this point on the lower edge of the snow terrace at 12.30 p.m. and had spent 6 hours climbing the hanging glacier (ice cliffs) including 2 hours lost on the first line attempted.

- that having a demoralizing effect. And yet we had to be nearing our goal, for we were after all constantly gaining height. I began to count the rope lengths so as to at least have a yardstick of our headway. I got as far as eleven, then we had reached our goal. At 6. 30 p. m. , sixteen hours after leaving the Schönbiel hut, we rammed our axes into the summit snow of the Dent d'Hérens. This magnificent peak was ours by its most challenging route.

Now, for the first time in the day, we treated ourselves to rest and refreshment. Then we devoted our attentions to the view and to day-dreaming. An almost mysterious tranquillity surrounded us. Not a breath of air stirred. Mountain upon mountain stretched out in silent majesty and glory, bathed in the warm rays of the setting sun which was veiled by thin cirrus clouds, the first signs of the storm to come next morning. It was time to depart.

The descent by the West Ridge to the Tiefmattenjoch seemed both relaxing and enjoyable. We rushed down the snow of the Tsa de Tsan* glacier by leaps and bounds, raced down boulder-strewn moraine slopes. Even so, the last light of the day had faded away by the time we sat safely within the sheltering walls of the Aosta hut.

* This is the Grandes Murailles glacier on present-day maps, but it was formerly known as the Tsa de Tsan glacier.

Guidebooks and Gradings

1925 WAS Welzenbach's most prolific year. He climbed 149 peaks and made 19 first ascents. An extra motivation for this prodigious output came through a contract he signed on 1st July to edit a new guidebook to the Wetterstein Range. This stipulated "... a complete revision of the 4th edition to take into account all new routes in the region. Herr Welzenbach will deliver the manuscript in a fit state for the printer by 31 December 1925."

Welzenbach qualified as an ideal guidebook writer with his ability to produce accurate and objective route descriptions uninfluenced by the earlier assessments of others. He possessed the rare talent to write up a climb informatively in broad outline without getting bogged down in trivial details. If the contract deadline for completion seemed to allow little time for research and for checking information, that was reckoning without Welzenbach's boundless energy. He oozed enthusiasm for the task which suited admirably his preference for concentrating upon one selected area at a time so as to climb everything worthwhile there. Of course, nobody had suggested that he need add any new routes himself, but he seized this gilt-edged opportunity to undertake a virtual second conquest of the Wetterstein. (1)

The publishers generously authorized Welzenbach to pay companions 10 Reichmarks per day for participating in the guidebook fieldwork. During a period of mass unemployment Welzenbach experienced no difficulty in finding climbers to check all the routes. He enlisted the help of his friends to repeat numerous climbs and with the extremists among them - notably Paul Bauer (2), Adolf Deye (3), Eberhard Müller, Hubert Rüsch and Karl Wien - he made a relentless series of first ascents, 17 in all (4), within four months.

That Welzenbach spent four weeks holiday in the Western Alps during this very period heightens the impact of his activities in the Wetterstein.

Several of Welzenbach's new climbs were achieved in the Zugspitze group, Germany's highest mountain massif. Here the Zugspitzeck West Face and Kleiner Wanner North Face, both 1000 metre high rock walls, provided serious undertakings with sustained difficulties. Despite this, Rüsch later related that they hardly used their rope on the Kleiner Wanner. On this occasion they moved together most of the time. Welzenbach firmly believed that it was far more sensible to climb unroped than to use the rope casually or carelessly. The same pair were more seriously tested by a severe storm on the upper half of the Zugspitzeck West Face, but under such circumstances Rüsch happily placed his faith in the contemporary conviction that "when with Welzenbach no accident can happen to you."

Welzenbach's finest first ascent of this campaign, of the Schönangerspitze North Face Direct, was made on 4th October with Paul Bauer. This forbidding climb was a longstanding problem that had repulsed several previous assaults by other mountaineers. Welzenbach's route description of the summit wall indicates the nature of the undertaking which is today graded VI-: "... A broken yellowish crack rises left up the vertical wall. Go up it for 8 metres (peg), then move right and climb a loose overhang to a poor stance (exceptionally difficult). Traverse first left using detached flakes, then right up to a steep slabby band (good stance). Follow the band to the right, narrowing to a ledge, up to a yellowish crack. Climb this for 6 metres to a steep scree-covered slab. Move right round a corner and climb a smooth 3-4 metres high groove directly to the summit." Come the 1970s and not a single word of the description has been changed in the current edition of the guidebook.

Undoubtedly the most unexpected and unusual partnership of the summer came into being on 18th June at the Knorr hut.

Here Welzenbach and Rüsch were accosted by the hut's adventurous waitress, Hanny Lechner. A native of Garmisch, she
insisted on joining them for a day's climbing. Despite initial
scepticism on the side of the guidebook party, she proved her
competence on two new ascents, the West Ridge of the Hinterer
Gatterlkopf and the North Ridge of the Mittlerer Gatterlkopf.
Welzenbach was sufficiently impressed to take her on another
altogether harder first ascent in the autumn, the North Face
of the Vorderer Gatterlkopf.

Elsewhere in the region Welzenbach's explorations included
two new routes on the Wetterspitzen, the North-West Face of
the Nördliche Riffelspitze and the North Ridge of the Oberer
Schüsselkarturm. The distinctly loose limestone rock in the
Wetterstein is the one drawback to all these routes. All in
all, 1925 became Welzenbach's most successful year for pure
rock climbs. The fruits of his unstinting labours were received by the climbing world with publication of the updated
guide to the Wetterstein 15 months later. It was lavishly
praised for its clarity, completeness and conciseness.

Work on the Wetterstein guidebook had made Welzenbach
reflect once more upon the need to update the system for grading
climbs. He had always interested himself actively in mental
and physical problems associated with mountaineering developments. He had already contributed a treatise on the correct
ethical use of rock pegs for Der Bergsteiger magazine in 1924.
This discussed the validity of an ascent forced by excessive
pegging - adjudged reprehensible tactics, the dangers of in-
competent climbers attempting overpegged routes otherwise
beyond their capabilities and the right of climbers to remove
pegs - viewed as desirable so that routes might retain or return
to their natural state. He had also outlined the history of
crampons for the magazine in 1925.

Back in 1922 Welzenbach had first entered the arena of growing controversy surrounding the contemporary system of
assessing climbs. He wrote: "In my opinion, climbing successes have almost reached the upper limit of what people can

achieve. The future will show whether this is so." He went on to summarize his belief that further advances would come through a greater accumulation of difficulties in the course of a route, while individual pitches would still be mastered by the means already developed by Hans Fiechtl, Otto Herzog and Hans Dülfer - a reference to the introduction of pegs and karabiners as artificial climbing aids, and to associated new techniques such as tension traverses and pendulum abseils. He envisaged the ascents of bigger walls with extreme pitches throughout, whereas many of the earlier face climbs had only involved short sections of extreme difficulty. These views naturally required some modification later, both in terms of improved equipment and revised concepts of what is technically possible.

There was an obvious connection between the proliferation of climbing guidebooks and the development of a grading system. With the publication of route descriptions a classification of difficulties was needed so that climbers could compare ascents with reasonable accuracy. The generalizations of late nineteenth and early twentieth century guidebooks, of the nature "an expedition which can be recommended only to first-rate mountaineers" (John Ball about the Dent Blanche in his "Pennine Alps" guide of 1873) or "the only satisfactory and safe way up the mountain" (George Abraham about the Weisshorn East Ridge in "Swiss Mountain Climbs", published 1911), were unsatisfactory if not meaningless in themselves. Approximate comparisons that one peak or route was harder or easier than another were found inadequate by continental climbers in particular.

In Britain, objections to the grading of climbs on a quasi-scientific basis were founded firstly upon concern that such a system would tempt ambitious but inexperienced youth onto routes dangerously beyond their capabilities and secondly upon the fear that such a system would enable mountaineers to compare their performances more accurately, so promoting competitive attitudes if not a cult of danger. For alpine climbing purposes in the 1920s, this reaction overlooked the fact that the then affluent English normally employed guides, while the generally guideless Germans required route descriptions that accurately assessed the difficulties. So the need for a method of classification of climbs that everyone could interpret reliably. Most continental climbers wanted evaluations of routes that would in the first instance serve as some sort of yardstick to measure themselves against and allow them to compare routes in one region with another. That climbers would also be able to compare their exploits was originally incidental. Despite later oft-repeated allegations, mainly from the British, that the grading of climbs incited undesirable competitive excesses between mountaineers and sometimes on a nationalistic basis, this effect has been grossly exaggerated and rivalries were anyway inevitable in a fast growing sport, irrespective of international strife.

In the early years of the twentieth century a fourfold adjectival grading system had evolved in the Eastern Alps. (5) Then Hans Dülfer proposed in a rough and ill-defined outline the system that Welzenbach later revamped. New climbs made by Angelo Dibona, Tita Piaz, Paul Preuss, Dülfer and Fiechtl among others outdated the original system before the First World War. All these new routes had to be accorded the fourth category, yet represented a range of three grades by modern standards. In 1914 Karl Planck and Dülfer commented in the Österreichische Alpenzeitung (Austrian Alpine Journal) that the fourfold scale of difficulties had become meaningless and needed extending if climbers were to be made aware of the precise nature of the harder routes. So a fifth grade was unofficially added by some but not all of those responsible for grading climbs. In the early 1920s "Der Hochtourist in den Ostalpen", a guidebook series to the Eastern Alps sponsored by the German and Austrian Alpine Club, had progressed to the fivefold adjectival classification system (easy, medium difficult, difficult, very difficult, extremely difficult) and for comparison included introductory examples of each grade from several regions outside the area in question.

Welzenbach realized the importance of assessing the technical difficulties of a climb more precisely than previously. He was convinced that accurate grading formed an essential prerequisite for mountaineers in planning their activities, especially when visiting a region for the first time. This belief inspired his treatise "A suggestion for standardization in the scale of difficulties", published in the May 1926 issue of the Österreichische Alpenzeitung and in Bergkamerad magazine. Here he presented his sixfold numerical and adjectival classification for all types of routes - not just rock climbs as has been misinterpreted by several mountaineering historians. (6) He formally added the sixth grade which he correctly felt the newer harder achievements of the previous few years made necessary. But he disputed Dülfer's claim that rising standards would require any scale of difficulties to be corrected "every 5-7 years". He re-affirmed his view: "... a significant raising of rock climbing standards is no longer possible ... in ice minor advances are still possible." He recognized that the sixth grade was already in use among some climbers and in some guidebooks, and did not claim to invent it as such. At the same time he criticized the absence of any uniform description of what it signified. What he deplored was the inconsistency in the use and definition of grades. His aim was to produce a uniform system and clear definitions that would eliminate the prevalent confusion. Although he evaluated his scale of difficulties by Roman figures from I to VI (as in the examination marking system used in German and Swiss schools), with lower and upper limit refinements of each grade denoted by plus and minus signs (this for pure rock climbs only), he also defined a sixfold adjectival scale (7) and formally recommended its use in preference to figures: "The 'live' word expresses much more than a 'dead' number". Welzenbach backed up his suggested grading scale with numerous examples divided into three tables for: 1. "Limestone climbs" - the pure rock routes of the Northern Limestone Ranges; 2. Gneiss and granite climbs" - rock routes in the Eastern and Western Alps; and 3. "Ice climbs" - ice routes in the Eastern and Western

98

Alps. Further, he elaborated how the scale should be used and the nature of climb each grade signified. At the bottom, grade I (easy) indicated terrain requiring the use of one's hands or, on snow, an ice axe for support. Anything easier than this was "without difficulty" and outside the scope of the grading system - but where applicable he suggested expressions such as "surefootedness necessary". By contrast, the top grade represented "the extreme limit of a first-class climber's capabilities". He was careful to point out that "continually changing conditions always lend some uncertainty to the judgements pronounced on high alpine routes" where "prevailing conditions can bring about an increase or decrease in difficulties, so that a list of graded examples has no absolute value but only a relative one".

Welzenbach's clear arguments and striking examples earned acceptance of his proposals not just inside Germany but also in Italy and France. The Italian Domenico Rudatis, a great enthusiast of the "Sesto Grado" (sixth grade) image and active in the Civetta group of the Dolomites, wrote in 1927 to Welzenbach: "Your scale of difficulties is without doubt the best one introduced up to now and I am in complete agreement with its principles." Indeed, the "Welzenbach Scale", as it became known, remained used throughout the Alps until the late 1940s. The Italians promptly applied the scale - very slightly adapted as the "Civetta Scale" - to the Dolomites, but Renato Chabod - who made the first ascent of the Aiguille Blanche de Peuterey North Face in 1933 with Aimé Grivel - later suggested that grading in the Western Alps should also take into account the length of a climb, altitude, objective dangers, etc. The French too acquiesced with Welzenbach's division of difficulties into six categories, but like the Italians had reservations about its rigid application to mixed routes in the higher alpine regions. Something was required to express the seriousness of a route which depends on the factors outlined by Chabod, as well as on how sustained a climb is, its remoteness, route-finding problems, the quality of the rock, exposure, belaying protection and the prevailing weather-dependent snow or rock conditions. Welzenbach had grasped all this and had himself emphasized this point: "When a climb is graded, apart from the pure technical requirements, allowance should also be made for its length, unfavourable conditions, etc. Judgement should be based not only on a technical point of view but by evaluating the overall demands of the route." It took until 1951 before the French found an acceptable answer to the grading problem and adopted a modified version of the Welzenbach Scale: this involved combining a sixfold overall descriptive grade (8) with the sixfold numerical grading retained for individual rock climbing pitches.

Until after World War II the British reacted less than enthusiastically to the numerical scale of classification. Comments in the Alpine Journals of the 1920s and 30s alleged that a comparative grading system was tantamount to a competitive one and must encourage climbers to take unjustifiable risks contrary to the ethics of mountaineering. That a comparative scale of values assisted climbers in judging what lay within their powers and so provided a potential safety factor was largely ignored.

In Germany and Austria modifications to Welzenbach's grading system were discussed over the years, most frequently upon the basis that the technical limit of difficulty was being extended by new achievements. Suggestions included increasing the number of grades to eight. In 1939 Fritz Kasparek, one of the Eigerwand conquerors, remarked in his autobiography "Ein Bergsteiger": "Despite many attempts to reform the system of evaluating difficulties, in my opinion there is only one scale of difficulties that ought to be applied to all climbs in the Alps. That is the scale in six grades as devised by Welzenbach."

An Austrian, Raimund Schinko, between piling up extreme first ascents during the 1930s in the Dachstein and Gesäuse among other regions, touched upon the nub of the grading debate. He proposed that a climb should be categorized with a free climbing grade and, if applicable, an artificial grade. Now, while Welzenbach's sixfold scale stood the test of time, there was one weakness in his descriptive criteria: "All routes that as a rule cannot be climbed without the use of technical aids belong to the supremely difficult sixth grade." Thus Welzenbach assigned grade VI to all routes - among others - that were only climbable by artificial means. This did not tally with his ideal of grade VI representing "the limit of human capability". It was soon seen that pegged routes can become routine exercises once a climber is practised in artificial techniques. Eventually grade VI was re-defined as free climbing to the absolute limit of what is physically possible, a judgement that kept faith with Welzenbach's original ideal.

In 1947 an international commission met in Chamonix and revised the Welzenbach Scale into the socalled Alpine Scale (Alpenskala). In 1971 the UIAA (International Federation of Alpine Clubs) attempted to standardize grading systems. The necessity to differentiate between free and artificial climbing was agreed upon. Their document re-affirmed that "six grades are sufficient to denote the difficulties involved in free climbing." Welzenbach's Roman figures from I to VI, with their sub-divisional refinements, were retained. For artificial climbing the grading is indicated by the letter A with qualifying numerals from 0 to 4 and the addition of a small letter e in the event of expansion bolts being needed (e.g. A3e).

In the last few years Reinhold Messner, among others, has advocated a seventh grade. He has argued that the limits of human capability have been stretched and that today's difficulties will be exceeded in the future. He has pointed out that rigid adherence to a sixfold scale of difficulty has resulted in routes being downgraded over the years (but not every ten years as Messner asserted). It cannot be disputed that many of the grade VI climbs of the 1920s have been demoted to grade V in the light of modern concepts. Such modification has been necessary in the main to accommodate rising standards within the six categories of difficulty available. On the other hand, some climbs have simply been devalued by the large number of pegs now permanently in place - an excellent example being the South Ridge of the Aiguille Noire de Peuterey, in Welzenbach's day the hardest rock climb in the Western Alps. Discussion about introducing a seventh grade in the Alps continues and in early 1979 the UIAA gave approval to the existence of a grade VII. For all that, the Welzenbach Scale still forms the basis of today's classification system for the grading of climbs.

Author's notes:

1. In an article about guidebook literature in the 1978 Yearbook of the German and Austrian Alpine Club, Welzenbach's efforts in the Wetterstein are singled out for praise as the classic example of new routes being discovered and climbed by an editor in the course of preparing his manuscript.

2. Bauer became the leading organizer of German inter-war exploration in the Himalaya and with Bechtold set up the German Himalaya Foundation.

3. Deye made several important new routes including the North Wall of the Torre delle Madri dei Camosci (Gamsmutterturm), Julian Alps, in 1929 with Rudolf Peters. He also made the first attempt on the Fleischbank East Wall in 1910 with Otto Herzog, and its second ascent just eight days after Dülfer and Schaarschmidt in 1912.

4. With Josef Dreher he added the 950 metres high South Face of the Mittlere Wetterspitze, now graded V-, in August 1926 to bring his grand tally of first ascents in the Wetterstein to 18.

5. In Britain Owen Glynne Jones invented a scale of four grades (easy, moderate, difficult, exceptionally severe) for his "Rock Climbing in the English Lake District" guidebook, published in 1897.

6. Two such instances in the 1970s are C.E. Engel's "Mountaineering in the Alps" (1971) and R.W. Clark's "The Alps" (1973). Both authors also wrongly credit Welzenbach with the invention of the grading system. In Britain Robin Collomb was first to recognize the all-purpose nature of Welzenbach's grading system and used it in some of his guidebooks after 1965, while there are notes on this subject dating back to 1948 in the Collomb diaries.

7. I = leicht (easy), II = mittelschwer (medium/moderately difficult), III = schwierig (difficult), IV = sehr schwierig (very

difficult), V = überaus schwierig (extremely difficult), VI =
äusserst schwierig (supremely difficult).

8. facile (easy), peu difficile (little difficult), assez difficile
(fairly difficult), difficile (difficult), très difficile (very difficult), extrêmement difficile (extremely difficult).

Consolidation, 1926

AFTER numerous ski tours during the winter of 1925/26, Welzenbach spent Easter in the Bernina Alps. His companions were Paul Bauer and Ludwig Böttcher. On 3rd April they climbed Piz Scerscen (3971 metres) by its North-West Spur along the Eisnase, a 60-70 degrees steep ice nose upon which the reputation of this magnificent ice climb hinges. Though Walter Risch is credited with the first winter ascent of this mountain as late as 29th March 1938 (by its North-East Face), elsewhere at this altitude claims to winter ascents made up to mid April and even later were often accepted. Welzenbach's party made no such claim. Two days later they climbed Piz Roseg. Such performances influenced Arnold Lunn to label Welzenbach as "among the leading winter mountaineers" in the British Ski Year Book for 1926, and to accord to the Munich Academic Alpine Club "the place of honour" in "the great role" played by the continental university clubs in the development of ski mountaineering.

Between his trip to the Bernina and his 1926 summer campaign in the Western Alps, Welzenbach spent several weekends in the Dachstein group and the Kaisergebirge. A stamina-sapping expedition in the latter region on 6th June brought some unwanted excitement towards evening. His party first climbed the Predigtstuhl by the West Wall (Dülfer Route, IV+), then traversed the Hintere Goinger Halt (III) and still found energy to tackle the Fleischbank. On the final descent they were caught by a violent thunderstorm at the Winklerscharte. Welzenbach noted: "... struck by lightning twice. Winkler Gully in torrential rain."

Through the introduction of more advanced ice climbing techniques a need for new and modified equipment arose. About this time Welzenbach appropriately developed his own ice hammer and so contributed to supplying the requirements he was largely responsible for causing. Coincidentally, he also conceived and produced his own bivouac tent, a three-cornered design simply held up by an ice-axe. Both these items were further refined and then marketed under Welzenbach's name by a Munich mountaineering equipment manufacturer.

Welzenbach produced no full accounts of his summer climbs in the Mont Blanc Range and the Pennine Alps. Fortunately, Eugen Allwein was persuaded nine years later to recall the events of their attempt on the South Ridge of the Aiguille Noire de Peuterey, after Welzenbach's death. And Fritz Rigele wrote an article about their ascent of the Breithorn North-West Face for the German and Austrian Alpine Club Yearbook.

The South Ridge of the Aiguille Noire de Peuterey had attracted attention before the First World War. The quality and difficulty of this pure rock climb were recognized by several potential trail-blazers, but it resisted numerous assaults. This route represented the most significant effort to raise rock climbing standards in the Western Alps to match the tremendous technical advances applied in the Northern Limestone Ranges and the Dolomites. Welzenbach and Allwein eventually retreated, but on 23rd October 1928 Jacques Lagarde, editor of the Guide Vallot, wrote to Welzenbach that he proposed to commemorate their attempt by naming the third tower - their high point - Pointe Welzenbach and requested his consent. It was given and so this summit became an enduring memorial on the map of the Mont Blanc Range. Two years later Brendel and Schaller accomplished the first ascent; and soon after the brilliant Italian climber Giusto Gervasutti singled out the South Ridge of the Aiguille Noire as "the only pure rock climb of first-class standard in the Western Alps".

Complete contrast marked Welzenbach's two climbs from Zermatt with Bachschmidt and Rigele. First the big ice climb on the Breithorn, second a serious rock route on the Ober Gabelhorn. Pure rock faces are not common on the 4000 metre peaks of the Swiss Pennine Alps. Ones with technical climbing interest are rarer still. Such prerequisites are united in the South Face of the Ober Gabelhorn. A broad rock wall giving some magnificent slab pitches, it had probably been climbed only two or three times by 1926 according to Rigele. In fact, three years before, Rigele and Welzenbach "had taken a great fancy to the face" but had been driven back from the foot of it by a sudden snowstorm. On this occasion Welzenbach led throughout the climb, "mastering one slab after another with exemplary skill", as Rigele put it. Going down by the Arben-grat they were amused at collecting an ice axe abandoned as an abseil point by two Zermatt guides unable to climb down the Grand Gendarme*. Earlier in the afternoon the selfsame guides, already on the descent, had been heard loudly inform-ing their clients that the party on the South Face below them would certainly not extricate themselves the same day and quite probably not at all. Upon being questioned and very shortly afterwards overtaken, the guides pretended the axe had been left behind by a Zinal party. Next day one of the guides called to pay his respects to Welzenbach's party at their hotel, praised their climbing achievements lavishly and sheepishly got round to the subject of his ice axe - in truth their story the previous afternoon had been concocted to preserve pride.

Frustratingly, bad weather held Welzenbach in check for several days. His leave drew to a close with uneventful ascents of the Weisshorn and the Zinalrothorn.

* A fixed peg abseil has since been placed at this point.
106

Pointe Welzenbach

EUGEN ALLWEIN

COMING down past the Combal lake after our ascent of the Peuterey Ridge of Mont Blanc in 1925, Welzenbach and I were captivated by the sight of a wild pinnacled rock fretwork forming the South Ridge of the Aiguille Noire de Peuterey. Once we had assured ourselves back home that this ridge remained unclimbed, we accorded it top priority in our 1926 programme - all the more so on discovering from our literary researches that it was already a longstanding problem. In 1913 some of the best climbers of that era had tackled the ridge; first Guido Mayer with Angelo Dibona had retreated from the wall of the second tower (1), and then Paul Preuss climbed the first tower - the Pointe Gamba. (2) Nothing was known about further attempts, but we heard rumours that the Courmayeur guides were interested in the ridge.

We arrived in Courmayeur late on 22nd July. The weather being superb and the rocks of the Aiguille Noire completely free of snow, next day - armed with food for a couple of days and with some rock pegs and karabiners - we straightaway went up to the small hut built three years previously in the Fauteuil des Allemands cwm. We were amazed by the grandeur of the scene that opened up before us. The South Ridge of the Aiguille Noire - We had not envisaged quite such an awe-inspiring prospect. First the smooth obelisk of the Pointe Gamba; above it four more equally mighty and considerably higher towers, the whole ridge soaring tremendously steeply to the south summit (3) of the mountain. Slowly it sunk into us that this would be no easy victory.

By 2.30 a.m. on a moonlit but suspiciously warm night we were moving slowly and steadily across the snowfields still covering the upper part of the Fauteuil des Allemands towards the couloir coming down from the Col des Chasseurs. We had kept the weight in our rucksacks to the minimum, taking only a little food as well as a couple of rock pegs and karabiners. We had left our bivouac gear behind on the assumption that if the ridge would go, then it had to be climbed in one day, for the weather showed signs of breaking. We reached the col before dawn by climbing a steep but easy gully, and immediately got ready to continue. By late afternoon we hoped to have completed the 1000 metres high ridge (4) so as to be able to descend to the hut during the evening, if need be with the assistance of the expected full moon. The weather would surely hold out that long.

At 4. 10 a. m. it was light enough to commence the climb proper. On Pointe Gamba we initially kept to Preuss's route, but higher up we hoped to bypass the summit by a traverse directly into the gap beyond it. The first pitch on the crest was not at all easy, then we moved together for some 50 metres up broken rocks on the ridge to the foot of a steep wall. Willo spent a long time trying to climb this directly, but had to give up and sent me to investigate the ground to the left of a corner. There two chimney-cracks led upwards, albeit with difficulty. On easier terrain we reached the shoulder of Pointe Gamba and began the traverse to the gap beyond it. We had to surrender a good deal of the height gained, descending grassy rocks to our right before reaching more broken ground to the left above us by a two metres high vertical step. This led further right by rising and descending movements into the couloir coming down from the gap beyond Pointe Gamba. (5) We only went up the couloir for a short distance, then climbed the rib on our right before moving across a large slab into a second couloir which we followed upwards. Leaving this likewise to the right, we crossed slabs and scree into yet another steep gully by which we eventually rejoined the ridge somewhat above the gap at 9. 30 a. m. We had taken four hours to round Pointe Gamba against our estimate of two hours at the most. If we intended

108

Aig. Noire de
Peuterey
South Ridge.

Features as
indicated:

A= Col des
Chasseurs

B=Pte. Gamba

C=Pte.Welzenbach

D=Pte. Brendel

E= Pte. Ottoz

F= Pte. Bich

G= summit

to finish the route today, we would have to move fast.

From here the ridge rises in three tremendous towers towards the summit wall in front of which a less prominent but obviously very hard fourth (6) tower extends. The route ahead held no possibility of an emergency escape at least till beyond the third (7) tower where a wide couloir looked as if it could be descended with some abseiling.

Stepped slabs, broken by grass ledges, led rapidly upwards. Further on we traversed first slightly then sharply right onto a subsidiary rib which higher up merged almost imperceptibly with the main ridge. Things now became serious. After a few more easy steps, the going got harder and harder. Keeping close to the crest of the ridge all the time, I led up to a somewhat flatter spot where we found a small cairn, probably dating from Dibona's attempt in 1913. Difficult rock steps alternated with very short easier sections of ridge, until we got to some 50 metres below the summit crest of the second tower (counting the Pointe Gamba as the first tower). There we were halted by smooth overhangs. Welzenbach did manage to gain a couple of metres by standing on my shoulder, but was soon forced to give up, so we were obliged to make a detour. Taking the lead again, I descended unpleasant shattered rock steeply to the right before succeeding in making an awkward right-hand traverse, straddling across into a couloir. We moved upwards again until an opportunity arose to traverse out right, then we climbed steep holdless slabs. With great difficulty I turned a two metres high overhang to its left - Willo had favoured climbing it directly by throwing the rope over the top block, but in attempting this awkward manoeuvre he wrenched his shoulder out of its socket. In those days he had suffered repeatedly from shoulder dislocations and due to the frequency with which these occurred he was fortunately so practised in treating it that he managed to jerk the arm back into its socket. Naturally I expected we would now give up, because you can hardly continue this type of climb with an arm that has just been dislocated. But Welzenbach didn't even contemplate such an idea and before

110

I had time to express my thoughts he was already beside me. We stopped for a few minutes so that he could exercise his arm, but then he was in a hurry to press on. From that point, however, he left me to lead throughout.

We went up a gully to reach the ridge near two gendarmes forming the summit of the second tower. We turned the first gendarme and climbed the second one by a hard pitch, then came a six metres vertical drop to the narrow ridge crest. The route ahead to the third tower looked full of problems and I again thought about suggesting a retreat, but we would have a look at it in any case.

After a difficult descent we reached a gap from the right and could then actually climb the next step by its knife-edge crest for a bit. The wall of the third tower now looked terribly smooth and we couldn't see any way of getting up it. After a short stretch on the ridge we accordingly moved onto the right-hand flank and climbed grassy ledges to the right until it became impossible to continue. But the cliff of the tower was no longer quite so offputting and we were able to climb steep slabs directly upwards. Several moves were very difficult - according to current (8) French literature these pitches are graded V - and on one occasion I even had to bang in a rock peg. Above we moved right again with somewhat less bother and climbed a short steep gully to rejoin the ridge right on top (9) of the third tower.

Our altimeter registered 3420 metres, so we had put a good two thirds of the ridge's vertical interval below us (10), but it was already 3 o'clock in the afternoon and the signs of on-coming bad weather were growing increasingly menacing. Black clouds were rolling in slowly from the west and a warm wind was howling across the ridge. In addition, the route ahead promised to be quite exceptionally difficult, if at all possible, and consequently we decided to abandon the climb.

Our tower, which the French named Pointe Welzenbach during Willo's lifetime, falls vertically to the next col. We believed that an abseil would be unavoidable here, but Brendel and

Schaller, the eventual first ascensionists of the complete ridge, in fact climbed down free. (11) According to them we had judged the difficulties ahead correctly - It was exceptionally difficult, and today the South Ridge of the Aiguille Noire still ranks as the hardest rock climb in the Mont Blanc Range. (12)

It goes without saying that, given the right circumstances, we had intended to tackle the ridge again, but Welzenbach's illness and my subsequent expedition plans (13) thwarted another assault. During this period several aspirant guides from Courmayeur repeatedly sought the glory of the first ascent for their native village, but all efforts foundered below the fourth tower (14) where the locals had built up quite a store of ironmongery by the time Brendel and Schaller (15) snatched the route at their first attempt on 26-27th August 1930 in 21 hours climbing time with a bivouac below the final wall of the south summit. (16)

Below our tower we found some melt water and took a short rest, the first one for 11 hours. We returned by our ascent route after all, as the couloir looked very problematic at close range. The retreat was difficult and took almost as long as the ascent. We abseiled all the harder pitches, in total 16. Often we missed the correct line on the complex terrain and only very slowly did we lose height. In the gap before Pointe Gamba it was already pitch black night, but soon the moon appeared enabling us to continue. At 1.45 a.m. we eventually reached the Col des Chasseurs and just before 3 a.m. the hut, almost 25 hours after setting off. Rain beating down woke us in the morning, so then at least we were glad that we had not let things lead to a bivouac.

Author's notes:

1. The second tower (nameless) is a subsidiary one, composed of two gendarmes, under the next main tower (Pointe Welzenbach).

2. First ascent of Pointe Gamba by Paul Preuss and Ugo di Vallepiana on 20th July, 1913. Mayer and Dibona joined the ridge beyond (N of) this tower.

3. Allwein is referring to Pointe Bich (3753m.).

4. Taking into account the various ups and downs, the vertical interval involved from the foot of the climb at 2675 metres is over 1200 metres.

5. In 1912 Mayer and Dibona had reached this couloir fairly directly. The now established route does so similarly from the foot of Pointe Gamba.

6. Allwein has knowingly ignored the Pointe Gamba in this survey of the scene. Consequently, the fourth tower he refers to ahead of them is in fact overall the fifth tower (now called Pointe Ottoz, 3586m.).

7. Allwein has now reverted to including Pointe Gamba in his calculations. Hence this third tower is Pointe Welzenbach-to-be.

8. Written in 1935. Nowadays this section is graded IV and the 1973 edition of the French guidebook rates the crux pitch, called the Welzenbach Slab though led by Allwein, IV+.

9. This seems inaccurate as the ridge crest is logically re-joined before the top. The ascent took place on 24th July 1926 and nearly 9 years elapsed before Allwein was requested to produce this account after Welzenbach's death.

10. The correct height of the third tower (Pointe Welzenbach) is 3355 metres. In terms of present-day time allowances for this route Allwein and Welzenbach were barely half-way to the top of the Aiguille Noire de Peuterey.

11. Nonetheless, it subsequently became standard practice to abseil down to this col, and it is considered that once a party has passed this abseil from Pointe Welzenbach it may find a retreat very problematic.

12. Valid in 1935. It has meanwhile become a modern classic climb. The variable number of pegs nowadays usually found in place has reduced the grade to D/TD accordingly. In its original state it rates TD+.

13. Allwein was a member of the 1929 German Himalaya expedition to Kangchenjunga.

14. Later named Pointe Brendel (3499 metres).

15. Two young Munich climbers. Both were killed in 1931, Brendel on the Predigtstuhl in the Kaisergebirge and Schaller on Kangchenjunga with the German expedition of which Allwein was also a member.

16. Pointe Bich (3753 metres).

Zermatt
Breithorn
North–West
Face.

Klein
Matterhorn
on right.

Zermatt Breithorn

FRITZ RIGELE

I WAS breakfasting at the Post hotel in Zermatt on a mediocre morning in August 1926, contemplating what a soloist could realistically undertake in the district. The week before I had been climbing with two friends in the Bernese Oberland, but I had now come to this mountain paradise without making advance arrangements to meet anyone. After some reflection I decided to make the Rimpfischhorn my immediate objective.

Just at that moment Willo Welzenbach wandered jauntily into the room and greeted me cheerfully. He took me over to another table and introduced me to a group of his friends from the Munich Academic Alpine Club. The general gossip was soon interrupted by Welzenbach's call to get down to brass-tacks and consider the pressing matter of the day's programme and what we were going to do next. Welzenbach assured us that he had something new up his sleeve. "Probably the North Ridge of the Dent Blanche," I queried dubiously. "No, the North-West Face of the Breithorn," came his swift retort. In answer to my objection that Bethmann-Hollweg had already done the route years ago I was enlightened in detail to the contrary, and I had to agree: Welzenbach was right. (1) There was yet another side to this ever popular Zermatt viewpoint that merited our attention.

To cut a long story short, I packed my things together and went ahead by myself to the Gandegg inn, situated at over 3000 metres, while Welzenbach and Fritz Bachschmidt who joined us as the third member of the party preferred to follow after lunch. Evening saw us gathered together at the inn which cannot be praised for the exemplary Swiss restaurant service to which I have otherwise been accustomed. Exorbitant prices were charged for this inhospitality (2) and we were not sorry to get away from the shabby establishment at 1. 30 a. m.

Our plan of action was to descend onto the south-west branch of the Gorner glacier (3) and ascend it to the foot of the 1100 metres high North-West Face. Our first problem would be various steep steps and ruptures on the lower part of the ice face where we would have to decide whether to continue up the ice face itself, which despite its steep angle could not throw up any desperate difficulties subject to firm snow conditions and proper cramponing technique; or whether, in view of the sérac barrier north-west of the summit dome where ice blocks jutted out threateningly, we should avoid the danger of falling ice by making for the rock barrier on the north-east side. In that case we should have to climb the ice spur supported by the rock barrier, cross the main bergschrund and overcome the very steep upper section of the ice face above. Even then one last big question mark confronted us in terms of the snow-plastered slabby summit barrier.

The day's first decision was to leave Welzenbach's tent sack behind. We doubted that there would be any sites on the face large enough to set it up and reasoned that the less we carried the faster we would move, an argument that appealed to our aversion to heavy rucksacks.

We were pleasantly surprised that the waning moon still lit up the scree and rock slope leading down to the glacier. There we roped up and just one hour after leaving the hut Welzenbach led the party onto the North-West Face of the Breithorn, his sharpened ten-point crampons already strapped on for action.

Almost immediately we encountered resistance, climbing left towards a steep ice ramp. Deep powder snow lying on the glassy ice gave us a great deal of hard work. The moon had by now disappeared and darkness surrounded us. As we pushed upwards, the steepening terrain loomed larger in front of our eyes. Welzenbach ploughed the trail in the deep fresh snow, chopping many a step in the smooth surface underneath. As we emerged from this dark bay of ice, the powder snow got

116

thinner until we clung like flies to the bare ice face. Then I led through and got to grips with an unusually steep ice bulge. I cut footholds and handholds and, thanking God my actions were done under the cover of night, I drove a seven inch long ice peg into the ice - not simply as a belay point but rather to serve as a handhold and then as a foothold. I did also clip the rope into a karabiner attached to its ring to protect myself and my friends from a free fall. While I banged in a second peg - reluctantly due to the severe morning frost and the hard ice, daybreak allowed us to survey our immediate surroundings. Climbing straight up was going to cost us a lot of step-cutting and ice pegs, not to mention sweat, but to our left we spotted a narrow ice ramp. It rose steeply and was ruptured by large crevasses, but looked easier and quicker to climb than the vertical wall above us. So I pulled the rope through the ring of the upper peg and lowered myself back down, sacrificing the lightweight aluminium peg given to me by Viktor Sohm for testing. (4) We ascended the ramp towards the adjoining rock barrier as the first rays of the sun caught the uppermost section of the face and threw a dazzling light on the summit sérac barrier. We saw the apparent explanation why the face had never been climbed despite its challenging position - Whoever is still in the firing line of the summit sérac barrier at 5.30 a.m. on a fine summer morning runs the risk of being struck dead by its crashing debris which is loosened by the first touch of the sun. The enormous ice blocks and avalanches at the foot of the face had already testified silently but dramatically to the accuracy of these reflections; and they also settled the question of which line we should take. We climbed several difficult schrunds to our left and reached the north-easterly rock barrier.

In dry conditions this rock barrier would not be excessively difficult, but coated in powder snow and adorned with icicles it seemed to be the crux. Welzenbach led it with composure and safety - the two most important qualities for a mountaineer. As last man on the rope I felt reassured watching his controlled movements. One at a time we followed very cautiously, groping for sound holds under the powder snow, mindful of the treacherous film of glassy ice that threatened to whip our feet from under us. Upon completing these delicate rock pitches we took our first rest on a short level section of the snow spur above, well and truly satisfied with our progress. All the mountains around us were glowing in the sun, but by contrast we still remained in the chilly shade.

Now it was my turn to lead again. At first the going was laborious breaking through the crusty surface of frozen snow at every step, but soon my ten-point crampons were biting into firm ice, ankles straining to place all the spikes into the steep slope simultaneously. A bit later we stood before what seemed a major problem - A bergschrund extended right across the whole face, its lower edge caved in, its upper lip presenting a six to eight metres high vertical ice wall. I baffled Bachschmidt by borrowing his ice-axe. Armed with two axes and exercising the utmost caution I crawled on my stomach, distributing my weight as evenly as possible, along a powdery snow bridge - there was simply no alternative - and saw that my hunch about the condition of the vertical wall was right. It was just soft enough to ram in an ice-axe, albeit not without a protracted effort, and yet sufficiently firm for the shaft to be used with complete confidence as a point of support for a rope belay, a handhold or a foothold - always assuming the wooden shaft had an adequate breaking strain. Slowly I cut bucket steps upwards, belayed by the rope looped over the ice-axe shaft which next became my foothold. For a bit I worked on ahead with the second axe, then I rammed it into the wall and flung the rope over it so that I could pull out the lower axe. I then repeated this little game until I had overcome the vertical step. I certainly can't deny that in effect I stooped to using the axe shaft as a wooden ice peg. Securely belayed from above, my two companions followed confidently even with only one ice-axe between them.

As we got higher, so the snow grew thinner and soon we came

118

onto bare ice. Due to my complete confidence in the security afforded by crampons I continued without cutting steps, straining ankle joints to their very limits to get all ten crampon spikes into the ice. Below us the wild ice face fell away abruptly into the bottomless shadowy depths. This induced Welzenbach to pull out his clinometer and declare as coolly as you please: "The angle is 60 degrees." After that I was quite relieved to see a small rock outcrop protruding ahead of us, and just below it melting ice had conveniently left a thin crevice that provided a welcome resting place for our feet. Balancing carefully on my crampons I wouldn't have fancied the awkward job of hacking out a stance. To ease the strain on our ankles we now changed our climbing style and nicked small steps up each pitch to a belay stance, sometimes finding a boulder jutting out as if for this purpose. Resting places of this sort increased as we approached the final problem on the route, the snow-plastered rock barrier immediately below the summit dome. But the nearer we got, the more feasible it looked and eventually it turned out to be nothing more than a harmless slope of shattered rocks caked in snow. Nothing else could delay our triumph and at 11.30 a.m., precisely ten hours after leaving the Gandegg, we stood on the summit - already trodden by thousands of mountaineers via its normal route (5), but never before climbed by its North-West Face.

Author's notes:

1. Welzenbach was wrong! He had not traced an account of Bethmann-Hollweg's climb and had been led to believe that it took a line further east nearer the Triftji Ridge. The ill-defined topography of the face offers a possible explanation of this misunderstanding based upon secondhand verbal information. The original route made an easier indirect start by a diagonal approach from right to left across the lower part of the face, formed by the headslope of the Triftji glacier: Dietrich von Bethmann-Hollweg with Oskar and Othmar Supersaxo, 3 September 1919. On the second ascent (1 August 1926) Welzenbach, Rigele and Bachschmidt took a more direct line nearer the left edge of the headslope and so they can at least be credited with an improved variant or more generously with the 'direct route'. This account by Rigele was published three years later in the

1929 issue of the German and Austrian Alpine Club Yearbook under the title of 'The Zermatter Breithorn: first ascent by the North-West Face'. The correct facts about the Bethmann-Hollweg ascent had still not been unearthed and further erroneous reports were issued in Swiss Alpine Club publications before Marcel Kurz, the renowned guidebook writer and topographer, eventually revealed the true details in the 1944 edition of 'Die Alpen'.

2. This was the case for many years.

3. The Unterer Theodul and Triftji glaciers merge and flow into the Gorner glacier from the south-west.

4. The ice peg was at a very experimental stage in 1926. Sohm was an Austrian pioneer of skiing and ski mountaineering.

5. On the way down the ordinary south-west flank route the party made a quick detour to bag the Klein Matterhorn.

Glockner Campaign, 1926

UPON his return from Zermatt Welzenbach's thoughts turned once more to the Glockner region. He now felt ready to tackle its biggest unclimbed faces. Whenever he visited an area, without fail he examined his surroundings for worthwhile future objectives. In this way he had spotted the potential of the Klockerin North-West Face while descending after his momentous success on the Grosses Wiesbachhorn two years previously. The fierce North Wall of the Grossglockner had won his admiration during a high level traverse in his youth and its challenge had later nurtured his ambition. The Eiskögele North Wall completed a formidable trio of objectives. Strangely, he had never even seen this face and was relying upon an enthusiastic report from a well-known Viennese mountaineer, Emil Meletzki, who considered it one of the greatest remaining problems in the region.

So knowing exactly what his aims in the Glockner region were, in the late summer of 1926 Welzenbach devoted himself with total commitment to the task of resolving them. His boundless drive during this tenacious campaign typified his approach to climbing and reflected his determination to carry out all his plans. Not that he needed any encouragement to visit this his favourite area in the Austrian Alps ever since his first summer expedition there six years earlier.

In his current capacity as appointed adviser to the Munich Section of the German and Austrian Alpine Club on their management of the Schwaiger hut, he was always furnished with a ready-made reason to spend a few days there. Ostensibly his visit with Karl Wein was for the purpose of scientific research. Yet while the pair of them were assiduously excavating holes in overhanging snow cornices on the Kaindl Ridge to the general amusement of tourists ascending the trade route on the

Wiesbachhorn, the truth emerged that they were plotting their assault on the neighbouring North-West Face of the Klockerin. No sooner said than done... And just two days later they got to grips with the North Wall of the Eiskögele. It took a nasty break in the weather to frustrate their designs on the Grossglockner North Face. With conditions ruined for some time they travelled home.

Next morning dawned fine and Wien received a terse telegram in Mittenwald from a restless Welzenbach in Munich: "Arrive Scharnitz one o'clock. You rope, me pegs. Laliderer North. Willo." That evening they reached the Falken hut, a six hour walk from Scharnitz. Next day they climbed the North Wall of the Laliderer Wand, probably the most famous climb in the Karwendel. Its immense wall is among the most intimidating features in the Northern Limestone Ranges, akin to the greatest cliffs of the Dolomites. Their fine form during a rapid ascent - in contrast to the subdued retreat with Merkl and Bechtold four years before - boosted confidence for a crack at the Grossglockner North Face, postponed for two weeks in the hope of the snow and ice clearing from the rocks.

Though there were few other climbers attempting comparably serious ascents, strangely and without knowing it, Welzenbach was twice nearly forestalled in his Glockner ambitions. Richard Gerin and Roman Szalay attempted the Grossglockner North Face in late August 1926. Despite dreadful conditions they battled their way up ice slopes treacherously covered by fresh snow to the foot of the summit rock wall. Here their hopes immediately foundered on the thickly verglassed rocks and they were forced to escape by the Bergler Couloir onto the North-West Ridge. This Austrian pair were understandably convinced that in such conditions nobody else would even try let alone succeed in climbing the face during the few remaining weeks of autumn, and they confidently looked forward to renewing their challenge early the following summer. They were to be as disillusioned by the action of 19th September 1926 as by 15th July 1924 when the North-West Face of the Grosses Wiesbachhorn had been snatched from under their noses. On that occasion, on the very evening after the first ascent and initially unaware of the day's events, they had met up with Max Hilber at Mooserboden in readiness for their proposed attempt. In both cases they had reckoned without Willo Welzenbach.

Klockerin North-West Face.

The Glockner Walls

WILLO WELZENBACH

IN OUR present age of over-exploitation of the Alps reports of new climbs are greeted with a certain amount of scepticism as a matter of course. This scepticism stems from the general belief that all worthwhile alpine problems have long since been solved; consequently anything new is automatically tainted with being artificial, far-fetched and meaningless. This biased attitude is greatest in respect of new climbs made in regions which are overrun each year by hordes of mountain walkers and in which pioneering activity dates back to the very beginnings of mountaineering.

The Glockner region, visited annually by crowds of tourists in numbers hardly encountered in any other area, serves as a perfect example of this prejudice. Precisely in this region secluded areas, almost untouched by man, abound away from the main stream of tourist traffic. You can find ascents that have not been repeated in several decades and until recently there remained untrodden faces of outstanding beauty and awe-inspiring grandeur that had gone unnoticed throughout the course of time. My experiences in climbing these faces have left me with some of my richest mountain memories.

North-West Face of the Klockerin

The special attraction of Mooserboden lies in the surrounding profusion of scenic contrasts that enrapture mountain and nature lovers alike: lush pastures (1) fed by rushing mountain streams, tremendous glaciers, glistening snow fields and towering rock faces. Amidst all this grandeur the awesome north-west precipices of the Klockerin, soaring 1000 metres above an isolated glacier cwm, stand out as the indisputable show-piece of

Mooserboden.

I had often admired this face, no less in the dusky grey of dawn than in the glittering light of the setting sun, and it always seemed as magnificent as it was frighteningly formidable. When Fritz Rigele and I were descending from the Wiesbachhorn in July 1924 after making the first ascent of its North-West Face, we had a view from the Kaindl ridge across the ice-coated slabs of the North-West Face of the Klockerin down to the snow gullies at its foot that were furrowed by rock-falls, and we agreed at that time that nobody would ever set foot on the face. A few months later I mentioned at a lecture that this flank was one of the big problems left in the Glockner region, but that it would remain unsolved for all time. I never dreamt that I would be privileged to find a route up this face just a couple of years later.

I had seen the face several times since, had thought about it even more, and slowly but surely I had changed my opinion. What I had originally considered impossible and irresponsible now seemed well within the range of my capabilities. It is a well-known fact that things which strike fear into us at first lose their terror as soon as you look at them from a set distance and reflect upon the circumstances thoroughly and uninfluenced by momentary moods or impressions. In this manner I had gradually convinced myself that the face could be climbed.

In late August 1926 my friend Karl Wien and I were based at the Schwaiger hut, devoting several days to a scientific investigation of snow cornices on the Kaindl ridge. (2) Though we had ample opportunity to study the face, we were too far away to spot potential problem pitches. So one muggy afternoon we trudged across soft snow slopes to the Klockerin and descended its west ridge for a bit. Then we lay on our stomachs on a flat slab protruding above vertical precipices and peered into the depths. What we saw shattered my confidence. Our gaze first lighted upon a smooth ice couloir sweeping down from the gap below the summit to a ramp coated in thin ice or elsewhere covered by dreadfully crumbling rock. And all we could see between this ramp and the gentle slopes of the Klockerin glacier far below was air, thin air. It was impossible to speculate whether and how this precipice could be overcome, and even assuming we succeeded, the upper parts of the face were undoubtedly going to present a severe challenge. We were at least happy to note that the face remained in the bitter cold shade till late afternoon and that, despite the hot sunshine beating down on the summit snows, not even the tiniest drop of melt water was dripping on the face and no rocks at all were being dislodged.

By the time we got back to the Schwaiger hut that evening, we had made up our minds to attempt the face the following morning.

We left the hut in the pitch black of night and descended endless zigzags towards Mooserboden, leaving the track behind a grassy hump (Point 2108 metres) about 100 metres above the valley floor to head across scree and moraines onto the Klockerin glacier. Meanwhile the new day had broken. The basin of this glacier is fed by snow and ice avalanches that tumble down the tremendous bounding cliffs in winter and summer alike.

We kept as far away as possible from the left-hand bank of the glacier to avoid the danger of falling ice from the hanging glacier on the Bratschenkopf. The going was tiresome on the scree and boulder-covered ice. Above a short steep section we reached the upper glacier cwm, covered by dirty avalanche snow. From here we had a good general view of the whole face. A small broken hanging glacier is embedded in the lower part of this imposing flank to the right of the summit line and a snow couloir falling from its left-hand edge to the glacier obviously provided a start to the route. We hoped to turn the wall towering above the hanging glacier by a rock rib on its left and then use the ramp above to make a rising traverse right into the summit couloir which had to supply our exit line.

After a short look round we entered the snow couloir by a convenient avalanche cone heaped up at its foot. Soon the angle

127

steepened to an enormous cleft marking the spot where the moving glacier broke off from the snow of the couloir. We crossed this bergschrund by a wedged block of ice and continued up the increasingly steep gully, keeping to its left side in case of falling ice from the hanging glacier. When we were about level with the séracs and the gully petered out below impregnable cliffs, we traversed onto the enclosing rock rib.

Here we went up nicely stepped rock with unexpected ease and I would go so far as to add that the climbing was really enjoyable. But the conditions soon changed. The rock became slabby and thickly verglassed as we gained height. We were held up quite a long time forcing one steep pitch glazed with crystal-clear water ice, before we drew level with the barrier girdling the face to the right of our rib. Above this vertical barrier we could now see that the angle relented temporarily. Everywhere the slabs were plastered with snow and ice, so that we were left with no option but to strap on crampons.

Now began a long rising traverse to the right along the impressive ramp. Mostly we cut no steps, just nicking out a few when we encountered smooth ice or had to cross narrow gullies and grooves. Gradually we neared the fall-line of the ice-filled summit couloir from which we were separated by a short wall. We made for a rotten rib coming down on the far side of this wall. Balancing in sloping steps on steep ground we removed our crampons and after this proceeded even more carefully upwards on this shattered rock. From the top of the rib a short traverse back left led to the foot of the couloir. It was chock-full of clear greenish-blue ice and rose unrelentingly to the summit gap where an ice wall gushed down like a frozen waterfall. Energetically I got to grips with the ice and hacked a zigzag line upwards. The sun was streaming through the gap above onto the uppermost rocks. First a few icicles broke off from their edge and rattled down the gully, then several tiny stones whizzed past our ears. We paid no attention to them. But when the air hummed with a rock the size of my fist hurtling between my friend and me into the depths, that was just too much for us. We traversed onto the right-hand wall and climbed its steep rock. Loose boulders heaped on one another called for the utmost caution. After a few pitches the angle of the rock eased and scarcely a stone's throw away I saw the West Ridge glittering in sunlight. We accelerated our pace up to the crest and followed the final metres of the ridge to the snow-capped summit of the Klockerin.

We enjoyed a long summit rest gazing at the vast glacier expanses glistening in the sun. Behind loomed the huge figure of the Glockner, the view of its shaded north-facing precipices claiming my entire interest as so often before. There indeed waited a virgin face, as majestic as the mountain to which it belonged, a face that occupied my every thought - the North Face of the Grossglockner.

It was late afternoon when we got ready for the descent to the Schwaiger hut. From the shale rocks of the Fochezkopf we once again looked across the icy flanks of the North-West Face of the Klockerin and we could hardly grasp that this wall had capitulated with so little resistance.

North Face of the Eiskögele

One day after our ascent of the Klockerin by its North-West Face we walked from Mooserboden across the Kapruner Törl to the Rudolfs hut. Our next objective was the North Face of the Eiskögele. Admittedly I had still never seen this face, but I had heard so much about it from authoritative sources who had even dubbed it one of the finest and final problems in the region.

Because the mountain is literally named the "ice cone" I accordingly visualized its North Face as an ice flank marked by threatening hanging glaciers and as a result I was amazed to be confronted by a sheer rock wall, merely crowned by a snow dome.

Towards evening we inspected the face with the hut warden's binoculars and what we saw inspired little hope in us. Seemingly smooth compact rock towered heavenwards. But the picture changed dramatically as the setting sun beamed its last rays across the ridge onto the face. Then suddenly a dark shadow was cast onto the face, starting just below the top at a gap on the West Ridge and extending diagonally left down to the centre of the face. Now, where there was a shadow, there also had to be of necessity a formation projecting it. Consequently we knew there was a rib parallel with the track of the shadow and behind the rib there logically had to be a couloir. We based our plan on these observations. We hoped to master the less steep lower section of the face without undue difficulty and on the upper cliffs we reckoned that the couloir or the sharp rib to its right should provide a line of ascent.

In the early hours of the following morning we encountered the unexpected as we were descending the path by flickering lantern light towards the Ödenwinkel glacier. The track led as a man-made staircase steeply down smooth slabs, but suddenly it ended abruptly, melting away at our feet into the pitch black of night. Below me I saw nothing but the faint impression of some moraine boulders a good ten metres lower down. The track had apparently broken away due to some sort of natural phenomenon and had not yet been rebuilt. Seeing no alternative and somewhat put out, we finally uncoiled the rope, looped it round an iron spike planted in the slab and abseiled onto the moraines. Then we stumbled down a diabolical boulder slope to the glacier.

Daybreak confronted us with our intimidating surroundings. We contemplated towering cliffs, imposing peaks and soaring ridges all at close range. A semi-circle of mountains, dominated in the centre by the beautiful form of the Eiskögele, encloses the upper basin of the Ödenwinkel glacier and its North Wall overshadows the head of the valley. Now standing so near to it, we could spot all its features and weaknesses, yet this in no way detracted from its forbidding and offputting effect. The total height of the wall from the level glacier floor amounts to some 800 metres. Of this, the steep crevasse-riddled glacier slopes girdling the foot of the face account for about

130

EISKÖGELE 3426m
ÖDENWINKELWAND HOHER KASTEN |3192

Ödenwinkel Glacier

Eiskögele North Face.

two fifths of the height, so three fifths remain for the rock wall itself.

At six o'clock in the morning we started up the steep glacier slopes, wending our way between the many gaping crevasses, lucky to find snow bridges in the vital places. On this terrain we rapidly gained several hundred metres height and came to a debris-strewn snow slope leading up to the bergschrund. Ascending from right to left we crossed this by a thin bridge and so reached a steep ice slope immediately below rocks. Nicking out an occasional step, we slanted in the same direction up to the foot of a broad ill-defined rib jutting out to the left of a recess in the summit fall-line. This rib rises to the centre of the face, petering out somewhere near the beginning of the couloir sweeping up to the right. It clearly presented the best line of ascent.

After taking off our crampons we moved onto shattered rocks. The terrain gave exceptionally unpleasant climbing. Nailed boots can hardly grip on holds and steps caked with frozen grit. About 100 metres higher a vertical step blocked our progress and forced us into the slabby recess indented in the face on the right of the rib, but after a few pitches we managed to traverse back onto the rib which we climbed with ever increasing difficulty as it gradually merged into a barrier of smooth slabby walls.

Here it finally became impossible to continue, but further right and level with our stance we now saw the foot of the couloir mentioned at the outset as rising to a gap on the West Ridge. Filled with black water ice it looked distinctly uninviting and there was not even the thinnest layer of snow to make things easier. A traverse of about 30 metres along narrow rotten ledges brought us to the start of the couloir. At first we were able to climb the left-hand wall for 30 metres until bulging slabs forced us to enter the ice gully. It was most exacting and delicate work hacking out a ladder of steps in this bone-hard ice. At every blow of the axe the sheet of ice lying on the smooth rock cracked ominously with such an uncanny hollow

132

echo that we were petrified by the thought that the entire layer of ice could be set in motion and plunge with us into the depths. Because of this we endeavoured to escape back onto the left-hand wall at the very earliest opportunity. There we powered our way some 60 metres upwards placing intermediate peg belays.

For a long while I had been toying with the idea of getting onto the sharp right-hand rib but time and again I had been deterred by a barrier of overhangs. Thanks to our steady progress upwards we were now above the level of these overhangs and it seemed that our best course lay in getting onto the rib. Accordingly we cut steps across the couloir to our right and started to climb boiler plate rock towards the crest of the rib. I still recall this section as being especially unpleasant and nerve-jangling. Pebbles frozen into the film of ice coating the rocks were all we could resort to for holds and steps. I heaved an enormous sigh of relief when I eventually found a small stance on the rib from where I could belay my companion.

Our assault now proceeded at the double. A few short steep steps merely checked our pace momentarily. Soon afterwards we exited onto the West Ridge and, as we sat down briefly, in some ways I felt as if my soul had been released from a nightmare.

In a matter of minutes we ascended soft snow slopes to the summit. (3) From its symmetrical snow dome you could not have had the faintest notion that we had just emerged from such a savage cliff. We did not rest long as we still wanted to traverse the Johannisberg and descend via the Obere Ödenwinkelscharte to the Rudolfs hut that same afternoon.

We glissaded down soft snow to the Untere Ödenwinkelscharte. From the extreme edge of this saddle where the slope plunges towards the Ödenwinkel glacier we viewed the wall we had just climbed. And we had to admit that if we had seen the wall beforehand from this point, we would probably not have attempted it, so offputting and downright desperate did it look. This impression was dramatized even further by the sun gleaming

GROSS GLOCKNER 3798 m.

DIRECT

WELZENBACH

BERGLER COULOIR

PALLAVICINI COULOIR

Grossglockner North Face.

through a fast gathering veil of föhn clouds.

In humid heat we laboured up rock and snow to the Johannisberg. Again we saw the Glockner North Face rearing upwards,
now much closer at hand than from the Klockerin. We also
observed that the upper rock wall remained sheathed in an
armour of ice despite continuous fine weather. Yet we found
this view irresistibly tempting and despite the unfavourable
conditions we planned to tackle the wall within the next few
days. On that occasion it was not to be, for the weather deteriorated during our descent to the Rudolfs hut and next morning we left the Stubach valley in torrential rain and dense
swirling mist, nonetheless firmly resolved to return at the
first opportunity to claim our last outstanding objective.

North Face of the Grossglockner

The Grossglockner truly deserves to be known as the monarch
of the Austrian Alps. Anyone who has ever seen the mountain
from the Oberwalder hut must recognize that rock and ice formations of incomparable splendour harmonize here into a setting
that is unequalled elsewhere in the Eastern Alps and compares
with the most savage landscapes of the Western Alps.

The idea of attempting to climb the Grossglockner by these
precipices is highly enterprising and it is quite remarkable
that Karl Hofmann contemplated this bold idea as early as
1869 (4), at a time when exploration of the Glockner region was
still in its infancy. Three problems stood out conspicuously:
the tremendous ice couloir sweeping down from the gap between
the Grossglockner and the Kleinglockner, running parallel to
this the North-East Ridge and further right the North Face. In
1876 the couloir was the first line to be conquered, climbed
by and named after Pallavicini. (5) Next in 1911 Richard Gerin
and Otto Pitschmann vanquished the North-East ridge, and by
a curious coincidence exactly 50 years had elapsed since the
ascent of the Pallavicini couloir when the North Face finally
capitulated to complete this triple saga.

Even in my mountaineering youth this wall had attracted my

135

attention during a first visit to the Glockner region shortly after the end of the Great War. On that occasion I did not dream of putting it on my list of climbs to be done. I simply admired its structure - the steep bluish ice of its grooved lower slopes, the ice-encrusted rocks higher up.

However, success breeds ambition. When the great Tauern climbs fell into our laps one after the other in the late summer of 1926, it became our dearest wish that we might conquer this last Glockner Face to crown our achievements.

On a chilly September morning a few weeks after our success on the North Face of the Eiskögele my friend Wien and I cycled from Bruck up the Fusch valley. Leaving our bikes at a shelter on one of the last pastures, we crossed the Pfandlscharte to the Franz Josefs Haus where we lazed away the rest of the day viewing the Grossglockner and studying thoroughly the icefalls of the Inneres Glocknerkar glacier that we should need to negotiate during the coming night.

It must have been about 2.30 a.m. as we left our room by its ground level window to save any bother and set off down to the Pasterze glacier on a moonless night. The stars were fast fading as we crossed the glacier and at daybreak we stood below the impressive ice-falls obstructing our approach to the Inneres Glocknerkar. As the dim light of dawn did not allow us a clear general view of the terrain ahead, to begin with we went directly up the ice-fall, hoping to find a route through haphazardly. In fact things went quite well for a time, but then the crevasses increased in number and size, and the ice-fall grew more chaotic until we seemed to have reached an impasse. Repeatedly repulsed by enormous chasms, we decided to escape right by a long traverse away from the ice-fall to the rock rib running down from the Glocknerwandkamp (6) to the Pasterze. Ascending steep firm snow on its left-hand flank we quickly reached the flat glacier terrace of the Inneres Glocknerkar.

Meanwhile the sun's first rays lit up the summit rocks of the Glockner and the crazy pinnacled ridge of the Glocknerwand. Soon the ice chute of the Pallavicini Couloir became bathed in

136

its glow, and before long its warmth brought the first rocks rattling down.

We sat down on the snow and eyed our face. It lay in the shade and a good thing that was too. At this time of the year at least the danger of stone-falls could not be very great.

What sort of technical difficulties could we now expect? Firm snow covered the ice gully at the start and that assured us of quick progress. But bare ice glistened in the central zone and that promised hard work. Higher up, as the slope steepened and approached the snow-plastered rocks, there appeared to be good snow again, or could it be loose powder? The latter would be most unpleasant. Lastly we considered the summit wall, its slabby rocks towering up and offputtingly steep. Could we master it? As yet that was an unanswerable question. For a short while we sat there wavering, undecided. Perhaps we ought to climb the Pallavicini Couloir which looked far more enticing and inspired substantially greater confidence than the North Face? Yet almost immediately we felt ashamed of our shilly-shallying behaviour, and pulling ourselves promptly together we hastened up to the bergschrund.

On the far side of this cleft our first difficulty already lay in wait in the form of a smooth ice wall, six to eight metres high. Belayed by my companion I cautiously stepped onto the remnants of an old snow bridge wedged tightly in the bergschrund and began to chip steps and holds in the sheer ice. Slowly I won my way upwards metre by metre. Close on half an hour had elapsed by the time we had overcome this vertical pitch and stood at the start of the evenly angled ice chute above.

Swirling snow flurries whipped up by the chilly morning breeze were streaming down the narrow grooves in the face. Luckily, snow ribs remaining intact between these fluted grooves enabled us to ascend at high speed and we led through alternate pitches. Crampons bit reassuringly into the bone-hard snow and only occasionally did we need to wield the axe.

Something like an hour had passed as we neared the central zone of the ice face. Now the route took on a different complexion. Gradually the snow ribs petered out and the angle steepened noticeably as we moved onto bare ice. Exhausting cramponing soon made our ankles ache so painfully that we decided to hack a line of steps up the shimmering ice. Wien undertook this task with great zeal, but all the same our tempo was slowed down considerably. Even when we once again had snow under our feet after a prolonged step-cutting session, we still couldn't feel pleased about it. The snow was only superficially consolidated on the surface and underneath it was in a somewhat powdery condition. Of course, the sun's rays never find their way onto the uppermost and steepest section of the face - at least not in autumn. Our crampon spikes could not get a proper hold in such loose stuff and as a result I decided to scoop out steps, each one with two blows of the axe, to give our feet a more comfortable stance and our ten-point crampons a secure purchase into the firmer ground underneath.

Laboriously we now climbed in a bee-line towards the summit cliff. The steep ice couloir sweeping down its centre looked so intimidating that we chose to make for the foot of a rock rib rising slightly right to the North-West ridge. The snow cover grew steadily thinner, our axes swung into hard ice and then we got onto the lowest rocks. They were slabby, steep and plastered in snow and ice.

In the absence of a suitable spot to take off crampons, temporarily we continued to climb with them on. A little higher we had spotted, so we thought, a platform where we planned to sit down in comfort. Unfortunately, at the position of the expected platform the angle of the cliff turned out to be merely a few degrees less steep with no more of a stance than elsewhere. Several times more we were fooled by similar illusory platforms until we got fed up, crouched down on a more imaginary than actual resting place, unstrapped our crampons, and ate - shivering all the while. Wherever else we looked the sun was shining - below on the glittering Pasterze glacier and almost within striking distance on the snow cap of the Glocknerhorn; only our flank lay in the bitterly cold shade.

We were soon glad to get away from our uncomfortable resting place and we continued up the rib to a vertical riser which we tried to climb in vain. Repeatedly we were beaten back by its steep smooth slabs. Eventually I noticed a narrow ice gully recessed in the rocks on the left of the rib. I was sure the gully would go, but descending into it proved problematic. To deal with this difficulty I pulled a long piton out of my pocket, drove it into a crack right to its head and abseiled into the gully. On steeply sloping slabs I made do with an awkward stance. It didn't take long before my friend joined me, but he then had desperate trouble pulling the rope down through the peg ring.

For about one rope length we now moved up on the edge of the rock and ice. We had to scrape out holds with great care on the snow-plastered rocks or cut steps single-handed in the ice. Above the level of the vertical riser we managed to move back onto the rib and climb its airy crest of slabs up to a delicate thin snow arête abutting against the uppermost rock wall.

Beckoning us close by, the North-West ridge gleamed in the afternoon sun. Slanting up left we climbed a few more steep rock pitches, traversing several ice gullies in the process, and then emerged onto the North-West ridge 40 metres below the top. Just a short clamber up nice warm rocks and we shook hands by the summit cross of the Grossglockner. (7)

We sat there a long while basking in the heat, gazing southwards to the jagged sea of the Dolomites extending across a blue horizon, northwards to the Salzburg Limestone Ranges glistening above lush green valleys.

The sun was sinking in the west as we descended the Hofmanns glacier to the Pasterze. After recuperating for a few hours at the Franz Josefs Haus we set off under a silvery moonlit heaven for Bruck to catch the night train back to Munich. We dragged our weary limbs up to the Pfandlscharte and at the saddle we again rested briefly. Sharply etched against the silvery grey of the night sky, the top of the Glockner jutted out above the pinnacled ridge of the Freiwandspitz. All our tribulations were forgotten thanks to the beauty of the world around us. A feeling of total satisfaction overcame us. After all, our dearest wish had come true; we had conquered the majestic mountain by its most majestic face... And we were accompanied down the pitch dark Fusch valley to the train by the happiness found in achievement.

Author's notes:

1. Flooded by the Mooserboden reservoir in 1955.

2. At the time Welzenbach was preparing a scientific thesis about snow structures and movements for his doctorate.

3. They took 7 hours from the hut to the summit, a remarkably fast time for a first ascent of this calibre and probably not bettered since.

4. In the same year Hofmann opened up the normal east side approach to the Grossglockner from the Pasterze glacier. Hofmann's "bold idea" did not however relate to the North Face. Admiring "these precipices" from the Johannisberg, he elaborated: "More than ever before the desire was aroused in me to make a direct ascent from the Pasterze (glacier) to the Glockner peak... A terribly crevassed ice slope would have to be crossed to reach the ice couloir rising about 3000 feet (Hofmann uses 'feet' and overestimated the height by one third) to the saddle (between the Grossglockner and Kleinglockner)... I can't say with certainty whether it would be prudent to set foot on the adjoining rock walls..."

5. Count Alfred Pallavicini with three Heiligenblut guides. For the Eastern Alps this success was comparable in historical significance with the first ascent of the Marinelli Couloir on the East Face of Monte Rosa.

6. The Glockner bivouac hut was erected on the crest of the Glocknerwandkamp at 3255 metres in 1958.

7. In the annual journal of the Munich Academic Alpine Club 1925/26 Welzenbach reported that they spent 8 hours on the face and 4 hours over the approach. With a clinometer he measured the angle of the lower ice slopes at 53 degrees, steepening to about 70 degrees by the summit wall. Heights such as the exit point onto the North-West ridge were based upon altimeter readings.

Illness and Comeback

1926 HAD witnessed a brilliant climax to Welzenbach's achievements in the Eastern Alps. Of the three big north wall climbs during September he rated the Klockerin the most imposing because of its enormous scale, the Eiskögele the most delicate due to the loose terrain together with a virtual absence of reliable belays. Perhaps as a warning to others, he emphasized that such ground demanded absolute reliability and total mutual confidence. Technically, he had no doubt in classing the Grossglockner, "a great mixed rock and ice route", as the hardest undertaking. These successes, added to the breakthrough in ice climbing techniques on the Wiesbachhorn in 1924, have permanently linked Welzenbach's name with the history of mountaineering in the Glockner region.

Everything had gone so well for Welzenbach during his Glockner campaign. He had always been in the right place at the right time. His ambitions satisfied in this region and his experience of big wall climbing invaluably widened, he now felt and seemed ready for the greatest faces of the Western Alps. Ironically, the hand of fate was set to strike him cruelly.

A weekend meet had been arranged at the end of October with Karl Wien and other club friends in the Kaisergebirge. During the train journey from Munich to Kufstein Welzenbach complained of intense pain in his right arm, and this got so bad that he travelled back to Munich the next morning. For the Saturday Welzenbach entered in his logbook: "Arm ailment", for the Sunday he merely noted: "Homeward journey alone due to severe pains". Below this he later added: "Beginning of November 1926 to end of May 1927 illness".

Welzenbach was now afflicted with a perplexing illness for six months, mysterious in its origin, difficult to diagnose with certainty, baffling to treat. The most plausible explanation of the medical cause is supplied by Welzenbach's history of ill-health during childhood. As a one-year-old baby he had contracted diphtheria. Still a young boy, he was laid low with osteomyelitis - inflammation and poisoning of the bone marrow. This developed into a minor tuberculosis of the bone. It left him frail, with weak arms in particular, and its aftereffects were sufficiently serious to earn him dispensation from sporting activities at school. It seems possible that the disease may have remained dormant throughout his youth and early manhood. Some sort of localized tuberculosis of the bone may then have recurred in late 1926. Welzenbach told relatives that he had banged his arm badly during a climb, and that this had resulted in a sore and increasingly painful elbow. A severe knock could not in itself account for his arm condition, but may have suddenly aggravated developing symptoms. The physicians soon decided that Welzenbach must be suffering from ankylosis - the bones on either side of the elbow growing together. This at any rate was the assumption upon which surgery was based. In Munich he was operated on by Professor Lexer who cut the bone and used grafts to re-create a joint, at that time an advance in surgical methods. The operation proved reasonably successful with his upper arm, but his forearm remained powerless. No improvement occurring, Welzenbach feared that his arm might become permanently paralysed. In a second operation in Leipzig Professor Sauerbruch managed to restore a little strength to his forearm.

For five months, meanwhile, Welzenbach was obliged to undergo treatment at a Swiss sanatorium in Leysin. At first his condition worsened, but even so his natural resilience was reflected in the letters he wrote left-handed to his parents and friends. He especially wanted to be kept informed about all the activities of the Munich Academic Alpine Club. In his first letter to Karl Wien, dated 15th December 1926, he described his own state of health briefly and promptly apologized: "Now I've written enough about myself, will make sure it doesn't happen again."

142

In the spring Welzenbach completed his convalescence at Samedan in the Engadine valley of Eastern Switzerland. On 14th May 1927 he wrote to his parents that he had experienced no adverse reactions to his most recent course of injections and that his tuberculosis was no longer active, adding: "The doctor told me that one can't even be sure whether my illness actually was tuberculosis. It seems unlikely that tuberculosis would have cleared up in such a short time." At this time, due to his disabled arm, he was obliged to forgo his earliest opportunity to visit the mountains of Asia. It grieved him to decline an invitation to join Willi Rickmer Rickmers' 1928 Russo-German expedition to the Trans-Alai Range in the Pamirs. He vented his bitter disappointment in the same letter of 14th May: "It is maddening to think that thanks to my previous alpine achievements I would have been a first choice... Borchers is very sad that I can't take part in the expedition." Welzenbach had little option in taking this decision. Apart from requiring further surgery to his arm, more to the point he could not now possibly afford the time for a six months long expedition. He needed to catch up with his work and his studies for the advanced civil-service examination. He was also preparing a scientific thesis on snow structures, advised and assisted by Professor Wilhelm Paulcke of Karlsruhe.

At Whitsun Welzenbach returned home. Reasonably as he was restored to health, he was left with a rigid right elbow joint. He immediately started intensive training on straightforward peaks in the Karwendel and the Kaisergebirge. Initially though, he was distressed and depressed by the limitations now imposed upon his technical capabilities as a result of his physical handicap. The illness had put extreme rock climbing beyond his scope and for a short while he feared being forced to modify the nature of his activities in the long term. However, nothing could keep him away from the mountains and his innate optimism quickly reasserted itself. With unflinching willpower he set about overcoming his disability. His sustained efforts despite considerable discomfort and pain reflected his tremendous strength of character and illustrated his enormous enthusiasm for alpinism.

Inevitably, Welzenbach's handicapped right arm made him depend far more on his legs and feet. Where others climbed using their hands on straightforward steep rock, he was in any case accustomed to proceeding in an upright position relying entirely on his exceptional surefootedness. He had always placed his confidence in technical competence and balance climbing rather than muscular strength. Such a technique was to prove itself well suited for the intimidating walls of rock and ice, with their treacherously unstable terrain, that were yet to become his principal objectives in the Western Alps.

Considering the length of his illness and the serious impediment of a permanently weakened right arm, Welzenbach staged an astonishing comeback during the summer of 1927. Disappointed with his first few performances on rock, he turned his thoughts to ice routes. Obviously he would not have forgotten his ice climbing techniques and on such undertakings he would not suffer as much of a disadvantage as on rock.

So it came about that on 16th July 1927, with Karl Wien, he climbed the Pallavicini Couloir on the Grossglockner. Together with the Grosses Wiesbachhorn North-West Face it shared and still shares the distinction of being the best known ice climb in Austria. Its first ascent in 1876 had been a remarkable achievement for the period. In an age of neither crampons nor pitons the leading guide, Josef Tribusser, cut the then record number of 2500 steps in seven hours. Just how far this climb was in advance of developments in alpine climbing techniques is illustrated by the fact that it was repeated only once in the next 45 years. What made this success of Welzenbach's all the more astonishing was that he accomplished it despite not having sufficient arm strength to ram his axe properly into hard snow, despite being unable to use his axe as a balancing support on rising traverse movements to the left. The climb supplied reassuring evidence that his superb footwork remained unimpaired. Naturally, on this occasion

144

Wien led throughout. Not content with making merely the 6th ascent of the Pallavicini Couloir, they added a direct finish by climbing straight up to the Obere Glocknerscharte, and a brewing midday storm. By this tactic they kept to the ice all the way. Their time of $5\frac{1}{2}$ hours from the Hofmanns hut to the summit of the Grossglockner was so fast that when they reached the Oberwalder hut in the early afternoon and the mist lifted, they saw "some of the visitors trying to spot the two people in the Pallavicini Couloir!"

After this climb Welzenbach wrote in the monthly mountain magazine, Der Bergsteiger, that he assessed the Wiesbachhorn North-West Face as significantly harder than the Pallavicini Couloir. He based this judgement upon the difficulty of the ice bulge on the Wiesbachhorn and went on to reaffirm that on this bulge ice pegs were used by Rigele and himself solely as a belay and not as an artificial climbing aid - a fact misinterpreted with monotnous regularity by climbing historians ever since.

Welzenbach's aims for his summer holiday in the Mont Blanc Range were amazingly ambitious in the circumstances. He had obviously been greatly encouraged by his experience with the Pallavicini Couloir. His first objective was the Hirondelles Ridge on the Grandes Jorasses. Descended in 1911 by Geoffrey Winthrop Young's party with Josef Knubel, it still awaited its first ascent. (1)   But here all the difficulties were on rock. Welzenbach coolly countered the misgivings of Karl Wien, again his companion: "You'll just have to lead all the hard pitches." And so on 1st August they set out from the Frébouze bivouac shelter. From the Col des Hirondelles they climbed as far as a U-shaped gap about half-way up the ridge. Wien was "astonished how quickly and competently Welzenbach was able to follow despite his rigid elbow joint". Above this point Wien was beaten back by "a shallow dièdre of smooth waterwashed rock" (the later Fissure Rey, V+). Of the hardest "25 feet of the crack" Young - a man not given to exaggeration - had remarked: "They seemed to all of us as we descended them as unclimbable by

145

any sane man as they had been pronounced by more competent judges inspecting them from below." Welzenbach and Wien were left with no option but to retreat.

Back at Courmayeur they joined forces with Eugen Allwein, Philipp Borchers and Erwin Schneider. Welzenbach excepted, this gathering constituted the complete climbing party for Rickmer Rickmers' 1928 Pamirs expedition. (2) They promptly returned to the Grandes Jorasses, but this time attentions were directed to a traverse of the West Ridge from the Pointe Marguerite to the Pointe Walker. It was an outing enjoyed by all, for the pleasant rock climbing and for the airy positions above the intimidating North Face.

Now Welzenbach felt prepared to tackle the boldest project of this campaign. Two years previously from the Aiguille Blanche de Peuterey he had marvelled at the ribs, buttresses and couloirs of the Brenva Face - one of the most impressive walls of rock and ice in the Alps. Meanwhile he had conceived the plan of trying to make a direct ascent from the south bay of the upper Brenva glacier to the summit of Mont Blanc. Several mountaineers had independently given serious consideration to a direct line up the face - these included R. W. Lloyd, Paul Preuss, George Mallory and in particular Thomas Graham Brown - but as yet nobody had made an actual attempt. All efforts had been concentrated on the original Brenva Ridge route which still enjoyed a very high reputation. First climbed as early as 1865, this route had only been repeated by twenty parties up to the end of 1926. Graham Brown, the eventual pioneer of three great climbs on the Brenva Face (3), was at the time unaware that any potential competition to his ambitions existed.

Welzenbach and his companions decided firstly to make a reconnaissance ascent of the Brenva Ridge. This would permit a more thorough examination of the most promising lines on the face proper. At the Torino hut they were obliged to sit out a series of snowstorms. When the weather cleared, they postponed their climb for a day due to avalanche danger.

Borchers and Wien volunteered to prepare the route across the Col du Trident to the upper plateau of the Brenva glacier, while Schneider and Welzenbach took to the snow arêtes of the Rochefort Ridge. In the early hours of 11th August the "bath-tub" steps cut up the ice slope to the Col du Trident ensured fast time being made to the Brenva glacier, so fast that they brewed tea for an hour awaiting the first glimmer of dawn. Aware of the impending threat posed by a thickening veil of clouds gathered over Mont Blanc, they climbed straight up the grooved ice of the broad Güssfeldt Couloir to join the Brenva Ridge about one third of the way up at its famous ice arête. Poor visibility caused brief problems in finding a route through the wall of séracs onto the easy upper snow slopes and also deprived them of a close-up inspection of the main face on their left. They crossed the summit of Mont Blanc battered by a growing storm in white-out conditions.

Looking back on this climb, Welzenbach took stock of the Brenva Ridge and similar great classic climbs. He reflected objectively upon revised concepts of difficulty in the light of technical progress and contemporary attitudes: "We had required slightly over four hours for the climb itself. Once one of the greatest undertakings in the Alps, it has now become a comfortable half-day outing. All the classic routes undergo this curious change to a certain extent. I have often considered the reasons. Is it the effect of continuous developments in climbing techniques and equipment aids, is it the result of a change in climbers' attitudes towards the mountains? There's a lot of truth in the first contention, but the second point is the decisive factor. The present generation tackles alpine problems more as a matter of course and with an absolute feeling of superiority. This mental approach inspires physical performances and is a prerequisite for success. But is this development to be welcomed or regretted? In terms of progress it is definitely welcome. Yet it is regrettable that all the classic routes of our alpine pioneers thus decline in importance and are robbed of their prestige. Perhaps after us - who think

147

ourselves so superior - another generation will come and be-little the routes which today seem like the ultimate achieve-ment."

Any ideas of a return to the Brenva Face during the remaining days of their stay were washed out by abysmal weather. Three weeks later Graham Brown and Frank Smythe found a direct line to the summit of Mont Blanc by their Sentinelle Rouge route. Welzenbach and Wien had also harboured designs on attempting the Aiguille Verte by an unspecified line on its North-East Face above the Argentière glacier. This plan too fell foul of the weather. On a murky morning at the Lognan inn Welzenbach decided to cut his losses and travel home im-mediately.

By Welzenbach's previous standards the summer's campaign would have rated as disappointing. As it was, he had satisfied himself that his climbing career was far from finished. Coming so soon after a prolonged illness and despite his disability, his courage won admiration in France and Britain. On 2nd Sept-ember 1927 J.P. Farrar, President of the Alpine Club from 1917-19, wrote expressing his delight that Welzenbach had not been obliged to give up climbing and adding what a grievous loss that would have been for everyone. Karl Wien commented that Welzenbach put such tremendous effort into his climbs that his companions could almost completely forget about his physical handicap.

Welzenbach began 1928 ski touring in the Samnaun group. In climbing terms this was set to be his most frustrating year, one of missed opportunities and without any lengthy mountain-eering trips. He had to face the consequences of his illness. Several minor operations on his right arm were still necessary and he had to prepare thoroughly for his autumn examinations. He found it impossible to conceal his bitter disappointment at having had to decline the chance to explore the Pamirs for six months. Most of his climbing companions either went to the Pamirs or joined an expedition to the Caucasus. In their ab-sence he spent far fewer weekends than before in the Northern

148

Limestone Ranges.

Welzenbach produced a number of contributions to mountain-eering literature, perhaps some consolation for his comparative inactivity. Apart from personal accounts - "North Walling in the Glockner Region" and "The Brenva Face of Mont Blanc" - he assisted Paulcke in the preparation of the 8th edition of Zsigmondy's classic book, "Die Gefahren der Alpen" (4), com-piled with Wien a survey of "The History of Mountaineering in the Glockner Region" for the German and Austrian Alpine Club Yearbook and again collaborated with Paulcke on the article "Snow, Cornices and Avalanches" for the Journal of Glaciology. This last piece of writing resulted in part from a fortnight's research in April with Paulcke studying avalanches on the Eiger glacier.

In March Welzenbach had set out one night to ascend the Grossvenediger on ski straight from the valley (this involved an unusually long approach and 2800 metres of ascent), but was forced to turn back in the morning due to bad weather. Occasional similar bursts of activity punctuated spring and summer. In early August he visited Zermatt very briefly and went up the Matterhorn by the Hörnli Ridge. More indicative of a future intention, albeit one never pursued further, is a note in his logbook for 2nd August: "Afternoon reconnaissance of Matterhorn North Face".

The disappointments of 1928 did not deter Welzenbach and were tempered by his improved professional qualifications and status. With hospital treatment and examinations a thing of the past, he managed two ten-day visits to the Western Alps in 1929. His confidence boosted by a bag of 34 summits in the Austrian Kitzbühel Alps - on one Sunday he took in 17 tops with Hans Reimer, he partnered Georg von Kraus in the Mont Blanc Range from 21st June to 1st July. They quickly recovered from being "repulsed by the North-East Face of the Aiguille Verte" on the 24th to climb the same mountain by its Whymper Couloir two days later - having traversed Les Courtes from the Argent-ière hut to the Couvercle hut in between. Their only other outing was an ascent of the Aiguille de Bionnassay by its North-West Face, a 1100 metres high snow and ice flank, in the record-breaking time of $2\frac{1}{2}$ hours from the Tête Rousse inn. (5) On a rare trip to the Dolomites Welzenbach climbed the Fünf-fingerspitze. (6) With Deitlhauser, Reimer and Tillmann he climbed the Kederbacher Route on the 1800 metres high East Face of the Watzmann in the Berchtesgaden Alps. This is the classic route on the highest rock wall in the Eastern Alps. Here they had a lucky escape when an enormous rock avalanche thundered down the cliff, boulders tearing their rope to shreds in several places. Two less fortunate climbers below them were swept down the whole face to their death.

Welzenbach's September visit with Heinz Tillmann to the Bernese Oberland centred specifically upon the longstanding problem of the Fiescherwand, a forbidding 1250 metres high wall of rock and ice; also the most extensive cliffs belonging to any one mountain in the region. By way of thorough pre-paration for this climb they first traversed the Eiger, obtaining excellent views of their main objective from the Mittellegi Ridge. In the event, a combination of unforeseen delays on the approach to the foot of the face and uncertain weather dissauded Welzenbach and Tillmann from pursuing their attempt. They alleviated their bitter disappointment by a typically positive on-the-spot decision to make the second ascent of the Fiescher-wand's North-East Rib. (7) In fact they found this a far harder alternative than they had bargained for. (8) It took them almost nine hours to climb instead of $4\frac{1}{2}$ as estimated. Uncertain weather and poor conditions then forestalled any ideas of another attempt. They settled for concluding their stay with a traverse of the Schreckhorn. Failure on the Fiescherwand Direct had whetted Welzenbach's appetite. Happily, Tillmann felt equally committed to the cause. Welzenbach gave notice of their re-solve: "We knew one thing: we would return and we would conquer the face."

1930 saw the publication of Welzenbach's thesis, "Investigat-ions into the stratigraphy of snow deposits and the mechanics of snow movements together with conclusions about processes of accumulation". Several years of patient and thorough research under the guidance of Professor Wilhelm Paulcke went into this highly acclaimed work. It had earned Welzenbach his doctorate at the University of Karlsruhe. In the course of climbs and ski tours his companions had frequently been called upon to cooperate in unconventional experiments, such as 'sawing off' cornices with their skis and setting off avalanches. Hans Reimer recalls how one such avalanche on the Unterberghorn near Kössen (east of the Kaisergebirge) flattened the trees in the basin below. After this incident they judged it prudent to make off quickly! Not surprisingly Welzenbach became known in mountaineering circles as the 'avalanche doctor'. The thesis itself was expounded in two unequal parts. Welzenbach outlined his investigations, experiments and results under subheadings dealing with snow, cornices and avalanches. Here he was particularly concerned to examine the long-term formation of snow and ice, and to assess their properties of strength. Proceeding from his own conclusions he was then able to draft practical ideas and suggestions about future protection against snowdrifts and avalanches. With the implementation of these measures his research had contributed to reducing the dangers of winter travel, most notably on alpine roads.

In terms of the regions Welzenbach chose to visit and the sequence of his activities, 1930 was a virtual replay of 1929. There were however two significant differences: he chased more ambitious aims and, despite several rebuffs on major undertakings, recorded one resounding triumph. His early summer campaign was again devoted to the Mont Blanc Range. Here he had previously concentrated on mixed climbs on the higher peaks, with the exception of the attempt on the South Ridge of the Aiguille Noire de Peuterey. It was quite natural that he had shown little interest in the pure rock climbs during his trips to the Western Alps, as the Northern Limestone Ranges within easy reach of Munich presented ample opportunity for such routes during the rest of the year. Now he wanted to sample the solid granite rock of the Chamonix Aiguilles. After a training exercise on the Aiguille de l'M, he traversed the Grépon with Rigele and Wien. Welzenbach revelled in the delightful and varied rock climbing on this superb Chamonix classic. Above all, he was surprised by the different techniques required for the cracks and chimneys of sound but smooth granite compared with limestone, a coarser rock profusely endowed with holds but far less reliable. He was also impressed by the exposure on this ridge.

For Welzenbach the Grandes Jorasses North Face presented the greatest goal in the Mont Blanc Range. At the time it was one of the "three ultimate challenges in the Alps", together with the Eiger and Matterhorn North Faces. As early as 1907 Geoffrey Winthrop Young had "spent more than one night and many futile days upon the beginnings of the central ribs up the north face", but "after a number of unfruitful years Josef (Knubel) and I (Young) gave up hope". In 1928 Rand Herron, Leopoldo Gasparotto and Piero Zanetti with the guides Armand Charlet and Evariste Croux were forced back from 200 metres up the Walker Spur. Charlet found the rock too smooth and steep for traditional free climbing and was rigidly opposed to employing artificial aids. Welzenbach had long since been convinced of its feasibility subject both to careful route planning and to timing an attempt to coincide with a low level of objective danger. He had already eyed the face with more than passing interest, notably during his ascent by the West Ridge in 1927 and again from the Aiguille Verte the summer before. On 4th July 1930 Welzenbach, Wien and Rigele walked up to the Leschaux hut to consider the possibilities at close hand. Welzenbach's cryptic logbook entry for 5th July reveals little: "Attempt Jorasses N Face". Karl Wien later explained the events. Sizing up the mountain from Montenvers, the party had straightaway recognized that conditions were incompatible with their intentions. The rocks were still plastered in snow. However, their observations were not fruitless. Their curiosity was aroused by the steep hanging ice flank sweeping down

152

from the Hirondelles Ridge and to the left of the Walker Spur towards the foot of the face. They had in fact spotted a fine line, now known as The Shroud, that was not to yield for 38 years and then only after a protracted struggle. (9) They set out expecting that one of two ice couloirs would provide access from the foot of the face to the icefields above. Wien reported: "Unfortunately we were bitterly disappointed in our hopes of finding practicable rock or ice on the eastern side of the face. The foot of the face is composed of very smooth steep slabs which were coated by a sheet of thin ice. We tried to cut steps up the steep ice which from a distance had looked like an ice couloir, but we discovered that here too smooth slabs lay just underneath the surface. The wafer-thin plaques of ice were not bound to the rocks and so gave us no security. As a result our attempt was repulsed in its beginnings. We all fully understood the situation and accepted the need to retreat."

Though Welzenbach never actually made another attempt on the Grandes Jorasses North Face, this was only due to adverse conditions during his subsequent visits to the Mont Blanc Range. It continued to preoccupy his mind. In early July 1931 Welzenbach and Merkl walked up to the Leschaux hut for a cursory inspection of the Jorasses, this a day trip between their two-part ascent of the Grand Charmoz North Face. Based at the hut they found Anderl Heckmair and Gustl Kröner who had been vainly besieging the Jorasses North Face for a fortnight, with three unsuccessful attempts to their credit. On 22nd July 1933 Welzenbach noted in his logbook: "Jorasses North Face reconnaissance". This time he was accompanied by Alfred Drexel and Erich Schulze, but again poor weather prevented more than a routine approach to the foot of the face. (10)

The conditions remained unsuitable for extreme climbs during July 1930, so Welzenbach's party contented itself with modest expeditions: the Aiguille du Chardonnet, the Tour Noir and a traverse of the Aiguille de Talèfre. In contrast to many similarly ambitious contemporaries, Welzenbach did not abandon the mountains just because his main objectives became untenable. He craved constant action and simply modified his plans according to prevailing circumstances.

On another fleeting trip to the Dolomites Welzenbach fitted in two fine climbs on the Langkofeleck (Spallone del Sassolungo) and the Grohmannspitze (Sasso Levante). In the Glockner region he carried out the long ridge traverse from the Hoher Tenn to the Grosses Wiesbachhorn and climbed both these peaks individually on a separate visit.

At the beginning of September he and Tillmann returned as pledged to Grindelwald. While they limbered up on the Wetterhorn, their minds grappled with the real reason for their presence - the Fiescherwand. The die was already cast...

Author's notes:

1. Made on 10 August 1927 by an Italian party (G. Gaia, S. Matteoda, F. Ravelli, G. Rivetti) with the guides Adolphe Rey and Alphonse Chenoz. Five days earlier Rey and Chenoz had climbed to the top of the crux pitch (the Fissure Rey that defeated Wien) on a reconnaissance while waiting for their clients who had gone down to Courmayeur to buy provisions in anticipation of a long siege on the ridge. Rey first led the crack placing 3 pegs which he used as hand and footholds, then left in place a fixed rope attached to the pegs abandoned by Knubel at the top in 1911.

2. Allwein, Schneider and Wien made the first ascent of Pik Lenin on 25th September 1928.

3. First the Sentinelle Rouge with F.S. Smythe, 1-2 September 1927; second the Route Major with F.S. Smythe, 6-7 August 1928; third the Pear with the guides A. Graven and A. Aufdenblatten, 5 August 1933. See his meticulously researched book "Brenva", published 1944.

4. Helmut Dumler's 1969 revision of this work was translated into English under the title "Hazards in Mountaineering", published in 1973 by Kaye & Ward.

5. Now a French Alpine Club hut.

6. Its official Italian name, Punta delle Cinque Dita, has never been adopted by the Germans or Austrians. This applies to all peaks situated in the part of Italy that was annexed from Austria after World War I.

7. Described in next chapter.

8. The outstanding Scottish climber Robin Smith described his 1960 first British ascent of this rib with Brian Wakefield to Dougal Haston as "3000 feet of tiptoeing from frozen pebble to frozen pebble with no protection and hardly daring to breathe too hard in case they (the pebbles) melted out."

9. First ascent by René Desmaison and Robert Flematty, 13-26 January 1968.

10. The first ascent, by the Croz Spur, was achieved 28-29 June 1935 by Rudolf Peters and Martl Meier. The Walker Spur was not climbed until 1938 by Riccardo Cassin, Luigi Esposito and Ugo Tizzoni.

Fiescherwand.
The third dark
mass to right of
route line at base
of wall marks the
buttress and rib
climbed by
Welzenbach in
1929.

The Fiescherwand

WILLO WELZENBACH

ORIGINALLY got to know the Bernese Oberland in winter. During March 1923 I roamed the vast glacier expanses of its south side on ski and trod the main summits. On that occasion I also ascended the Gross Fiescherhorn for the first time from the south by the Walliser Fiescher glacier, and from its summit I looked northwards over a bottomless abyss. I must confess that these precipices filled me with horror at that time.

A few weeks later I read an article in Guido Lammer's book "Jungborn" (1) about his ascent of the Mönch. In his description, initially published in 1886, Lammer reflects on the challenge of the Fiescherwand, writing: "I consider the unsolved problem of a direct ascent of the Gross Fiescherhorn by its immense and intimidating wall above the Grindelwald-Fiescher glacier to present the finest, also the most exacting challenge in the Bernese Alps, and only the most resolute mind and most persevering aspirant will succeed in accomplishing this tremendous feat." Having read this, I began to consider the problem mentally. I reasoned that if Lammer had debated the possibility of an ascent of the face as early as 1886, then it could not have looked so impossible that a mountaineer of the modern school could not risk such an undertaking.

A year later, at Easter 1924, I caught a glimpse of the face for the first time in the course of the rail journey up to the Jungfraujoch. There was a short stop at the Eismeer station, so I got out of the train and looked through the window-opening cut out of the rocks. The mountains were enshrouded in mist. But the raging gale suddenly tore a gap in the mist, revealing for a few moments a rock and ice face that rose incredibly steeply from the glacier snows to dizzy heights. As I was picking out obscure gullies and cracks on this wall, already forcing a route up its horrifying cliffs in my mind, clouds swirled in and whisked this scene of inconceivable magnitude and wildness away into unreality. This brief sight left me with a tremendous impression of the face; it seemed formidable and forbidding, and yet especially desirable precisely because of its inaccessibility.

I did not visit the Bernese Oberland again for several years. I strove after major objectives in the Pennine Alps and in the Mont Blanc Range, in the Bernina and in the Tauern. Nevertheless, irrespective of my other alpine aims, I always remembered this particular face and I was determined to attempt it as soon as an opportunity arose.

In the late summer of 1926 I heard about the attempt that Dr. Kehl, the well-known Berlin alpinist, had made with the Grindelwald guide Ammatter. (2) I learnt that other famous mountaineers were interested in the face: namely, Yuko Maki of Japan, the conqueror of the Mittellegi ridge; Smythe, among the best known of the young English guideless climbers; and, last but not least, the late Captain Farrar (3), the great Englishman whose activities reach back to the classic age of mountaineering.

With so many serious rivals around, hasty action was called for. But in the autumn of 1926 news reached me that the Fiescherwand had been conquered: Amstutz and von Schumacher, university graduates from Bern, had forced a route up the face in a fifteen hour effort on 3rd August 1926. This information meant a great personal disappointment, because it seemed that an objective hankered after and cherished for years had escaped me.

The feat of the Bern pair constituted an outstanding achievement, for they were the first to break the spell of the Fiescherwand and to set foot on its forbidding precipices. However, their route was not entirely satisfactory; it led up far to the right of a direct line to the summit by the rock rib already mentioned by Farrar and culminating about 800 metres away from the summit at Point 3804 metres on the north-west ridge.

The north face direct of the Fiescherhorn consequently still awaited its conqueror. This realization revived my interest in the face. Yes, I might say that this problem had now doubled its appeal in that the route taken by the Bern pair only further underlined the enigma of a direct ascent to the summit. At that time I became even more firmly set in my resolve and I told myself over and over again: The Fiescherwand Direct must yield.

Towards the end of 1926 I was suddenly afflicted with an ailment to my joints. I had to spend several tedious months in a Swiss sanatorium being nursed back to health. Day after day I looked out longingly at the mountains, but I had really given up any hope of ever being able to climb them again. In the summer of 1927 I returned home, a stiff arm the remaining consequence of my illness. Admittedly, I still often thought about the Fiescherwand, but it seemed to have retreated beyond reach into the distance as an unattainable object of my dreams. Eventually, thanks to the surgeon's scalpel, my arm once more became tolerably mobile. I had learnt to use it again by many months of single-minded application. By training ever so hard I became more and more capable of overcoming this physical handicap and could even forget it.

Meanwhile my mountaineering activities took off afresh. Whereas in 1928 I found the Swiss ridge of the Matterhorn hard, in the early summer of 1929 I already managed a traverse of the Courtes, an ascent of the Aiguille Verte and the Aiguille de Bionnassay by its north-west face. In the autumn I again started thinking about the Fiescherwand and this rekindled my old climbing passions. I wanted to take a close look at the face that had been occupying my every thought.

I therefore decided to travel to Grindelwald with my friend Tillmann, a fellow member of the Munich Academic Alpine Club, having quickly gained his support for my plan. To start with we wanted to undertake a none too strenuous training climb that should simultaneously also enable us to see and survey the

Fiescherwand. What could be more appropriate than the Mittellegi ridge on the Eiger? We took ten hours over the ascent from Grindelwald to the Mittellegi hut, but this long-winded approach was offset by one big advantage. We had the Fiescherwand before us the whole day and we could study all its couloirs and ribs as well as the stonefall and avalanche lines. The next day we needed merely two and a half hours for the once so feared ridge. It was a superb ridge, amazingly exposed. To our left the view down the almost vertical cliffs of the south face onto the crevasse-riddled Grindelwald-Fiescher glacier; to our right steep ice slopes down to the green meadows of Alpiglen. Yet this route no longer has much in common with climbing in the true sense of the word. It was gymnastics, pulling up on fixed ropes that lead in an almost uninterrupted sequence towards the top. The main tower that for decades had defied all attempts thus offered no resistance. Resting by the summit cairn, we gazed across to the wall of the Fiescherwand, menacing by its mere presence, and southwards to the towering giants of the Pennine Alps. We descended the southwest flank (4) to the Eiger Glacier station and ambled down to Grindelwald in the evening twilight.

The constant view of the Fiescherwand from the Mittellegi ridge and the continual mental preoccupation with the problem had built up a nervous tension that pressed for a solution. For us it was therefore a foregone conclusion to put the Fiescherwand next on our programme so as to settle the outcome quickly.

North of the Fiescherwand there extends in its foreground the greenish ridge of the Zäsenberg which is surrounded like an island by the surging ice of the Lower Grindelwald and Grindelwald-Fiescher glaciers. The Zäsenberg seemed the perfect bivouac site for Fiescherwand aspirants. But Tillmann countered: "Let's go to the Schwarzegg hut instead, we can have a proper night's sleep there and if we set off in good time tomorrow morning, then we can be at the beginning of the route just as early as if we bivouac on the Zäsenberg." I could not ignore the logic behind these words, so we went to the

Schwarzegg hut. Twelve hours later I certainly regretted this decision bitterly.

We set out from the hut at 2.30 a.m. (5), crossed the Lower Grindelwald glacier just above its large icefall and intended to follow its left bank downwards for a while before crossing directly westwards onto the slopes of the Zäsenberg. But already fate was against us. In the dark we slipped and slithered around on the steep moraines, then returned to the glacier only to be forced back left by sudden drops and deep crevasses. We lost precious hours clambering among steep polished rock slabs and greasy mud-coated ice without finding a way out in the dark. Day was already dawning when we reached the open slopes of the Zäsenberg. We ascended scree and broken rock slopes, and at last crossed gently inclined glacier terraces to the level snow basin at the foot of the Fiescherwand.

Now that we finally faced this steep wall, almost 1300 metres high, the conquest of which we had desired for so long, it inspired cold fear in us, so frighteningly inaccessible did it look.

If you approach a limestone cliff in our native mountains, however off-putting it may look from afar, it will reveal its secrets as you get nearer. Gullies, ledges and cracks will become discernible, and after prolonged observation your eyes will work out a way to the top. But here, as frequently in regions of gneiss rock, it was just the reverse. The nearer we got to the foot of the face, the steeper it seemed to tower above us, the more devoid of holds the smooth slabs and the glistening ice appeared to the eye.

Above the yawning bergschrund the lower half of the face rose in flights of slabs. The rock grew steeper and steeper with increasing height, suddenly leaning back so as to disappear half-way up below the summit snow face. At its steepest point the rock was verglassed and coated by powder snow. We gazed up at the smooth snow flank higher still and the gleaming ice bulges, captivated especially by the ice barrier crowning the face. Freshly fallen ice and huge avalanche cones at the foot of the face testified to the forces of nature raging hereabouts.

For a long while we sat at the edge of a thin snow bridge that arched over the bergschrund, and stared up at the face. Ought we to risk it? It attracted us enormously, but then the voice of common sense reasoned: Even if you get up above the rocks of the lower third of the face, you will very probably be repulsed by the verglassed slabs in the central zone where Dr. Kehl was also compelled to abandon his attempt. Yet conversely we reasoned: A great deed has never been achieved by hesitation - and my companion crossed the bergschrund to the rocks on the far side. But soon he paused, looked upwards once more and we conferred again.

I glanced at my watch, it was already 8 a.m. I looked up at the sky and saw fish-shaped cloud banners extending across the northern horizon, a sure sign that a change for the worse was to be expected in the day's weather. We reconsidered the matter: If we started the climb now, in view of the anticipated difficulties we would most probably be caught by a storm in the central zone. A bivouac would then be inevitable; and if the bad weather persisted, then tomorrow we would have to battle for our lives to get off the face. At this point common-sense prevailed. Tillmann returned slowly across the berg-schrund and we ambled down the steep avalanche cone to the level snow basin at the foot of the face.

If it is depressing to have to retreat defeated from a face after a tough struggle, the knowledge of not having dared to fight at all is far more shameful. Quite logically our minds now focussed upon how to make amends for our reverse and somehow still use the day profitably. Our eyes fell upon that impressive ridge, prominent on the right of the face and conquered three years previously by Amstutz and von Schumacher. Its attraction was too great. We already visualized ourselves climbing its airy crest in warm sunshine. We estimated its height as 1000 metres and reckoned we could reach its exit by 1 p.m. - up to which time the weather would hold out, we hoped. Those were our calculations, but we were grossly underestimating the difficulties of this route.

Without further delay we crossed to the steep rock spur at the point where the rib rises from the glacier. It was 8.30 a.m. by the time we stood below our new starting-point. All haste was called for. We bombed up steep ice gullies left of the crest and then made a rising right-hand traverse by ice ledges to the steep friable shale on the west side of the rib. No step and no hold was reliable there. Boulders crashed into the depths beneath our feet, holds crumbled in our groping fingers. We pressed on upwards without a stop to put this unpleasant section behind us quickly. Above, while we were resting briefly on a rock ledge, an ice avalanche thundered down the face to our left, below which we had stood a few hours previously, toying with the idea of starting up it.

The rock became sounder, the ridge rose steeply. Only then did we rope up. Difficult but magnificent pitches led endlessly upwards, and it was already 2 p.m. when we reached the steep snow ridge rising elegantly to the slab defences of the summit wall. According to our calculations we should have been at the exit by 1 p.m.! Yet a hard piece of work still lay ahead of us in overcoming an almost vertical section of the face. We stopped to put on crampons. Ghostly shreds of mist were streaming up from the Grindelwald-Fiescher glacier. From the south-west thick damp mist was building up over the main ridge and soon enshrouded the Fiescherwand. Slowly it began to snow.

Hurriedly we climbed the steep snow ridge towards the final rock wall. It was delicate and exacting work, for the snow, being wet and heavy, had no adhesion to the underlying ice. At the same rate that we gained ground, the weather got worse. Eventually we stood below the final wall. Tillmann set about it, but his initial exertions were in vain. The rocks were sheathed in ice, steps and holds were filled in by fresh snow. Once again Tillmann tackled this pitch which was blocking off access to a groove continuing above. With the utmost effort he managed to hammer a peg into a thin crack, clip a karabiner on and pull the rope through. Desperate pull ups and lay backs ensued, nailed boots scraping against the smooth wall, then he disappeared from view into the groove. The rope ran out slowly, I could hear nothing but the howling of the storm and the gentle sound of the snow settling. At last, through the raging gale, I heard Tillmann's voice calling me on.

My fingers numb, tensely I worked up the rocks. The snow ran down under my shirt-collar and up the sleeves of my jacket. My disabled arm was threatening to fail me. Taxing myself to the limits, I struggled into the groove and jammed myself between its icy walls. The tricouni nails on my boots bit into the thin ice, I dug my fingers into the snow, I moved upwards bit by bit. I negotiated about ten metres in this manner before the groove eased off somewhat. I moved round a corner and joined Tillmann.

We had now done the hardest part of the route. The roof of the cornice crowning the face hung out barely 50 metres above us. We climbed the last few rope lengths on steep but sound rock. Soon we were crouched in the hollow below the cornice. A couple more blows of the ice-axe by Tillmann broke through this final hindrance and we stood on top on gently inclined slopes. At that moment the mental tension of the previous hours ended abruptly like a nightmare.

It was 5.10 p.m. There was no longer any question of ascending to the summit of the Gross Fiescherhorn. We would be lucky to reach the Bergli hut or the Jungfraujoch station in the mist and the blizzard.

We started down, breaking in up to our knees in the soft snow at every step. It was dusk when we reached the level ground of the Ewigschneefeld. Trudging on endlessly, we came upon an indistinct track and followed it without knowing its source or destination. According to the compass it was guiding us to the Ober Mönchjoch. The terrain steepened again, our halts grew more frequent. Then the ground flattened out and the track began to descend; we had crossed the Ober Mönchjoch. We staggered along in the flickering light of our lantern until a shimmering glow broke through the mist, becoming brighter

164

and clearer, finally revealing the entrance to the Sphinx tunnel which led us inside the mountain to the Jungfraujoch station. (6)

A few days later, the weather having become too unsettled for big routes, we climbed the Schreckhorn by the Anderson ridge. When the mists parted briefly during the descent, I had my final glimpse of the Fiescherwand for 1929. We did not find it hard to leave Grindelwald the next morning, as fresh snow had fallen low down in the woods and the mountains were enshrouded in sombre clouds. But we knew one thing: we would return and we would conquer the face.

A year elapsed, and once again I travelled with Tillmann to the Bernese Oberland. A blazing hot day saw us on top of the Wetterhorn. Amongst all the formidable mountain peaks round us, again it was the Fiescherwand that held us irresistably spellbound. We recognized that we were addicted to the face and convinced ourselves that this time we would emerge the victors.

Next day we ascended boulder-strewn grass slopes from the Lower Grindelwald glacier to the Zäsenberg, enjoying one of those fine days that autumn so willingly bestows upon us. There we sought out a suitable bivouac site. After an evening of cooking and eating we slept about as well as one might expect in an improvised bivouac.

On the morning of September 5th we left the site late, actually much too late for the major undertaking we planned. Tillmann contended that the night is made for sleeping and not for stumbling about on pathless terrain. It was 5.15 a.m. when we set off from the bivouac, and 7.15 a.m. by the time we arrived at the foot of the face. Today we felt well acquainted with its prospect. Once viewed with fear, now we eyed it with cool objectivity and soon believed we had worked out a practicable line.

The rocky lower part of the face is seamed by a series of parallel ribs. If we started up the face at the foot of the third rib (7) from the right, we reckoned on being able to traverse left by a steep snow slope from it to the fourth rib which begins

165

at a somewhat gentler angle above an exceptionally steep ice wall. We could then climb this rib until it ended in almost vertical slabs. There we would have to cross verglassed rocks further left on to the fifth rib which rises directly upwards as a steep but apparently sound rib to an icefield embedded in the face left of the summit line. If we next managed to traverse this icefield to the right and so climb the barrier above, then the summit face would be reached and with that the route to the top open. If we could master the majestic face by this audacious route, then one of the greatest problems in the Bernese Alps would be resolved.

We dallied no longer. Without further deliberation we ascended the avalanche cone to the bergschrund and crossed it by a firm snow bridge at the start of the third rib. We were on the face. In order to move as quickly as possible, we did not use the rope for the time being. Ankles flexed till they hurt, our crampons (8) bit into the blank ice. We climbed diagonally left. Only from time to time did a blow of the axe nick out a step. The chips of ice hailed down into the depths and disappeared in the yawning bergschrund at the foot of the face. Tillmann, who was leading, soon disappeared from view behind some rocks jutting out of the ice. When I rounded the corner, I saw him in the bed of the steep narrow ice gully that comes down between the third and the fourth rib, sitting in a hollow grooved out of the ice like a grotto. I traversed into it over rotten brittle ice. Squeezed together we roped up in the hollow.

A narrow gangway of friable rock, leading left out of the gully, opened up the route to the fourth rib. We climbed its ice and rock until the rib merged into the near-vertical slab section in the centre of the face. Here steep icefields directed us left towards the fifth rib which juts out as a distinct ridge and rises through this zone of slabs. We started up this hard section without cutting steps, relying purely upon the strength of our ankles and the quality of our crampons. The ice grew steeper and steeper, and worse and worse. After a few rope lengths our ankles could no longer bear the increasing strain. Painstakingly Tillmann had to cut steps up a section of brittle, rutted water-ice before we reached the fifth rib at last. It soared upwards as an unusually steep ridge, but with good holds. Precisely because of this steepness it was almost completely free of snow.

We removed our crampons and pressed on upwards. The climbing was superb. It was gone midday by the time we reached the end of the rib and stood at the beginning of the icefield embedded in the face at this point. Above us, rock and ice loomed up at an impossibly steep angle to dizzy heights. Only to the right did a route through the ring of cliff bounding the icefield seem feasible.

I now went first to relieve Tillmann who had led thus far. Cutting steps I climbed diagonally right towards the rock buttress bordering the far side of this icefield. We belayed each rope length carefully, gaining ground but slowly. This traverse was the sole section of the route endangered by stone-fall. Due to the warm weather stones began to break off higher up the face and whizzed down the steep ice slopes past us, vanishing among the cliffs a few rope lengths below. Gradually the rocks drew nearer. We managed to surmount the rock barrier by snow ledges and ice gullies, then moved up on to a steep boulder at the start of the snow face.

Here we took our first brief rest. It was 2 p.m. We were in the happiest of moods as the hardest part seemed to lie below us, and the route to the summit lay open above. For all that, our joy was to be short-lived. Dark thunder-clouds were brewing up behind the Mönch and Eiger, and the summit of the Fiescherhorn also became wreathed in cloud.

In great haste we set off again, still hoping to beat the bad weather to the start of the ice ramp that rises to the right towards the ice barrier crowning the face and the summit. The snow which was in good condition on the lower part of this flank deteriorated progressively as we gained height. In places it was so rotten that we broke in at every step; elsewhere it covered the ice underneath so thinly that we were saddled with the tiring task of cutting steps to provide reliable stances. To complete our pot of woe, a sudden and violent storm set in. Mist enveloped us, and all at once it began to snow heavily with thick driving sleet. Snow falling on the upper part of the face streamed down like a river and filled every freshly cut step in a moment. Wearily we worked our way upwards in the snow flurries. Finally nearing the ice ramp, the snowfall eased off, the mist lifted, and briefly we even got a peep at a spot of blue sky.

A steep ice gully brought us to the start of the ramp. We continued up this, uniformly monotonous. To us it seemed that the face just did not want to end. We changed the lead every two rope lengths; we were already too exhausted for either of us to lead for longer. We recorded our progress by keeping an eye on the mountains in the vicinity. Whenever we checked our position we seemed to have got hardly any higher. But eventually we were as high as Point 3804 metres - the top of our route the previous year. The face now narrowed noticeable. Height-wise we estimated another 200 metres to the summit, then 150 metres, 100 metres, finally 50 metres. At that point we decided to make a rising traverse left out on to the north-east ridge which rises as a knife edge to the summit.

As soon as we got on to the ridge we were battered by the full force of the storm from which we had been shielded on the face. We still had to summon up one final big effort to battle up the few remaining pitches to the top. At 7. 30 p. m. we trod the highest point, just as the last glimmer of daylight died away behind brewing banks of mist. (9)

There was no happy and tranquil rest on the storm-tossed summit. After a few minutes to put on some warm clothing that would protect us from the piercing cold of the gale, we set about getting down the steep crest of the north-west ridge in the darkness. We paid no attention to the yawning precipices on either side of the ridge. One thought only motivated us: "Downwards. " We groped our way down as there was no question of lighting the lantern in the raging storm. At last the terrain levelled out and we came to the snow dome where our ascent of the previous year had ended (Point 3804 metres). Meanwhile the storm had eased off somewhat, black clouds began to part, the moon peeped through the dispersing clouds and caused ghostlike reflections to dance on the white expanses of glacier. We followed an indistinct track down snow slopes to the foot of the Walcherhorn and the upper basin of the Ewigschneefeld.

From the year before we still had bad memories of the long grind across the Ober Mönchjoch to the Jungfraujoch. This time we therefore chose to cross the significantly lower Unter Mönchjoch, from where we hoped to reach the Bergli hut in a short time. Wearily we trudged up wide snowfields towards a low saddle on the ridge running right, which, in the pale twilight of the night, we imagined must be the Unter Mönchjoch. The moon was once more hidden behind black clouds, but now and again distant lightning lit up the inky night. We drew nearer and nearer to the saddle without finding the tracks of earlier parties as expected. We already suspected we might have gone wrong, but just then we came upon a broad beaten trail which we followed up a short snow slope to the Unter Mönchjoch. On the other side of the saddle we hurried down snow slopes, followed by a snow ridge and a rock rib. Then we saw the roof of the Bergli hut suddenly emerging out of the dark a few metres below us. At 11.15 p.m. we entered the wooden refuge, exactly eighteen hours after setting off from our bivouac site.

In sultry heat the following day we descended the icefalls to the Grindelwald-Fiescher glacier, and crossed its sodden snowy morass towards the Zäsenberg where we were going to collect our bivouac equipment. Again the Fiescherwand rose up before us in its immense magnitude; again we scrutinized its cracks and gullies, its slabby walls and fluted ice. But this time not with the eye of the hunter, endeavouring to discover its secrets, rather with the eye of the connoisseur proudly satisfied at having solved the problems of this face.

Author's notes:

1. Lammer (1863-1945), a fanatical Austrian advocate of extreme guideless and solo climbing, revelled in flaunting danger for its own sake. He wrote with relish of his perilous adventures, including several important first ascents, in "Jungborn" which became a mountaineering bestseller in the 1920s.

2. They started somewhat left of the summit fall line, but were repulsed a mere 250 metres up by verglassed slabs on the lower part of the face - W. W.

3. J.P. Farrar reconnoitred the face with the guides Peter Almer I and II in 1924, and reported that he considered possible the ascent of the striking rock rib sweeping down from Point 3804 metres north-west of the summit to the Grindelwald-Fiescher glacier. The foot of this rib is marked Point 2780 metres on current maps.

4. Though Welzenbach does not mention it, interestingly he and Tillmann did not in fact adhere to the normal descent route by the south-west flank throughout - this in any case takes the west ridge at first. Instead, they kept as near as practical to its right-hand (north) edge to get as many complete views as possible of the North Wall (Eigerwand) and so assess its feasibility for a future attempt. Tillmann recollects Welzenbach's reaction to the Eigerwand: "Willo commented that it looked like five Fleischbank East Walls piled on top of one another. He was convinced that a problem of such dimensions would require a five day siege on the part of the first ascensionists. At that time, still suffering from his arm disability, he was not prepared to risk such an undertaking, especially as he already had his eyes set on several other big unclimbed north walls in the Bernese Oberland. Moreover, he expressed concern that in the event of bad weather a retreat appeared very dubious."

5. 4 a.m. according to the original report in the Munich Academic Alpine Club Journal. Other times given as footnotes to this account are also taken from this publication, 1928/29 and 1929/30 issues.

6. Reached at 9.30 p.m.

7. The main rib sweeping down from Point 3804 metres to the Grindelwald-Fiescher glacier at Point 2780 metres is regarded as the first rib and is the line of the Amstutz-von Schumacher ascent, 3rd August 1926. Its second ascent by Tillmann and Welzenbach, 14th September 1929, is the climb described first in the present chapter.

8. They were using ten-point crampons. Twelve-point crampons, with two extra spikes protruding at the toe end, were an innovation of the late 1930s, making possible the technique of

170

front-pointing without cutting steps.

9. Welzenbach commented in the Munich Academic Alpine
Journal for 1929/30 that their time of $12\frac{1}{4}$ hours from the bergschrund to the summit could be reduced with better conditions,
pointing out that they were slowed down by stormy weather on
the upper part of the climb.   10-15 hours is the modern guidebook estimate despite knowing the line to take, improved equipment and more advanced techniques.   In retrospect, Welzenbach
remarked of the Fiescherwand: "A very difficult and dangerous
mixed route.   Sustained.   Poor belay protection."

Into a New Decade

THE Fiescherwand success inspired Welzenbach to pursue a remarkable series of north wall climbs in the Bernese Oberland. But for a complete break in the weather, he and Tillmann would have probably added the Gletscherhorn North-West Face to their tally straightaway. On 11th September, joined by Rüsch, they abandoned their attempt from the Rottal hut due to appalling snow conditions. For the same reason they retreated from high up on the Jungfrau. These instances illustrate that Welzenbach did not set out with the intention of forcing climbs irrespective of the dangers involved. He was never afraid to exercise his judgement in favour or against continuing a climb after a coolly calculated appraisal of the prevailing circumstances. In the Bernese Oberland, unlike in the Mont Blanc Range or in the Eastern Alps, there was no competition to pressurize his decisions. During the early 1930s Welzenbach remained the only serious challenger for the big north walls of the region. The Fiescherwand, the first stepping-stone in his campaign, remains the undertaking most respected by the modern mountaineer, feared for a combination of technical difficulties, unrelenting steepness and ever-present objective hazards.

During the following winter Welzenbach made several probable first ski ascents with Hans Reimer, notably in the Münstertal Alps belonging to the Swiss National Park. On 2nd February they were caught by an unforeseeable freak avalanche skiing down from the Wank, an easy ski top in Bavaria, to the Ersterbergalm. Welzenbach ended up head downwards with his skis entangled in a bush, but was able to struggle free. Reimer had come to rest on the surface at the edge of the avalanche.

In the literary field Welzenbach contributed one chapter entitled "Ice Climbing" to a 917 pages long "Alpine Handbook", published during 1931 in two volumes by the German and Austrian Alpine Club. In subsections he dealt with the composition of a party, all the features of glaciers and of snow and ice, rope management and ice techniques. Above all though, he stressed the differences between climbing on rock and on snow or ice. He was clearly concerned about a contemporary tendency to underestimate the dangers and difficulties of snow and ice climbing. He contended that "whereas the rock climber sets out aware of the difficulties to be encountered, not too seriously worried about objective dangers like stonefall and storms, the ice climber has to do battle with the uncontrollable forces of nature in addition to the technical problems posed by the mountain". He backed up his assertion by explaining the inherent hazards of crevasses, cornices and glissading together with the potentially serious combined effects of cold, heat, height and the length of an expedition in terms of snow and ice routes. Welzenbach drew his conclusion: "This illustrates that ice climbing demands far greater experience and ability than rock climbing. Exploration of the glaciated high regions of the Alps must be the preserve of the accomplished mountaineer."

Three times during the spring of 1931 Welzenbach's ski mountaineering trips took him to the Ortler Alps in the South Tirol. A winter ascent of the Königsspitze (Gran Zebru) was the most notable achievement. He now struck up a firm partnership with Willy Merkl. On Whit Sunday, 24th May, they attempted the Ortler North Face, an intimidating couloir line and nowadays commonly considered the most serious if not the hardest ice climb in the Eastern Alps, rivalled only by the neighbouring majestic Königswand. The contemporary Italian guidebook, a product of an earlier school of climbing unenlightened in its attitude to daring trends in ice climbing, did its best to frighten off would-be assailants of the Ortler North Face. It was depicted as "an enormous couloir situated between threatening rock banks and under the constant menace of the immense overhanging sérac bastion of the Upper Ortler glacier". Scathingly the editor continued: "Only those persons

173

desirous of uselessly exposing their lives would dream of an ascent by this funnel, swept continuously by stone and ice avalanches." Equipped with a good assortment of pitons, Welzenbach and Merkl set out to discover the truth for themselves. They climbed over half the face, but at 3300 metres and still 600 metres below the summit they decided to retreat because of bad ice conditions in the couloir and snow-plastered rocks on either side. Both factors had slowed their progress. Above all, they were aware of increasing avalanche danger as the day progressed. In withdrawing they demonstrated that their daring was matched by circumspection and the sound judgement of experience. News of their assault precipitated some urgent action. Young Hans Ertl (1), also from Munich, conqueror of the Königswand the year before and thirsting for further adventure, was momentarily shattered upon learning about Welzenbach's interest in the Ortler North Face, a challenge he had viewed as his secret preserve. He ranted: "Welzenbach had been on the North Face. On my face! I suffered sleepless nights... They had lost too much time through cautious stepcutting, by noon the snow got too soft, the ice too rotten, time too short, anyhow the mountain had won this time. But I knew that someone like Welzenbach would never admit defeat. I knew that he would return. I also knew that I would not give my face away without a fight. Now or never..." Desperate, Ertl hunted for a partner immediately and teamed up with Franz Schmid. On 19th June they cycled the 200 kilometres to the Ortler Alps in 22 hours, on the 22nd they battled up the face in $17\frac{1}{4}$ hours (2). They had forestalled their opposition, and just five weeks later Schmid conquered the Matterhorn North Face with his brother Toni. Strangely, true to Ertl's prediction and despite missing out on the first ascent, Welzenbach did return - 14 months later. His logbook for 14th August 1932 reads: "To the foot of the Ortler North Face. Weather and ice conditions very unfavourable. Traverse towards Marlt Ridge, Rumpf falls! Descent..." In between these episodes Welzenbach had climbed the Ortler in mid winter.

Ertl's self-congratulatory and over-dramatized accounts of his conquest of the Ortler North Face in the Munich Illustrated News and other magazines unleashed a controversy between him and Welzenbach in the Österreichische Alpenzeitung (Austrian Alpine Journal). Welzenbach took Ertl to task for inaccuracies, deception and self-contradiction. Among other points, Ertl grossly overestimated the steepness of the climb; he quoted the start as 50 degrees, 300-600 metres up as 60 degrees (bumped up to 'vertical' in another publication), 800 metres up as 70 degrees. Welzenbach had measured the angles at these points with his clinometer as 34, 45 and 52 degrees respectively. He countered Ertl's claim that other alpinists had always avoided vertical ice and sérac barriers by quoting examples dating from the Hochferner North Face in 1929 back to the first ascent of the Ice Nose in Piz Scerscen in 1877. Welzenbach was angered by Ertl's untrue statement in one magazine that he had used new ice climbing techniques to negotiate "huge ice overhangs" on the Ortler North Face, when elsewhere he had admitted avoiding overhangs, and that he supported his claim with an action photo captioned as taken by Franz Schmid during the ascent but upon questioning confessed to be posed on a glacier at a different date. It was unfortunate that Ertl marred what was indisputably an outstanding first ascent by publishing inaccurate or at best misleading accounts and by blowing his own trumpet with false claims made at the expense of his forerunners.

At the end of June 1931 Welzenbach and Merkl turned their minds from the Ortler Alps to the Mont Blanc Range and the North Face of the Grands Charmoz. For Welzenbach this was a cause that had drowned in torrential storms the previous July. Then with Karl Wien, he had got no nearer than Montenvers. Not even a reconnaissance had been feasible. Now he was determined to concentrate his entire efforts upon this objective. Neither he nor Merkl can have imagined just how much determination and effort they would be forced to draw upon.

Author's notes:

1. Film cameraman on the 1953 German Nanga Parbat Expedition, later a jungle explorer and farmer in South America.

2. The Alpine Journal ungraciously acknowledged this climb with "regret" and, totally opposed to climbs of such an extreme nature, refused to name the successful pair: "We purposely omit the names and nationality of these desperadoes - as well as any details of their insanity."

Storming the Charmoz

WILLO WELZENBACH

THE North Face of the Aiguille des Grands Charmoz is the show-piece of Montenvers, a 1100 metres high granite wall rising incredibly steeply above the ice stream of the Mer de Glace. The telescope on the hotel terrace must have been focussed thousands of times on the Charmoz. Hundreds of climbers have probably examined its cracks and gullies, and toyed with the possibility of an ascent. Nevertheless this tremendous flank remained unconquered until recently.

I first saw the North Face of the Charmoz in 1927 when I crossed the Col du Géant from Courmayeur to Montenvers. There I met an acquaintance, Dr. Alfred Grünwald who perished a few days later with his companion Max Bickhoff in a storm on the Col de Bionnassay. Dr. Grünwald told me about the attempt made by two well-known French climbers, Paul Fallet and R. Tézenas du Montcel, in 1926. From the foot of the face they had climbed a steep gully to the right-hand spur. (1) They had traversed back onto the face half-way up it and had then started up the summit couloir. Little more than 100 metres (2) below their goal they were defeated by the conditions. Severely harassed by a blizzard, avalanches and stone-fall during the descent, they only escaped narrowly with their lives.

From my own reading I also knew that the Irishman V.J.E. Ryan with the Swiss guides Franz and Josef Lochmatter had climbed the uppermost part of the North Face on the occasion of the first ascent of the North-West ridge (3) in 1905. This party turned the impassable ridge steps above the shoulder (Point 3117 metres) (4) by means of the smooth rocks of the North Face to the right of the ice couloir issuing from the gap in the summit ridge.

Stimulated by the news of the French attempt, I studied the face thoroughly and reckoned that it would go in favourable conditions. It seemed to me that from the highest point previously reached it must be feasible either to get onto the Ryan-Lochmatter route or to force a direct line to the summit.

Unfortunately my lame arm prevented me from making the attempt that season. Several years went by without an opportunity to test my plan. In the summer of 1930 I returned to Montenvers and enjoyed some good days out on the Chamonix Aiguilles, but just when I was ready to come to grips with my main objective - the Charmoz face, gales raged over the ridges and fresh snow plastered the mountain flanks.

It was early summer in 1931 before I succeeded in putting this long-cherished ambition into action with my friend Willy Merkl. One glorious evening in June we drove in my small sports car from Geneva along the Arve valley to Chamonix. Next morning saw us at Montenvers. The North Face of the Charmoz looked more majestic than ever, coated in sugary fresh snow after the thunderstorms of the past few days.

So as not to waste our first day we decided to go up to the Thendia glacier during the afternoon and explore the approach to the foot of the face. At the edge of the glacier we sat down amongst enormous moraine boulders and gazed up at the face. The lower part is composed of steep slabs broken by cracks and gullies. We suspected that this section would call for a very sustained effort, yet we were convinced of its feasibility. Above these slabs an ice-field in the centre of the face rises to the summit cliffs. This ice-field would likewise pose no insuperable difficulties, but then came the problematical upper section of the face. From the top of the ice-field an exceptionally steep ice couloir soars up the summit cliffs, seeming practically overhanging from our viewpoint. This ice couloir is bounded to its right by slabby walls, to its left by a smooth rock pillar scored by icy ledges. Our minds were preoccupied with one disquieting question - Would we manage to force a route either up the ice couloir or up the flanking rocks? There was no straight answer to this - Only an all-out attempt could decide the matter. Slowly we ambled back to Montenvers in the late afternoon.

Early on June 30th we left the hotel, twinkling stars heralding a fine day. We descended the track to the Mer de Glace and followed the bank of the glacier until right under the face whose outline stood out ghostlike against the night sky. We scrambled up grassy broken rocks and boulder slopes to the lateral moraine of the Thendia glacier. In the grey dawn we trudged up steepening glacier snow towards the tip of the avalanche cone extending below the foot of the face. Just as the sun was rising over the Aiguille Verte we crossed a fragile snow bridge onto the rocks.

The face rises in steep smooth slabs above the glacier and the first few rope lengths immediately above the bergschrund caused us a fair bit of bother. Maybe we did not move off the snow onto the rocks at the best point, but at all events the climbing was reminiscent in terms of difficulty with modern routes in the Kaisergebirge. Merkl skilfully warmed up the slabs in his light rock climbing boots while I followed in nailed boots. Next came some rising traverses - crossing streaming wet gullies, ascending steep snow tongues, climbing grooves, overcoming smooth steps. Slowly we gained height. The sun had meanwhile reached its zenith and was scorching down over the pinnacled summit ridge onto the face. The snow on the rocks began to melt, water trickled down every crack, avalanches rumbled down the gullies, rocks whizzed past our heads into the depths.

We needed all our skill to get up a slabby buttress with only the thinnest of holds, then in the late afternoon we stood on the final rocks below the ice flank. The layer of snow on the ice was dreadfully slushy and its condition now seemed exceptionally dangerous. The slightest disturbance might well have caused such wet heavy snow to avalanche off the underlying ice. Because of the danger we dared not proceed with the ascent and

179

instead decided to spend the night at this spot. Next day we anticipated continuing on frozen snow.

We prepared our bivouac for the night on a narrow outward-sloping ledge, hammered a few pegs into the rock (5) and tied on firmly to safeguard ourselves against falling off while asleep. When the last glimmer of daylight had faded away, we draped the tent sack over ourselves and tried to doze off. But we had to endure an unsettled night there, high on the North Face of the Charmoz. Every so often we were jolted out of our drowsing by a rock whirring past, then an avalanche thundered down the ice-field and passed barely one rope length away from our precarious site before disappearing down a gully into the depths. Sometime near midnight we were jolted awake by a terrific crashing noise. Startled we lifted the tent sack off and witnessed a spectacle of savage nature at its most magnificent. An enormous rock pillar had broken off from the cliff which rose almost vertically from the Thendia glacier to the Cornes de Chamois on the north-east ridge of the Charmoz. Like the aftermath of a bomb exploding, an avalanche of rock fragments roared down and crashed into the depths. In the dark we only saw a tremendous fireball of flashing bits and pieces, followed by a cloud of dust that enveloped the face in a thick smoke-screen.

We were more than glad when it grew light and we could get ready to leave our uncomfortable perch. We brewed some tea and warmed ourselves in the rays of the rising sun before commencing the ascent of the ice flank. We cramponned quickly up frozen snow tongues and by 8 o'clock stood at the top edge of the ice-field and at the foot of the narrow ice couloir which leads up to the gap in the summit ridge.

To avoid the ever present stone-fall danger in the couloir, we decided to tackle the rock wall on the right. We hoped to get onto Ryan's route and reach the summit by it, but in trying to find his line of ascent we were forced out too far to the right and reached the ridge just above its big step at Point 3265 metres. There we came upon a prominent cairn that must have

180

been built during an earlier attempt on the upper section of the ridge. It seemed to mark the highest point so far attained. A cursory inspection convinced us that the ridge above was probably impossible and would at best present exceptional difficulties. (6)

As it happened an imminent storm deemed it ill-advised even to attempt the ridge or return onto the face in search of the Ryan-Lochmatter route. Reluctantly we decided to descend the North-West Ridge without having reached the summit. We got down the big step below Point 3265 metres by a series of abseils on the north flank then traversed horizontally back to the ridge. Just as we arrived on the shoulder (Point 3117 metres) a thunderstorm broke in full force. We crouched for shelter in our tent sack while freezing rain and hail beat down and brilliant flashes of lightning vibrated on the nearby rock teeth.

When the storm abated we started down the slabby step that falls from the shoulder to the gap before the Doigt de l'Étala, the last pinnacle on the ridge. We were standing on a narrow ledge a little above this gap preparing for an abseil when a second storm struck with greater ferocity than I have ever experienced in the mountains. We just had time to attach a belay to a gendarme before the tempest burst with all its might. Water flowed in torrents down every crack and gully on the mountain and in no time we were absolutely drenched. We had to cling desperately to the rock to avoid being thrown off the the mountain. Thunder and lightning alternated without pause and we had to close our eyes against each blinding flash. This barrage from the elements defied us to survive for more than an hour.

Eventually the fury of the storm abated sufficiently for us to force our way down to the gap. It was already late in the evening as we set about traversing the Doigt de l'Étala, but we still held out hope of reaching Montenvers via the Col de l'Étala that same night. The ridge seemed endless and we had lost so much time that we were caught by dusk on the rocks of the

Doigt de l'Étala. We realized that we could not complete the descent and had to bivouac again on a narrow ledge soaked and frozen to the marrow. We lay awake all night shivering with cold. It poured with rain till midnight, but towards morning the weather improved noticeably and by first light a steely blue sky spanned the Chamonix Aiguilles. After doing some vigorous exercises to warm ourselves a bit, we set off down to the Col de l'Étala crossing the west flank of the Doigt de l'Étala (first scaled in 1925) slightly below its highest point. At the col we stretched out in warm sunshine on a flat slab and enjoyed a carefree rest that had long been denied us. It was late in the morning before we left our sunny spot. Two abseils in the couloir dropping to the Nantillons glacier delayed us briefly, then we rushed down soft snow slopes and boulder-strewn moraines onto the high level path leading round the hillside back to the hotel at Montenvers.

During the next few days we looked at the Charmoz face with mixed feelings. On the one hand we were pleased with our achievement, on the other we were not completely satisfied with the result. After all, our ascent did not end at the highest point, but on the north-west ridge some 160 metres below the top. The thought of an incomplete victory preyed on our minds. Consequently we decided to renew the ascent and try to finish the route by a logical line ending at the summit in a second undertaking. Meanwhile we used this rainy spell for an excursion to the Leschaux hut. (7)

When the weather improved a few days later we prepared for our second assault on the Charmoz face. On the morning of 5th July 1931 we set off from Montenvers under a cloudless sky with the barometer standing high. To avoid the lower sections of the face which were now acutely endangered by avalanches and stone-falls we settled on climbing by the Col de l'Étala and the North-West Ridge to the shoulder at Point 3117 metres where we would bivouac. The next day we planned to traverse onto the face and force a continuation of the line of our first attempt to the summit. Whereas we had descended

182

westwards from the Col de l'Étala to the Nantillons glacier three days previously, this time we climbed to the col from the Thendia side by a broken rock face. We followed familiar ground on the ridge with many superb pitches and reached the shoulder by evening. There a level ledge (8) just below the crest on the sheer Thendia flank served as one of the most impressive bivouac sites I have ever known, breath-taking scenery all around us.

I slept little that night. Much of the time I lay on my back and gazed up at the sky. Somehow I sensed the threat of disaster - the sky seemed too clear, the stars too twinkling. Yet all my misgivings vanished with the dawn of another brilliant day.

At 6 a. m. we began to cross the face. Three hours later we stood at the edge of the couloir on the spot from where we had moved right towards the North-West Ridge on our first attempt. Very hurriedly we made a rising left-hand traverse of the couloir (9), intermittently raked by stone-falls, and climbed an indistinct ramp. But even there we were not safe from bombardment. To escape this continual threat, we slanted further left along outward-sloping rock bands, glazed with ice, onto the crest of a huge pillar.

The fine and apparently reliable early morning weather suddenly began to deteriorate. Black cloud streamers were boiling up above the summit ridge of the Charmoz and distant thunder heralded the approaching storm. We increased our pace in the hope of reaching the summit before the storm broke, but immediately realized the fruitlessness of such action. All at once the storm struck. For three hours we were exposed on a tiny sloping stance without shelter to the lashing rain and battering hailstones. Again and again fresh squalls raged across the ridges. Our attempts to climb higher in search of a better stance were frustrated by difficult rock. Not until late afternoon when the storm relented a bit could we force the route further but we could no longer get to the summit that evening. Typically, we were compelled to bivouac on a narrow rock platform at the foot of a vertical step just below the connecting ridge rising from the Aiguille de la République to the Charmoz. We never dreamt we would be trapped for sixty hours on this airy spot 1000 metres up the face.

We cleared the snow and ice away, squatted on our rucksacks and pulled the tent sack over our heads for shelter from the heavy showers of rain. Throughout the night one violent thunderstorm followed another with barely a pause. The time passed slowly as the gale howled and the rain beat down on our flimsy fabric awning. Towards morning the depressing drumming of rain turned into the gentler pattering of snow. At daybreak we surfaced for fresh air. The snow flakes were swirling round our tent sack in a wild dance. Dank mist blotted out the view. Any hope that the weather might improve during the day diminished by the hour, while the savage storm raged round our tiny platform relentlessly.

The day drew to a close without any sign of an improvement, and we had to settle down for a third night on the mountain. Sleep was virtually out of the question. Our limbs ached from the enforced squatting position on this narrow ledge; our feet were cold, our clothes damp. Masses of snow streamed down the rocks onto us, piling up on our little platform and restricting our meagre space even further. By dawn we were practically buried in snow. Some great mental effort was needed to crawl out of the tent sack and clear away the deep drift so that our imprisonment on this confined spot might become a bit more tolerable.

Several disturbing questions continually plagued our minds – How long would the storm last? Would we still be able to climb the final difficult rock wall to the ridge once the weather improved? If we failed in our attempt to reach the summit, what lay before us? We would have to set about descending the face, now plastered in snow, glazed with ice and peppered by avalanches. We shuddered at the mere thought of such a retreat.

We had consumed almost all our rations yet we suffered no pangs of hunger. All appetite had deserted us, but we were

184

tormented by thirst. There was nothing left to drink, we had no stove and could only suck snow which burnt our tongues and made our craving thirst worse.

The hours passed interminably slowly. Neither of us spoke much; we had withdrawn into our own thoughts. Now and again we made notes in our diaries. We were still less worried about our own plight than by the agonizing conjecture about what might be happening meanwhile in Chamonix or back home. We suspected that our absence would give rise to considerable concern amongst our relations and friends, and we envisaged preparations being made for a rescue operation. During climbs all over the Alps we had both overcome many tricky situations without ever needing outside help. The thought of a rescue operation being mounted on our behalf was unbearable.

Towards evening the milky light given off by the mist suddenly brightened. We stuck our heads out of the sack and saw a tiny patch of blue sky overhead. Swirling mist dispersed, sinking lower to reveal the shapely snow peak of the Aiguille Verte towering above a billowy sea of clouds in the evening sunshine. At that moment we could have jumped for joy, but our happiness was destined to be short-lived. Fresh banks of mist surged up the mountain flanks, the breach in the clouds filled in again and straightaway we were engulfed by another violent blizzard. That evening turned into one of dreadful disillusionment. All hope of a sudden weather improvement had apparently disappeared.

An interminable fourth night began. Sitting it out on such a constricted spot had become an almost intolerable ordeal. For days we had been unable to exercise our limbs and every muscle in our bodies ached from huddling together cramped up on our tiny site. Towards midnight the snowfall eased, the wind died down and at the same time it grew considerably colder so that we froze terribly. We treated the sudden drop in temperature as a portent of better weather and awaited the morning with renewed optimism.

At daybreak the sky was clear and the valleys free from mist, but a bell-shaped veil of cloud already capped the summit of the Aiguille Verte. To us this spectacle was an unmistakable sign that the improvement was only temporary and that another storm could be expected within a few hours. It seemed obvious that we had to force our way to the summit ridge during this short respite or otherwise our fate would be sealed.

It took ages to loosen our limbs a bit, salvage belongings from the snow and get ready to climb. Then we began the ascent. We faced the very hardest work possibly imaginable. Every handhold and every foothold had to be dug out of the fresh snow; the rock underneath was caked with ice. We hammered one peg after another into the rock, battling upwards metre by metre. The knowledge that the fight with the mountain was for our lives gave us the strength to achieve what had seemed next to impossible upon leaving our bivouac. After four hours we emerged onto the ridge rising from the Aiguille de la République to the Charmoz, and we had cracked the worst of our problems. Not a moment too soon, for already the next snow-storm broke upon us. A horizontal section of jagged ridge led to the final wall of the summit tower. We summoned one last big effort to overcome this wall, then at 3 o'clock in the afternoon we had won through - the North Face of the Charmoz was ours. Due to the desperate weather conditions we had struggled for nine whole hours on the last 100 metres.

We stopped barely a minute on the storm-tossed summit before commencing the descent to the Nantillons glacier. One thought only governed us: Downwards! By snowed-up gullies and verglassed chimneys we reached the Charmoz-Grépon couloir. We descended extra carefully to reduce the risk of the loose layer of fresh snow in the couloir avalanching under the weight of our steps. Thick mist enveloped us and obliterated any view. Laboriously groping our way down, for a while keeping to the rocks on the Charmoz side of the couloir, seeing nothing, we frequently got stuck and repeatedly had to retrace our steps to look for the right route. Late in the evening we leapt over the enormous bergschrund onto the Nantillons glacier.

Navigating by compass we picked our way downwards, stopped time and again by crevasses that forced us into detours. By chance or by instinct - I don't know which - we came upon the small shelter (10) at the top of the Rognon des Nantillons, a steep rock island jutting out of the glacier. Here we rested awhile and then clambered down rocks in the gathering gloom to the glacier tongue below. Exhausted we staggered and stumbled down boulder-strewn moraine slopes to the path which guided us safely to Montenvers. At 10.30 p.m. we entered the hotel, exactly 110 hours after our departure.

At Montenvers our fate had already caused great concern. There was great joy at our return and we were treated with exceptional kindness. From the manager down to the valet everybody attended to our physical needs. Now we also learnt of the major alarm that our absence had aroused not just in Chamonix but back home too. (11) Further still, we were told that a rescue team was already on its way from Munich to Chamonix. Immediately we made repeated efforts to phone and send a telegram. Eventually, at 11.30 p.m., I succeeded in getting through by phone to friends in Munich. After more phone calls they managed to have the rescue team's vehicle intercepted en route and recalled.

Well after midnight we at last fell into a badly needed sleep. In the early hours we were awoken by voices. It was Heckmair and Kröner, colleagues belonging to the same alpine club section, who upon learning of our disappearance had selflessly hurried over from the Leschaux hut (12) to be ready to search for us.

We spent an enjoyable day recovering at Montenvers. Driving homewards from Chamonix the following evening, we stopped on the Col des Montets for a brief backward glance. Once again it rose before us - the Charmoz face where we had been trapped for five days. The events of these days now seemed like a dream - the promising assault, the desperate struggle, the final conquest. We were glad and proud that we had withstood the rigours of the weather and had battled our way unaided out of a virtually hopeless situation - one that would have meant certain death for many.

Author's notes:

1. This is the spur dividing the two branches of the Thendia glacier.

2. Probably nearer 200 metres.

3. Not accepted as the first ascent of the north-west ridge which was eventually completed in 1950 by Pierre Allain and M. Schatz.

4. Welzenbach obtained this and other altitudes quoted from the Carte Albert Barbey (X. Imfeld, M. Kurz), La Chaine du Mont Blanc 1:50,000 map.

5. Excavating some rocks to improve the site, Welzenbach shattered the shaft of Merkl's peg hammer (noted in Merkl's account).

6. See note 3. The North-West Ridge is graded TD and includes a pitch of VI.

7. Welzenbach does not mention that at the Leschaux hut they met Heckmair and Kröner who rather tactlessly revealed their intention of making the first ascent of the Charmoz North Face. It is likely that knowledge of this plan gave Welzenbach and Merkl an added and far more urgent incentive to renew their own assault on the face and finish the climb promptly.

8. A Leica camera, loaned to Welzenbach by Hans Reimer, was knocked off the ledge, but happily it landed on another ledge ten metres below and was retrieved in working order after a time-consuming rope manoeuvre (private report from Hans Reimer).

9. The couloir was climbed to gap 3429 metres on the summit ridge later the same season in the course of the second ascent by Anderl Heckmair and Gustl Kröner, 31 July - 1 August 1931.

10. Long since defunct. An open stone-walled enclosure remains.

11. Headlines such as "Munich mountaineers missing in the Mont Blanc Range" had appeared in European national newspapers.

12. In fact, Heckmair and Kröner ran out of food at the Leschaux hut and, unaware of the drama unfolding on the Charmoz, descended directly to Chamonix where they heard that Welzen-

188

bach and Merkl were missing. They immediately re-ascended
to Montenvers in the night to be ready to search for them next
morning.   At 4 a. m. they found Welzenbach and Merkl safely
returned, and were invited up to their room for celebration
drinks.

Grands Charmoz
North Face.

Aig. de la Rép-
ublique to left of
upper icefield.
The route went
into the second
broad couloir
right of this sharp
pinnacle and fin-
ished up the rocks
to its left.

Aftermath of the Charmoz

AS A life-and-death struggle, Welzenbach and Merkl's epic of endurance on the Grands Charmoz made international front-page headlines. Few believed they could survive the terrible series of storms and escape unscathed, let alone complete the ascent unassisted. Afterwards it aroused considerable and often contradictory comment - some of which was nationalistically biased - among leading contemporary climbers and critics. It thus became Welzenbach's most controversial climb.

The siege tactics employed by Welzenbach and Merkl unleashed a furious debate about the acceptability or otherwise of their mountaineering ethics. It was overlooked by many non-German commentators that their methods were imposed rather than chosen. Some objected in any case to what they saw as a race for the big north walls in the 1930s. Armand Charlet, a great French guide but austere and unaccommodating in outlook, echoed such sentiments with specific reference to the Munich School, complaining: "This is not alpinism. This is war." The Alpine Journal published a day-by-day description submitted by Welzenbach, but its uncharitable editor Colonel E. L. Strutt could not refrain from appending his personal note with a sarcastic sting in its tail: "We must express our thanks to Dr. Welzenbach for his interesting note and, beyond congratulating him on having extricated his party from a series of seemingly hopeless situations, refrain from comment. Dr. Welzenbach has kindly supplied us with complete details of his route, under the circumstances not perhaps the least remarkable achievement of the week."

By contrast, Lucien Devies represented the more magnanimous views of fair-minded mountaineers in a letter to Welzenbach: "After these long days of growing alarm we have learnt with great joy about the successful outcome of your magnificent performance. We can't congratulate you enough on your heroic deeds. " In a subsequent survey of Welzenbach's activities Devies quoted the Charmoz climb to illustrate his "powers of resistance, nerve and total composure". He recollected in this instance that though "people lost hope of seeing them again... though exhausted by the appalling conditions and lack of food, they knew how to conserve their energy so that they were able to utilize a brief respite in the weather and force the last 100 metres by an extreme effort".

24 years later, in 1955, Joe Brown (fresh from the conquest of Kangchenjunga), Don Whillans, Nat Allen and Eric Price found themselves in similarly stormy circumstances on the Charmoz North Face, on this occasion self-imposed: "Bad as the weather was we were in a mood to climb" - Brown. After Allen had survived a fall while traversing below the long summit ice couloir, the crestfallen party retreated subdued: "We had had enough" - Brown; "My nerves are shattered" - Price at the time; "The descent was dangerous... With tremendous relief we reached the rock" - Whillans. Such short-term reactions indicate what iron nerves it must have required on the part of Welzenbach and Merkl to sit out the storm waiting for better weather. Eventually, after several days trapped by the vicious elements, they realized a move had to be made irrespective of the weather. In this case they decided to force their way to the top. Their ability to finish the climb under conditions of such unbelievable severity, without the advantages of modern more sophisticated equipment, testified to their exceptional strength and willpower. Three years later it was maliciously suggested in some quarters that their experience on the Grands Charmoz gave them a feeling of indestructability, causing them to underestimate Nanga Parbat and defy the Himalayan weather.

A separate dispute centred around whether an interrupted climb counted as a proper first ascent. In this case the ascent of the face had been completed in two stages, 30th June-1st July and 5th-9th July. After their retreat by the North-West Ridge, on their second assault they did not repeat the two-thirds of the face already climbed. Instead they returned by the North-West Ridge and from its shoulder traversed to the very spot at the foot of the ice couloir reached on their first attempt. Thus they had climbed every inch of the North Face. The completion of a climb in two sections is hardly elegant, but by today's standards this is certainly acceptable if not ideal. At that time there was a lack of precedents and this allowed a small petty-minded minority to dispute its validity. Since then several major alpine firsts have been achieved in this manner - probably the best known being the West Face of the Drus in 1952 and the winter ascent of the Eigerwand in 1961 (this did arouse contention both because the German foursome allegedly tried to conceal the two-part aspect of the climb and because a railway tunnel was used to get back onto the face).

One slight criticism of Welzenbach and Merkl's route can be made. On the top section of the face they were forced to traverse left and so finished on the upper part of the North-East Ridge. The best and most aesthetic line takes the ice couloir straight up to the gap a little left of the summit. Welzenbach was fully aware of this, but rejected the couloir "to avoid the ever-present stone-fall danger". In the prevailing conditions he judged it safer to keep to the rocks.

In the Chamonix Aiguilles the Charmoz North Face was the last of the great classic faces to be conquered and its ascent closed an era. The harder climbs in the years to follow resulted from more advanced climbing techniques and improved equipment.

The Charmoz was Welzenbach's only climb in the Western Alps during 1931. His summer and autumn outings were otherwise restricted to the Wetterstein and the Kaisergebirge, except for the already mentioned second attempt on the Ortler North Face. Then, in November, he and Hans Reimer climbed the North Face of the Namloser Wetterspitze in the Lechtal Alps.

During the winter and spring he carried out ski tours most weekends. In this field he was now more active than at any time since his illness. Apart from the local mountain ranges he visited the Stubai, Ortler and Engadine regions. An ascent of the Ortler, by no stretch of the imagination a ski peak, on 26th January with Willy Merkl was the most unusual undertaking during this period. That it was a long day out is emphasized by Welzenbach's concluding comment in his logbook: "Nighttime ski descent from the Tabaretta hut."

Training climbs in May and June took him back to the Wetterstein and the Kaisergebirge. He was now preparing for his return to the north walls of the Bernese Oberland. Just as he had persistently pursued the greatest climbs in the Glockner region six years earlier, now he proposed to wage a similarly relentless campaign on another series of major objectives, all ahead of their time in concept and difficulty. Here too he was destined to become the principal pioneer of big wall climbing.

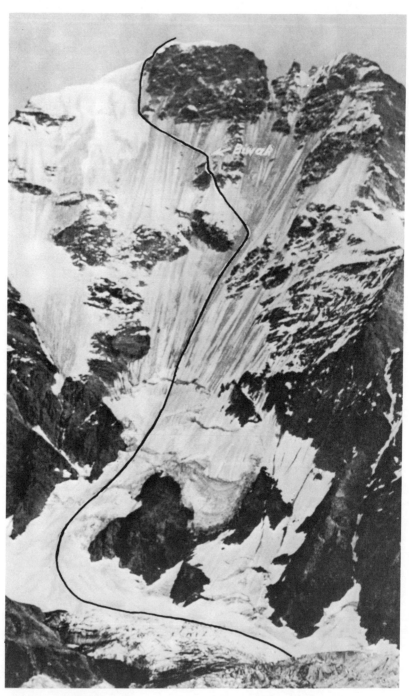

Grosshorn North Face.

Bernese Ice Walls

WILLO WELZENBACH

U NTIL quite recently the Bernese Alps held in store alpine problems of enormous magnitude and impact that had not been touched upon by the course of time. In a period of little more than a decade an unparalleled amount of pioneering activity was concentrated upon these remaining problems in the Bernese Oberland. After unhurried pre-war alpine developments it was left to a new generation to crack these problems after the Great War.

It would be going too far to list the names and climbs of all the pioneers involved. But I would especially like to pay tribute to the successes of Dr. Lauper and his companions on the north walls of the Jungfrau, Mönch and Eiger, climaxing recently in the conquest of the Eiger North Face (1).

At the same time the present writer and his friends were fully active. The North Face Direct of the Gross Fiescherhorn in 1930 served as the prelude. That year unfavourable weather prevented us from carrying out other ambitious plans, but in 1932 we more than made up for what we had omitted. In so doing we switched our main efforts to the area above the Lauterbrunnen valley which terminates to the south in a phenominal wall of rock and ice. This sheer wall, culminating in numerous peaks, offered unclimbed mountaineering objectives that rate amongst the greatest to be found in the Alps.

The following accounts are devoted to the story of their conquest.

NORTH FACE OF THE GROSSHORN (3754 metres)

We chose to direct our first assault at the 1200 metres high north wall of the Grosshorn. The gigantic wall of this mountain constitutes one of the finest show-pieces in the icy surroundings at the very head of the Lauterbrunnen valley. In my friend Erich Schulze of the Munich Academic Alpine Club I found an enthusiastic and reliable companion. Alfred Drexel and Dr. Hermann Rudy, both members of the same club section, also joined the party.

Early in the summer the weather remained constantly bad, so we postponed our departure week by week. Finally our patience broke and one afternoon we sped off in my streamlined DKW, hoping that the weather might care to improve at last for us to realize our aims.

On 19th July we walked from Stechelberg up the White Lüt-schine valley. It was raining and thick mist concealed the heights above us. Our destination was the Oberhornalp near the Oberhorn lake, the ideal starting-point for north side ascents on the Breithorn - Grosshorn - Mittaghorn chain. Just before dusk we found the shack from which we intended to make our assault on the white wall of the Grosshorn.

For six days we besieged the face in this hovel lacking even the most basic amenities. For six days rain beat down on the shingle roof. For just as many days we paced round in circles, stooping to avoid disagreeable contact with the charred beams. Occasionally the dense banks of cloud parted fleetingly to reveal our objective, the unremittingly steep ice flank of the Gross-horn North Face soaring more than 1000 metres above the Schmadri glacier. It rose before us, unbelievably beautiful, forbidding yet enticing, until the mist clamped down again to hide this splendid prospect.

One night it finally cleared. We set off under a twinkling starry sky, but by the time we wanted to strap on our crampons at the avalanche cone below the face, murky clouds were streaming in again. We had to abandon our attempt before even starting.

It was Monday 25th July. Once again we were granted a superb morning. At 2.30 a.m. we left the Oberhornalp. We ascended rock slopes and moraines southwards to the Breithorn glacier. By the meagre light of our lantern we crossed this from west to east and went up steep debris covered ground to the grassy moraine cwm of the Schmadribrunnen (2), lying between the snouts of the Breithorn and Schmadri glaciers. At dawn we stood on the avalanche cone at the foot of the face, about 2550 metres, for the second time. The summit towered 1200 metres above us.

For the first time we had an opportunity to study the face at close quarters and to examine our proposed route. An arm of the glacier, hemmed in on both sides by rock buttresses, extends up the lower part of the face to the final bergschrund (about 2900 metres). Above it, an exceptionally steep ice face - marked by rock buttresses in places - rises at a practically constant angle to the base of the summit cliff. The natural route of ascent had to lead from the avalanche cone at the foot of the face in a direct line with the gap between the west and main summits, as far as above the rock buttresses marking the face half-way up. We still could not make up our minds about the continuation from there to the top. Should we climb to the gap? That would undoubtedly be possible. But would we then succeed in overcoming the vertical step on the unclimbed ridge up to the main summit? Or should we tackle the summit wall directly? Given dry rocks, yes! But what would we find now after a week's bad weather had plastered the mountain flanks with fresh snow? Or ought we to turn the summit wall to its left? At any rate that route had to be feasible. We would take it if the summit wall proved unassailable.

Crouching on a block of ice, we put on our crampons and started up the face as two pairs. Briskly we climbed the initial snow slopes, grooved by shallow avalanche channels. Some large crevasses slowed down the pace for a short while. At 7.15 a.m. we reached the final bergschrund which presented serious difficulties. Schulze nicked out handholds and footsteps in the ice wall on the other side, moved up gingerly, rammed his axe into the uppermost lip of the crevasse and heaved himself up.

Now the ice face rose to the summit rocks, the same face that we had believed we could crampon up in a few hours. We hoped to find firm snow, but we met with solid ice covered only by a finger-thin layer of loose snow. A bitter disappointment.

Step by step we battled against the inflexible elements, zigzagging up the steep face. With every blow of the axe thin lumps of glassy ice flaked off and whizzed down by breath-taking leaps and bounds into the sudden depths. As comrades we shared in this tough work. After every two rope lengths we changed the lead. Frequently thin strips of glistening powder snow hissed down the ice over us; each time such a rampant little powder avalanche swept down we had to pull ourselves together urgently and concentrate our undivided attention on maintaining our balance.

Approaching the rocks in the middle of the face, the angle steepened by several degrees. We climbed the narrows between the rock buttresses and reached an enormous rock nose jutting out of the ice face at this point. Its crest barely had room for the four of us. Our legs dangled above the void while we ate a small snack and discussed our position. It was 2 p.m. Would it still be possible to get off the face during the day? There was no question of climbing the summit wall. That much was clear to us. But what if we tried the ice flank to its left? If the ice conditions turned out to be more favourable on the upper part of the face than lower down, then perhaps we might yet still succeed in reaching the top by nightfall.

While the others were still deliberating, I carried on. Again one step followed the other. To save time and strength I now began to cut the steps smaller and further apart than previously. Although we were gaining height, the summit seemed to remain as far from our grasp as ever. Working left towards a steep gully cutting through the second buttress zone on the face, we battled up verglassed rock and climbed an exacting rock crest with delicate moves to the left of the gully. For one rope length we continued up a steep snow rib, then paused. We had overcome the second rock zone.

In the course of our all-absorbing struggle we had not noticed the hours flying by, nor the banks of cloud drifting in from the west, nor dusk creeping up from the lowlands. Gradually the sky lost its evening glow, becoming dull and grey, then the last glimmer of daylight died away on the mountain tops.

In darkness we dug a hollow in the snow rib. Solid ice soon resisted our efforts and we had to be content with minimal space. We blocked up the entry to our hollow with a bivouac bag hung up on two ice axes rammed into the snow. The freezing cold penetrated our shelter, and to warm ourselves we prepared tea on a small meta stove which we held in turn on our laps. Due to our body heat the snow around us began to melt. A stream of icy water trickled down our backs and collected into little puddles at our feet. In no time our clothes were thoroughly drenched.

As morning dawned, the joyous anticipation of escaping from our dreadfully oppressive confines made us energetic. Stepping out into the open, grey mist enveloped us and snow whipped into our faces. Our soaking wet clothes rapidly became frozen stiff, our hands and feet terribly cold.

At 7 a.m. we began our second day's work. In thick mist, with visibility restricted to the length of the rope, we climbed the ice wall diagonally left. Once again the hours went by at lightning-speed. Towards midday a dark formation emerged through the mist. It had to be the rock spur bounding the summit cliff on its left. We rounded the foot of the spur and climbed on the left-hand side of the rocks, tracking in softer snow, now using our axes as a belay only. We saw nothing, we just knew that we were getting higher. Gradually the angle eased off and the rising wind betrayed the proximity of the ridge. For a few more rope lengths we plodded upwards, bearing right, then stopped hesitantly. We had to be close to the summit.

Now and again we thought we recognized the line of a ridge to our left, and we suspected that it must be badly corniced. Should we press on? Should we look for the top? Should we

Gspaltenhorn North-East Face.

commence the descent over unfamiliar terrain without any visibility? There did not seem the slightest chance of finding the way down to the valley in these conditions. So now, early in the afternoon (3), we started to construct a snow cave for the second time, on this occasion large and spacious. We certainly had plenty of time.

The night seemed to last forever. When the new day dawned, the mountains were clear of mist. True, an icy gale howled over the summit of the Grosshorn and the sun's rays would not warm us for a long time yet, but for all that we felt happy and flushed with the joy of victory. We now saw our summit barely a rope length away. All our trials and tribulations were forgotten. Our dream had turned into reality and our battle had ended in victory.

It was too cold for us to want to stop on the summit. By the steep south ridge of the mountain, crowned with cornices, we descended to the valley in the same number of hours as we had required days on the face. We came down through open pastures to Fafleralp and along a broad track reached Blatten in the Lötschen valley. That was on the third day after setting out from the Oberhornalp.

We crossed the Petersgrat back to the Lauterbrunnen valley. Stopping off at the Oberhornalp, we gazed at our route up the majestic ice face of the Grosshorn and discussed other challenges still waiting to be met. However, for further exploration of big routes the weather remained too unsettled, and the snow and ice conditions were too bad. So we headed down the valley with the avowed intention of returning to reap the rewards denied us by fate this time.

NORTH-EAST FACE OF THE GSPALTENHORN (3436 metres)

Situated at the head of the Sefinen valley, the North-East Wall (4) of the Gspaltenhorn ranks as one of the most tremendous precipices in the Bernese Alps. The vertical interval of the face amounts to 1650 metres and the summit towers 1900 metres above the valley floor at the Kilchbalm.

It is not at all surprising that this titanic wall had already attracted the attention of adventurous campaigners before us. Dr. Walter Amstutz and Gottlieb Michel attempted the face on 9th September 1928. They climbed the distinct buttress rib rising right from the foot of the face towards the north-west ridge. As the first ascensionists they proposed that this rib be named the Kilchbalm ridge. At the point where the rib peters out in the face several hundred metres below the main ridge, they traversed right and reached the Büttlassenlücke by the upper slopes of the Hirtli glacier. Owing to bad conditions the Amstutz - Michel party found it impossible to tackle the 800 metres high summit cliff.

In the annual bulletin of the Bern University Alpine Club I had read a note about this attempt on the Sefinen wall of the Gspaltenhorn which had aroused in me intense curiosity. I obtained a photograph of the face, studied it carefully and eventually formed the opinion that, given favourable conditions, an ascent to the summit could be mastered. As I saw it, from the spot where the Kilchbalm ridge levels off, it should be possible to reach the summit cliff by a left-hand traverse. It then had to be possible to attain the highest point by a system of poorly defined ribs in a direct line with the summit.

One matter still worried me however. The face is composed of limestone, that same friable, badly stratified rock with poor holds of which the Eiger is formed. I recalled the numerous attempts that had preceded the conquest of the Mittellegi ridge and feared that the structure of the rock could cause us serious difficulties.

I had already projected an assault on the Sefinen wall of the Gspaltenhorn after our conquest of the Grosshorn North Face in the early summer of 1932, but the inclement weather thwarted that plan. In September I returned to the Bernese Alps and this cherished dream guided me into the Sefinen valley.

On a wonderful afternoon we - my friend Schulze and I - wandered along the gently ascending path above the Sefinen

202

Lütschine stream. Coming to a curve in the valley, a magnificent sight burst upon us. A forbidding skyhigh wall - the North-East Face of the Gspaltenhorn - towers above the head of the valley, culminating in a brilliant white trapezoidal summit pyramid. To the left this face links up with the long snow-capped ridge of the Tschingelgrat, to the right with the steep precipices of the Büttlassen. With its overwhelming impact this mountain massif totally dominates the valley floor of the Kilchbalm.

Leisurely we ambled on to the head of the valley where we looked around for a bivouac site. On the north side of the valley we discovered a huge smoky cave, partly filled with fragrant hay gathered by shepherds on the steep hillside. For facilities it had a fire-place and a few improvised benches, while a trickling spring by the entrance supplied us with water. It was one of the finest bivouacs I have ever experienced. Sitting in front of a glowing fire, we smoked Swiss cigars and discussed the problems of life.

4 o'clock next morning - Sombre clouds enveloped the mountain flanks; only the valley floor was clear of mist. Quickly we crawled back into the cosy hay.

7 o'clock - We awoke to bright sunshine and a clear blue sky. Fate had fooled us. Going without breakfast we set off 15 minutes later and hurried up steep rock-strewn grass slopes towards a cirque filled with avalanche snow and situated to the right of the Kilchbalm ridge below the icefall of the Hirtli glacier.

We soon realized that all our haste was futile and that we would never succeed in conquering such a tremendous wall that day. Anyhow, we decided to reconnoitre the beginning of the route and the lower part of the face in preparation for a later assault.

The Kilchbalm ridge swept down as an imposing buttress to the screes at its base. We recognized that our route, like that of Amstutz and Michel, would have to take the ridge in its lower part, because the steep slabby recess in the face to its left

203

rising above huge avalanche channels is insurmountable. Where had the first ascensionists started up this buttress ridge? What line had they taken? We had no idea and we did not possess a route description. We therefore had to work out our own line up to the somewhat gentler section of the ridge. It mattered that this line should not throw up any great difficulties, as we needed to climb it before daybreak if we wanted to master this tremendous face without a bivouac.

We crossed the scree left to the foot of the buttress cliff and attempted to climb it directly. This was most unpleasant and we experienced major difficulties on smooth vegetated rock running with water. It was certainly nothing to be climbed at night, so we retreated and traversed a long way to the right below the rocks, then returning left by a higher rising ledge towards the crest. The terrain, though easier, was still too hard for a night-time ascent. We withdrew once again and for a bit we ascended on the right of the buttress by the avalanche cone embedded below the icefall of the Hirtli glacier. Soon we found a better stratified rock zone in the flank bounding the north side of the Kilchbalm ridge to the right of two deeply cut almost parallel chimneys. Perhaps easier access to the ridge would be possible here?

I crossed the snow cone to the bottom of the chimneys. Schulze stayed behind for the time being to retain a better view of the face. He would direct me by shouting out advice. I climbed ledged rocks westwards, and got into a system of cracks and gullies up which I made quick progress. I was already nearing the ridge when my advance was temporarily checked by steep slabs. But I had seen enough. In light rock climbing boots it would undoubtedly be possible to reach the ridge by these slabs and a continuing line of chimney-cracks above.

Satisfied with the result of our reconnaissance, we returned leisurely in the evening twilight to our bivouac site. Next morning we descended to the valley to meet Drexel, and that same afternoon we went back together to the Kilchbalm bivouac.

7th September - At 2 o'clock in the morning we left our overnight quarters. Thanks to the reconnaissance we managed to find the route to the beginning of the climb surprisingly well. Still in darkness - it was 4.15 a.m. - we started to climb. Slowly it brightened in the east. A silvery glow emanated from the grey limestone in the early morning light. Reaching the highest point of my reconnaissance, we changed from nailed boots into light rock climbing boots, and went up the line of chimneys spotted two days previously. Just below the crest of the ridge a difficult overhang barred our exit. Drexel led this pitch and lowered one end of the rope which we pulled up on quickly.

Here for the first time on the ascent we saw the stupendous summit wall of the Gspaltenhorn. We still did not grant ourselves any time to examine it at leisure because we wanted to put the Kilchbalm ridge below us. In quite superb climbing we stormed up the crest of the ridge which is composed of sound slabs. None of us even considered roping up. And for what purpose in any case? Why should we let frustrating rope management mar the pleasure of such splendid climbing?

Gradually the Kilchbalm ridge eased off a little. We could already see the snow dome that crowns the ridge shimmering close at hand. Schulze had hurried on far ahead of us and was sitting on a knoll, his eyes glued to the summit wall. Soon we reached him. It was only 7 a.m. We had ample time and could afford to enjoy the magnificent morning at leisure while studying the route ahead.

A deeply cut scoop separated us from the summit wall which rose in an almost vertical face to the north-west ridge. To reach the base of the wall we either had to descend by a series of broken rock gullies into the scoop or had to make a long traverse by uncomfortably steep ledges across the face on its west side. We reckoned that either route would go.

But what was the state of this summit wall? From our position we already realized that it was composed of rotten, boiler plate rock. Every ledge was snow covered, every gully and

205

crack was blocked with ice. Clearly we faced some hard work.

Schulze had descended a little below the ridge and had traversed on to the face to reconnoitre the route. He disappeared from sight behind a corner and we only heard the din of the stone-fall sent down by his movements. Gingerly we followed him, still uncertain whether we ought to be moving in his tracks. Rounding the corner, we saw that he was already near the snow couloir on the right-hand side of the summit wall.

There now remained no further doubt as to which route to take. We followed Schulze's track to the edge of the couloir swept by stone-fall, crossed it in great haste, then climbed rock ribs in the centre of the face. Meantime, Schulze had chosen to continue by a significantly harder line. He had ascended the couloir and much higher up he struggled across verglassed rocks out of the gully on to our rib. We were eventually reunited at an inadequate stance where we debated our next course of action. Ought we to rope up? Ought we to belay rope length by rope length? No, it would have served no purpose. The rock was so friable and devoid of holds, covered with snow, ice and pebbles, running with water and so exceptionally steep besides, that methodical belaying would have been impossible. Looking after the rope would have increased the stone-fall hazard and slowed us down. Moreover, in the event of one of the party falling it would have probably sealed the fate of us all. We therefore decided to dispense with the protection of the rope.

Exercising the most meticulous caution we continued upwards. Our movements resembled creeping more than climbing. Each of us took a different line so as to minimize the danger of knocking down rocks which might strike a companion. Occasionally bombardments of rock whizzed down from the heights, crashing to either side of us on steep slabs and scattering splinters into the depths below. It was a nerve-racking struggle, but at least we saw our success in terms of height rapidly gained.

The trapezoidal summit pyramid drew nearer. We were

already as high as the big tower on the Gspaltenhorn North-West ridge and we observed a party engaged in descending its glistening summit snow ridge.

With increasing height the system of ribs merged into a zone of steep slabs, only developing again at a steep step just below the snowy summit pyramid. The slabs were plastered with snow and ice. Here we would so willingly have changed from our light rock climbing boots, now totally unsuitable, into nailed boots, but we did not find a stance or any opportunity at all to do so. We had to carry on in our light boots, clearing holds and steps out of the snow with our axes, and cutting tiny nicks in the curst of ice on the rocks in order to provide some sort of surface grip for our soft felt soles. We turned the final steep riser, level with the highest step on the north-west ridge, by a recess in the face to our right and traversed back along its upper edge.

The climbers on the north-west ridge had meanwhile spotted us. They waved excitedly and shouted their approval at our success. A step composed of friable, flaky rock still had to be negotiated by some mind-shattering moves before we reached the uniform ice flank. Below it, standing on one leg at a time, we were at last able to put on our nailed boots. Ice axes swung into action again. We nicked out one step after the other, until the last one had been cut at 3 p.m. Delighted with our conquest, we shook hands by the summit cairn of the Gspaltenhorn.

For a long while we gazed at distant ranges and also at another face that we coveted - the North Face of the Lauterbrunnen Breithorn. There the problem of a direct route still awaited a solution. We had barely escaped the horrors of the Gspaltenhorn wall and already yearned for new adventures. But the longer we scrutinized the face, the more we formed the opinion that this tremendous wall of rock and ice must at all events hold in store very considerable or perhaps even insuperable difficulties.

Undecided about our next objective, yet well pleased with the day's work, we descended the north-west ridge to the Bütt-

Biwak

Gletscherhorn North-West Face.

lassenlücke. Looking back from there at our face, we could scarcely believe that we had succeeded in finding a route up its inhospitable flank to the summit. We rushed down snow fields and scree slopes westwards into the Kien valley, the last glimmer of daylight fading away on the snow crests of the Blümlisalp before we found overnight quarters at the Alp Dürrenberg.

NORTH-WEST FACE OF THE GLETSCHERHORN
(3983 metres)

While returning from the Kien valley across the Sefinenfurke to the Sefinen valley on the day after our assault on the Gspaltenhorn, the northern precipices of the Gletscherhorn were revealed to us in their full magnitude. Its face rises steeply to inaccessible heights above the very head of the Rottal valley, and it forms the eastern extremity of the stupendous rock and ice wall extending from the Wetterlücke to the Lauitor.

Two years earlier I had first besieged the Rottal face of the Gletscherhorn after the ascent of the Fiescherhorn North Face. On that occasion I abandoned my plans due to bad weather and deep fresh snow.

This time too the conditions did not exactly look promising. We could see black ice shimmering on the face. None the less we reckoned that we would achieve success more easily on the Gletscherhorn than on the intimidating north wall of the Lauterbrunnen Breithorn. But we already knew for a fact that mastering the face would exact a lot of time and all our endeavour.

On the following morning - it was September 9th - we ascended from Stechelberg to the Rottal hut. Our time was limited by Drexel already having to leave for home in two days time due to business commitments. In view of this we decided to start up the face as late as noon and bivouac as high as possible on the rocks in order to be able to reach the top in good time the next day.

From the magnificently situated Rottal hut we viewed the scene of our prospective struggle. Just below the summit a hanging glacier is recessed in the face. About half-way down the face there is a practically vertical rock barrier. The lower part of the face is cut by a huge, steep couloir that carries all the stone-fall and ice avalanches from the entire upper half of the face. We had to avoid this couloir if we didn't want to risk our lives. A broad, poorly defined rock rib, rising to the north-east of the central couloir towards the vertical rock barrier in the middle of the face, seemed to offer the best line of ascent up the lower half of the face. We would have to negotiate this barrier to the left at its lowest point in order to reach the steep ice on the upper part of the face. The exit from the face would no doubt have to be made to the right of a steep rock bastion extending below the north-east ridge.

We still tarried for a little while, observing the sky. Only a few hours before the sun had been shining out of a far too clear sky, but now it was hidden behind black cloud banks. Slowly it began to rain. Should we dare to put our bold plan into action just the same? Yes! Today was Drexel's last chance of tackling the face before the end of his holiday. Our decision was determined by this fact.

We left the hut at midday and crossed the virtually level catchment-basin of the Rottal glacier without difficulty to the foot of the face. The summit of the Gletscherhorn towered more than 1200 metres above. How long would it take to master these 1200 metres? And when would we attain the highest point?

At 1.30 p.m. we stood right by the main couloir below the bergschrund. It was a ferocious and discouraging sight. Overhanging ice bulges and vertical rocks scoured smooth by avalanches combined with the bergschrund to present an apparent impasse. Drexel was already preparing to commence battle with an ice buttress that seemed a dubious possibility. Then we discovered a spot further left where it was possible to make a convenient straddle across from the snow on to the rock on the far side. We climbed the initial steep wall on poor holds to somewhat gentler terrain.

To begin with we climbed the crest of the ridge directly for a few pitches, then moved up right towards an indistinct steep gully which the rib divides into a broad east branch and a narrow west one. Thanks to sound rock with good holds we made brisk progress. About 100 metres higher the gully merged into a rotten rock band extending through a section of brittle shale. We proceeded with infinite caution, cutting steps with our ice axes in the flaky rock and clinging with our fingers to the loose grit. Strenuously we sweated our way some 150 metres up the band until rock in steps led straight up again.

The weather deteriorated as we got higher, grey mist sweeping in from the west to blot out the valley below. The light spots of rain at the start had long since developed into an icy drizzle, and we could hear a storm raging over the summit ridges. Snow falling on the upper part of the face was whirled up by the strong gale and came cascading down, accumulating into torrents of snow that thundered down the steep gullies into the depths.

The conditions really did not seem suitable for assailing one of the highest walls in the Western Alps, but for all that we were not giving up a struggle that easily. We wanted to await the following morning before deciding whether to continue the attack or - if there was no alternative - to retreat.

As early as 3.30 p.m. and about 400 metres up the face we sought out a bivouac site. We didn't want to risk climbing too high, so that an eventual retreat the next morning would be neither too long nor too dangerous. Seeking shelter from the storm, we chose a shallow recess in the steep rock. However, it was such a confined space that only two people could squeeze into it. Drexel consequently volunteered to spend the night alone on a ledge below an overhang a few metres above. Schulze and I cleared ice out of the recess, banged a peg into the rock, tied on securely as a safeguard and draped one of our two tent sacks over us. Drexel took the other one.

The bivouac was bitterly cold and long. We two did not, I admit, suffer that much because we were somewhat protected from the storm in our recess. On the other hand, our position was more unpleasant, sitting on a smooth sloping slab devoid of holds. At every movement we slid down lower until the thin belay rope cut into our bodies. We never knew which position would be most expedient to adopt to get some long-desired rest. A disagreeable cross between sitting and lying was our lot that night. In this respect Drexel had a rather better deal. He could at least stretch out comfortably on his ledge, but by contrast he suffered badly from the cold and the storm despite his Mosetig sack.

On top of the intense impressions made by this storm-swept night, another matter occupied our troubled minds. The evening before we had received the news that one of our best friends and dearest climbing companions, Dr. Leo Maduschka, had perished in a vicious storm on the tremendous north-west face of the Civetta. As a consequence, it was without our customary adventurous spirit that we had started up this face. Our thoughts belonged to our dead friend who had been obliged to pay for his great mountaineering passion with his life.

We had to endure fourteen hours at our cramped bivouac site. Unable to sleep, we listened to the music of the storm and to séracs crashing down. Time did not pass any quicker at the thought of what lay in front of us or on account of our uncertainty about a successful outcome to the undertaking.

With the approach of day the force of the storm abated. At dawn we peered out of our tent sacks to a clear morning. There were just a few streaks of cloud hovering above the Jungfrau. We were quickly up and ready to go. Now we adopted the motto: Fight through to victory. At 5.45 a.m. we left our bivouac site. We climbed steep rocks, icy and snowed up, towards the left edge of the rock barrier blocking access to the upper half of the face. After a tough struggle we overcame this obstacle at its lowest point and then the route above lay open to us.

A steep ice slope, marked by isolated rotten rock outcrops, rises from here to the vertical rock girdle just below the northeast ridge. We would no doubt have to force our way off the face by the right edge of this final rock bastion, unless we succeeded in reaching the summit directly.

After a brief halt we proceeded with renewed vigour. Drexel led the next few pitches. He worked with dogged endeavour at the ice which was as hard as glass. It needed hours of step-cutting to advance a few rope lengths. The rock outcrops protruding from the ice here and there gave us little respite, being so crumbly that extremely cautious handling was essential.

Embroiled in our work we had not noticed the weather worsening. Mist was brewing up on the mountain flanks and blotting out the view. A gale force wind had suddenly sprung up, sweeping powder snow across the bare ice. The situation now called for us to get off the face as quickly as possible. We suspected that a bulge at the right edge of the rock bastion extending below the north-east ridge concealed a steep gully that would probably make it possible to exit on to the ridge. Drawing nearer, our supposition was confirmed and we traversed snow-plastered rocks to the foot of the gully. For two or three rope lengths we worked our way strenuously yet delicately up this slabby gully, until we managed to move right up steep verglassed rock on to the crest of the ridge.

It was 3.45 p.m. Close by we saw the summit beckoning us through the swirling mist. One last short effort, then at 4.15 p.m. victory was ours.

Laboriously we battled our way down to the Lauitor, then we bounded down the steep glacier slopes between the Rottalhorn and the Kranzberg to the Jungfraufirn. Exhausted, we trudged through soggy snow in the evening dusk up to Jungfraujoch hotel.

Next morning, as it was fine and clear, we decided to traverse the Jungfrau back to the Lauterbrunnen valley. We sat for a long while on top of the Jungfrau, admiring the awe-inspiring wall of the Gletscherhorn, happy to recollect our tough struggle and conscious of our hard-won conquest. Then we headed downwards by the classic route of the Rottal ridge.

In Lauterbrunnen we said good-bye to Drexel, homeward-

Lauterbrunnen Breithorn North Face.

bound, and made preparations for our final encounter which was to be directed at the Lauterbrunnen Breithorn.

NORTH FACE OF THE LAUTERBRUNNEN BREITHORN
(3785 metres)

The Lauterbrunnen Breithorn is the most beautiful peak on the mountain chain ringing the Lauterbrunnen valley. Its ice-coated north wall sweeps up 1300 metres from the Breithorn glacier.

The structure of the face is unique. A symmetrically shaped summit wall, divided by narrow rock ribs and ice gullies, is based upon two enormous supporting buttresses which project from the lower part of the face on both sides of the summit fall line. A bay, somewhat like a gorge, is recessed in the face between these buttresses. From the bottom of this bay a steep glacier arm, fed by avalanches coming down off the face, issues forth.

This majestic flank had already been the objective of a bold undertaking at an earlier date. Dr. D. Chervet and Dr. W. Richardet forced the first route up the north side of the mountain on 12th August 1924. These climbers had evaded the lower cliffs by ascending the Breithornjoch route much further left to the Upper Breithorn glacier. (5) There they traversed right to the base of a well defined rib on the upper part of the face which they followed to the east summit. So it seemed that the problem had at least been partly solved; all the same the face still aroused my keenest interest. I considered it one of the highest ranking objectives in the Bernese Alps to open up a route on this wall and in particular to find a direct line from the steep recessed cliff at its foot to the highest point.

In July 1932 we had spent many days at the Oberhornalp besieging unconquered faces in mist and rain. Whenever the clouds had lifted to reveal the North Face of the Lauterbrunnen Breithorn resplendent in fresh snow, avalanches cascading off it down to the valley, we had buried all our hopes of ever being able to force this coveted ascent. From the Gspaltenhorn we had once more viewed the face, forged and again rejected plans, cherished and again buried our hopes. Yet how could all such dithering help? Only a determined attempt could bring about a result.

On September 12th we went up to the Oberhornalp in the afternoon. With the rain beating down on the roof of the shack, we dossed down in the hay in low spirits. The early hours brought no improvement in the weather; thick mist enveloped our surroundings. At 9 a. m. it suddenly brightened up and we treated this as a signal to set off quickly. We wanted to utilize the fine weather and even if we should no longer succeed in conquering the face today, we certainly wished to reconnoitre it in preparation for a conclusive assault.

Ascending moraine slopes southwards, we reached the Breithorn glacier and crossed it to the foot of the steep glacier arm issuing from the lower part of the face. Here we strapped on crampons and began to climb steep, crevasse riddled ice slopes. After some 200-250 metres the angle of the ice eased off a bit. We paused near the lowest cliffs towering up as smooth slabby walls.

An inconceivably savage amphitheatre of rock surrounds the observer at this point. Slabby walls, scoured smooth with dripping water, soar upwards on all sides in the shape of a horseshoe and seem quite unclimbable. Perplexed, we let our gaze wander across the cliffs. Should we attempt the slabs, often swept by stone-fall, in the bed of the gorge? Hopeless! Or should we climb the rock buttress to the right? Here there appeared to be a way up, but this route would not have led to the summit and it looked even less direct than the Chervet-Richardet line of ascent. Again we scanned the face. In the apparently vertical wall of the rock buttress jutting out to the left we now spotted a horizontal band which ends at a step just short of merging into a ramp of slabs rising towards the bed of the gorge. At the end of this ramp it undoubtedly had to be possible to exit from the gorge on to the upper part of the face by a steep couloir rising slightly to the left. If we managed to reach the above-mentioned band by a system of cracks, and then the steep couloir beyond this band and the ramp, we would probably have discovered the key to the ascent.

We were still considering these possibilities when a terrific roar suddenly shook the air. Rocks swept down the face, debris crashing on to the steep glacier ice and bounding down the precipitous slopes below. We ducked for cover behind some low ice blocks. Slowly the howling of the rock salvos ceased and the immediate danger had passed.

We left our stance at the double and traversed left to the foot of the cracks and gullies leading up to the start of the horizontal band. We crossed the bergschrund effortlessly and gained height unexpectedly rapidly. Soon we stood on the broad band below a line of roof overhangs where we built a prominent cairn. Along the progressively narrower band we went up to the dreaded step at its end. This too was easier to negotiate than we had anticipated; we just had to climb a short vertical pitch on to the ramp which we climbed with increasing difficulty until it petered out at the foot of a vertical step. To the right of this we saw the steep couloir that held the key to the ascent. We had to reach the upper part of the face by it if our attempt was not to fail.

Thus far we had climbed unroped. Even now we still tried to find the best line independently. Schulze investigated the steep ground to the left of the gully and stuck persistently to the slabby rocks thereabouts.

Meanwhile I attempted to climb the deep couloir, streaming with water, directly. I inched my way upwards on tiny outward-sloping holds, considering every move carefully. Again there came an ominous humming noise from the upper part of the face. I was standing in the most dangerous position, in the narrowest section of a funnel attracting all the volleys of rock crashing down into the depths. I pressed my body closely against the slippery rocks, my forehead resting in the running water. Some alarming moments followed, while the bombardments thundered narrowly past my head into the depths. In great haste I battled up a few more metres to a meagre stance and leaned forward to look round a smooth bulge for a few seconds. I decided that the route would go here and had consequently found the key to the ascent. I beat a very hasty retreat with renewed rock salvos rumbling down the couloir.

I soon rejoined Schulze who had given up his attempt as hopeless. We got out of range of the stone-fall and reviewed the situation. It was 2 p.m. At this advanced hour of the day there was no question of still conquering the face. Two alternatives lay open to us. We could either get as high as possible and bivouac, or descend to the hut and try to achieve the ascent at one go the next day. We reasoned that the stone-fall danger was now greater than at any other time of the day. Further, the weather remained unsettled with veiled cirrus clouds building up. If we were surprised by the onset of bad weather during a bivouac, our situation could become really desperate in view of the expected difficulties. Following these considerations we decided to retreat and descended unhurriedly, reaching the Oberhornalp with the evening shadows.

When we looked out of the hut soon after midnight, the weather remained unchanged. Nevertheless we set out at 2.30 a.m. Thanks to our previous attempt we found the route in the dark without any problems and at dawn we were already on the scree band by the cairn we had built the day before. We dallied a short while here, still hesitant. Should we dare to continue in spite of the menacing weather? Yes, for the time being in any case, as we could always turn back a bit later.

We climbed the ramp to the point where it was necessary to traverse into the wet gully. Here we put on the rope and our light rock climbing boots.

Schulze led into the gully. At first the rope ran out slowly, then more and more quickly. I had only a few coils left in my hands and Schulze still hadn't found a stance. "Rope out," I bellowed. "Follow without a belay," came the reply. Cautiously I moved up the wet, holdless rock, continually aware that the slightest negligence would be fatal for both of us. Schulze

218

had long since disappeared from view, and I could only tell through the rope running out jerkily that he too was climbing. For a short time the rope stopped running, then it was taken in quickly - Schulze had found a belay stance. In no time I joined him and we stormed up the gully system at a furious pace, because already rock salvos had begun buzzing down from the summit wall. Moreover, we were moving on most unpleasant terrain, wet rock alternating with glassy ice and bone-hard snow. Our light rock climbing boots were soaked through, so we stopped on a narrow ledge to change into our nailed boots and strap on crampons.

We looked back well pleased with our progress so far. The lower cliffs lay below us which meant we had mastered the principal difficulty. Better still, the weather seemed to be improving with only a few isolated clouds drifting across the intense blue sky.

Confidently we set to work again and climbed a steep snow cone towards the second rock girdle which is level with the overhanging ice bulges resting on rock buttresses on both sides of the face. We overcame this barrier by a groove, beginning with a waterwashed overhang and a difficult vertical step. We then stood at the foot of a poorly defined rock rib leading straight to the highest point by a line to the right of the rib used by Chervet and Richardet.

700 metres still lay between us and the summit, and this rib was to tax our abilities to the limits. I only want to give a general impression of it. We were faced with some extremely hard rock and ice climbing. Rotten shale requiring the most delicate handling alternated with steep almost holdless rock demanding great technical skills. Loose powder snow on smooth slabs gave way to glassy ice that we mastered with a strenuous session of step-cutting. During this ascent we changed our boots more than half a dozen times, often only standing in a tiny step in the ice or clinging to steep slabs. Just as often, on poor stances, we had to strap on crampons and undo them again, take off our heavy rucksacks to fumble for gear and

stuff away items finished with. Often we gazed upwards at the glistening summit cornice, our enticing goal beckoning us in bright sunlight, yet it was only terribly slowly that we drew nearer to it. All 1300 metres of this face had to be fought for.

100 metres below the top the crest reared up defiantly to present a final obstacle. It rose almost vertically as rotten stratified rock. At a narrow stance immediately below this sharp riser Schulze hammered a peg into the rock, clipped on a karabiner and pulled the rope through as a belay. With infinite caution he edged up metre by metre, then he disappeared behind the sunlit crest of the rib. I soon rejoined him on an exposed platform close to the top. We stormed joyously up the last rock pitches to set foot on our splendid summit at 3. 35 p.m.

It was certainly the most enjoyable summit rest of this successful summer campaign in the Bernese Alps. We were thrilled to bits at our unprecedented triumph. To add to our pleasure, fortune let us savour an unrestricted view southwards to the high peaks of the Pennine Alps towering in their shining white mantle above a surging sea of clouds, and south-west to the snow dome of Mont Blanc.

Eventually we set off down the west ridge to the Wetterlücke. Wearily we rounded the south foot of the Tschingelhorn towards the Petersgrat. Pale moonlight gleamed on the glacier while we crossed the broad snow expanses of the Kanderfirn to the Mutthorn hut.

Next day, motoring down the valley in a hurry, we stopped briefly at a bend in the road to look back at the mountains that had granted us such exceptional experiences, recollecting our toughest struggles and the jubilation upon our successes. We headed homewards, knowing we had not battled in vain, convinced we had achieved values that make life worth living, that give our existence a lasting meaning and that raise man from everyday life to true humanity.

Author's notes:

1. The Lauper Route acknowledged here actually uses the

north-east face, while the famous Eigerwand or improperly so-called North Wall in fact leads up the north-west face. Welzenbach was writing for the 1933 German and Austrian Alpine Club Yearbook, the above-mentioned Lauper Route having been climbed in 1932, whereas the first proper attempt on the Eigerwand was not until 1935.

2. The Schmadri hut was later built here.

3. Time given as 2.30 p.m. in Munich Academic Alpine Club Journal report.

4. Welzenbach referred to this route as the North-East Face, but the modern guidebook labels it the North Face. Strictly speaking, the upper part of the cliff falls north, the lower part north-east.

5. The Breithornjoch was first reached from the north and traversed by O.K. Williamson and H. Symons with Jean Maître and Pierre Maurys on 26th July 1905. The Upper Breithorn glacier is a hanging glacier terrace above the Wärmietehoren.

Bernese Appraisal

WELZENBACH had set his mind on the great unclimbed faces of the Bernese Alps and each success inspired the next. He also had logical and practical reasons for concentrating systematically upon as many as possible of the most challenging objectives in one area. Often the observations made during one climb acted as a virtual reconnaissance for the next. Here in the Bernese Oberland, from the summit of the Gspaltenhorn Welzenbach mapped out his plans for the assault five days later on the Lauterbrunnen Breithorn and during the descent of the same mountain he grasped the opportunity to size up the North-West Face of the Gletscherhorn. Advantage could also be taken of knowledge gained of the prevailing conditions on one face by carrying out a similar type of route in the vicinity soon afterwards. By returning even within the same season he would arrive with a good idea of general problems, such as the state of a glacier and the amount of old snow or ice on the rocks.

Welzenbach's comparative affluence in a secure professional post allowed him to journey anywhere in the Alps without worrying about the expense. On several occasions he used this privileged position to make short visits to the Western Alps. If, as on his first 1932 trip to the Bernese Oberland, a persistent spell of bad weather wrecked his plans, he could cut short his stay and return later in the season. Precisely such tactics paid off handsomely here.

Bad weather in itself often failed to deter Welzenbach. Much depended upon what it did to the climbing conditions. Poor conditions were acceptable provided they were not unduly dangerous. Welzenbach's party patiently besieged the Grosshorn, their first objective, sitting out six days of rain and making one false start. Then they did not shirk from cutting 3000 steps in hard water ice over two days, hardly helped by an uncomfortable bivouac in sodden clothes followed by steady snowfall and negligible visibility on the upper part of the route.

On the Gletscherhorn - with limited time at their disposal due to Drexel's imminent departure - Welzenbach's party intentionally set out to bivouac 400 metres up the North-West Face despite rain and mist. Fully aware of the poor conditions, they wanted to maximize their chances of snatching the route by being in position in the event of an improvement. The decision to attack or retreat could wait till the morning. A storm-swept night spent separately, cramped on two ledges, was rewarded with a fine dawn. A prompt start for the summit was made unhesitatingly. Slowed down by snow-plastered and verglassed rocks, their opportunism and resilience ensured a remarkable success even though another storm broke towards midday. This encouraged Welzenbach to choose a line of ascent up the left-hand side of the face onto the North-East Ridge almost 100 metres below the summit. Even in such difficult circumstances Welzenbach managed to pick a line that avoided exposure to the objective dangers of the sérac wall directly below the summit. It comes as no surprise that his climbing friends always relied on his unsurpassed route-finding ability.

The Gletscherhorn had extended Welzenbach far less than his physically draining efforts on the Grosshorn. Yet technically it is now considered the most serious and difficult of his 1932 climbs in the Bernese Alps. Even so, as a measure of the high standards involved, the Grosshorn is currently compared with the Triolet North Face in the Mont Blanc Range and with the Dent d'Hérens North Face. All are rated TD (très difficile = very difficult) by the French adjectival scale for alpine climbs - this being just one grade short of the ultimate by modern concepts and a step into the unknown in their day.

Throughout his 1932 campaign, only once was Welzenbach blessed with fine settled weather - on the Gspaltenhorn North Face. That year it was also his only Bernese climb not on the great Lauterbrunnen Wall. In remote surroundings this awe-

223

inspiring precipice towers higher than any other Swiss face except the Eigerwand. Welzenbach's first attempt became a thorough reconnaissance once he realized they had started too late to conquer the wall within the day. With no reason for urgency, on this occasion he preferred to prepare for another assault rather than commit himself to an unnecessary and unavailing bivouac. It demonstrated his readiness to exercise caution if he believed such behaviour would promote his cause. Success on the Gspaltenhorn came just two days later and was most unusual in its method: the party climbed the entire route unroped (after soloing one chimney pitch Drexel lowered a rope which Welzenbach and Schulze used as a fixed line). Welzenbach explained: "The face is composed of limestone. The Kilchbalm ridge gives quite good climbing on sound rock, but the summit cliffs degenerate into dreadful crumbling boiler plate rock mixed with ice. As it would have hardly been possible to belay on the face and rope management would just have increased the objective dangers from stone-fall, we dispensed entirely with the rope. Only by this means were we able to conquer the tremendous face in such an exceptionally short time."(1) Although the party took 13 hours from their bivouac to the summit, their actual climbing time is given as $8\frac{3}{4}$ hours. The Gspaltenhorn climb may have been Welzenbach's least elegant route in the region, but it was undoubtedly a masterpiece of fast free climbing and intelligent route-finding.

Of the Lauterbrunnen Breithorn North Face, his final success of the season, Welzenbach admitted: "In its lower part the cliff is very exposed to stone-fall." And it has since acquired a reputation as the most dangerous of the Lauterbrunnen Wall climbs. Here again Welzenbach encountered uncertain weather and the first attempt was abandoned rather than risk a storm-bound bivouac. With the route reconnoitred, the following morning Welzenbach and Schulze set off confident of forcing the route quickly despite ominous clouds. In the event the weather held, but as on other occasions it does seem that the threat of a storm, together with the inherent objective dangers, positively

224

stimulated Welzenbach to greater efforts and a quicker pace. This was not a bad thing because on the big walls of the Bernese Alps speed was the essence of success. Unsound rock, steep ice and poor protection are common features on most of these faces. Fast climbing meant that Welzenbach and his companions spent the minimum of time exposed to the inescapable objective dangers.

Through his string of brilliant successes Welzenbach had realized the enormous potential for ice climbing in this region, pointed out at the turn of the century by the Conway - Coolidge guidebook. His list of achievements in the Bernese Alps left just one great challenge unsolved for his successors, that of the Eigerwand. Welzenbach's sound reasons for neglecting the Eigerwand have been explained (2) - For him the time was simply not yet ripe. And it would be wrong to think that he did not spot the potential of the Eiger's North-East Face. However, he was aware of Hans Lauper's longstanding designs on this route and their mutual respect excluded any kind of encroachment on one another's objectives. The two men corresponded about their own climbing activities and about mountaineering matters in general. Lauper had revealed his plan for August to Welzenbach who applauded its accomplishment (3) in a letter dated 31st August 1932: "I should like to express my heartiest congratulations on your splendid feat on the Eiger. I too thought that the route you took was possible..."

During the following winter and spring Welzenbach's ski touring activities were restricted to weekend excursions in the Eastern Alps. In July 1933 his holiday plans in the Mont Blanc Range were frustrated by unsettled weather and several heavy snowfalls. Forced to abandon plans to tackle first the Brenva Face and afterwards the Jorasses North Face, with typical foresight Welzenbach hit upon the idea of his party defecting to the southern part of the Bernese Alps. He rightly anticipated more feasible conditions on the Nesthorn North Face, a route he had marked down mentally the previous year. And so this was to become the last of his great Oberland ice climbs; a

225

series of climbs that pushed forward concepts of what was possible and inspired others to follow his example in future years.

Author's notes:

1. Munich Academic Alpine Club Journal 1931/32.

2. See footnote no. 4 in W. W's account of ascent of the Fiescherwand.

3. Lauper and Alfred Zürcher with the guides Alexander Graven and Joseph Knubel on 20th August 1932.

Nesthorn

ERICH SCHULZE

IN THE summer of 1933 Welzenbach, Drexel and I set off by car from Munich on the evening of 11th July, intending to spend our holiday in the Mont Blanc Range. The following night we reached Chamonix at 1 a.m. and from our room at the Hotel des Étrangers I saw Mont Blanc for the first time in the morning.

This trip was my fourth with Welzenbach to the Western Alps. I am indebted to him for a series of magnificent ice climbs in the Western Alps that highlighted the many marvellous experiences he shared with me in the mountains, and I was happy to be able to pursue new objectives in his company now.

However, as can happen, our plans were virtually wrecked by bad weather and storms. All the same we did at least manage to carry out some climbs on three successive days.

On 17th July we left the Leschaux hut at 1.30 a.m. and ascended the Mont Mallet glacier. While we were tracking in deep snow towards the foot of an ice flank (1), we saw a party of four following us at a fast pace. We had just crossed the bergschrund at an exposed spot when one of the four gentlemen, all members of the Groupe de Haute Montagne (2), asked permission to overtake. They seemed to be moving extremely well and we had no reason to object, yet this was very nearly our undoing. We had climbed two-thirds of the flank and Drexel was cutting steps where our predecessors had clawed their way up relying entirely upon their crampons. Suddenly I heard Welzenbach gasp out clearly and urgently, "God forbid!" About fifty metres above Drexel I saw the leading French climber tumbling rapidly towards us. Despite our comparatively good stances it was obvious that we could not hold this man who would certainly also pull off his second. We would be snatched from our steps and the downward slide would commence... if the impossible had not happened. Their second man had jammed his ice-axe into a slit in the ice, and this held the fall of his companion - despite the steep angle of the slope and the absence of a single step in the bone-hard surface. All three of us breathed a huge sigh of relief at the passing of such a frightening moment. After that we overtook the French, the shock having apparently turned their legs to jelly. A delightful snow ridge led steeply to the foot of Mont Mallet and, being without our light rock climbing boots, we climbed the summit rocks in our stockinged feet. Two hours later we stood on the Aiguille de Rochefort and in the afternoon we went along the ridge past the Dent du Géant.

While Drexel rested at the Torino hut next day, Welzenbach and I paid a visit to the Madonna on the Dent du Géant. In fine weather it was an amusing and harmless climb up thick fixed hemp ropes.

The snowfall of the preceding days, combined with the present effects of the sun, was causing so many avalanches on the Brenva face that we changed our plans for the third day and settled for the long traverse of Mont Blanc. Despite a starlit sky that evening we failed to find the hut, so we bivouacked in the open. It was fine and cold, circumstances that did not encourage us to tarry towards morning. By 6 a.m. we were already on top of Mont Blanc du Tacul. There Welzenbach decided to turn back and descend by the Mer de Glace to Montenvers. Drexel and I took up the battle with the deep fresh snow and waded up steep soft slopes to Mont Maudit. We reached the summit of Mont Blanc at 5 p.m. and got back to Chamonix exhausted about 11 p.m.

By this time our hopes of good conditions in the Mont Blanc Range were shattered. Nevertheless we waited for an improvement until Welzenbach suggested visiting the Bernese Alps again. This promptly agreed, we drove via Geneva, Martigny and the Rhone valley to Brig, and that evening walked up to

Belalp to stay overnight there.

Next morning we left the hotel laden with a lot of equipment and reached the enchanting Oberaletsch hut in a few hours. Our objective for the following day was the North Face of the Nesthorn. During our ascents of the previous year we had already seen the symmetrical, triangular shape of the face from the summits of the Grosshorn, Lauterbrunnen Breithorn and Gspaltenhorn.

After a short night's sleep we set out at 2.30 a.m., crossed the undulating Oberaletsch glacier and proceeded westwards up the Beich glacier to the bottom of the face. Viewed from this point the deeply recessed 950 metres high face does not exactly look inviting. We were all now aware that, despite being shorter than the other walls we had climbed in the Bernese Alps, it would present difficulties just as great and could be ranked equal in status. Towards 5 a.m. we strapped on crampons. Already the summit was glistening in the sun.

As almost always, Willo had figured out the route in advance. It was straightforward and at the same time magnificent, just like so many of his new climbs. A direct line from the foot of the face to the highest point, minor deviations only seeming necessary on the bottom third. There we would have to turn the hanging glacier at its lowest point which also seemed the easiest place. Above, we should climb the ice flank directly towards the summit. On the upper part of the face a band of slabs presented a problem and it remained to be seen whether we could master them. After this key section the main task seemed completed.

Slowly we started up the avalanche run-out. Day was already upon us and the surrounding mountains of the Bernese Alps were beautifully clear under a cloudless blue sky. We crossed the bergschrund without any of the anticipated difficulties, but instead we encountered hard and tedious work on the next section up extremely steep ice-cliffs. The ice was exceptionally hard and the snow cover so thin that every single step required numerous blows of the axe.

Nesthorn North Face.

Drexel took over the lead as he could cut steps longest without a pause. Welzenbach belayed him while I acted as photographer. After overcoming twenty extremely steep metres our advance was barred by vertical ice cliffs. A left-hand traverse was necessary and the subsequent pitches demanded meticulous care. A slight bulge at the foot of an outwardly arched sérac supplied the line for this traverse. Drexel had to squat to cut steps in this bulge and could not stand up at all due to the ice wall jutting out above him. Willo did have a good stance and would have been able to hold a fall, yet this did not permit Drexel to move any less cautiously, because at best a fall would have obliged us to abandon our attempt. And it is no pleasant matter to retreat down such steep ice slopes. After something like an hour the 15 metres traverse had been prepared for Welzenbach and me to follow with the heavy rucksacks. We were happy to get some movement back into our limbs after the wait at this exposed stance. Despite Drexel's thorough work we still found the traverse awkward with rucksacks, particularly as Drexel did not have anything like as safe a stance at the other end of the traverse as we had had at the start. After another ten minutes we were all together again, tightly huddled in an almost vertical grooved ice gully.

Drexel being somewhat exhausted by the last few hours, as third man at the back of the rope so far, I now took over the lead. Next we had to tackle this 15 metres high ice gully. These 15 metres were not unlike bridging up a dièdre, only I had to cut steps and holds all the way. It takes a long time before a hold in ice inspires confidence in its reliability. A short ice-axe would have been advantageous here, but failing that Willo handed me a big peg hammer with a curved pick which simplified my task considerably. Another hour saw the gully below us (3) and just above it came the last bergschrund above which the ice face rose at an increasingly steep angle. The snow cover made step-cutting easier than before but, as a consequence of climbing directly upwards, the second and third men on the rope had to endure a steady barrage of snow and ice chips. In this respect the leader definitely had the more pleasant position.

At the start we had reckoned that if necessary we could escape right or left onto the ridges confining the face, should we be repulsed by the central zone of slabs. Here, though half-way up the steep ice face, we realized that we had deceived ourselves. Both to the left and right our route was bounded by rock slabs so steep and smooth that a traverse in either direction seemed impossible, especially as vertical séracs and ice cliffs towered above the rock slabs below the ridge on the east side. We now knew that there was only one way up - the route already outlined well in advance by Willo who took over the lead on the ever steeper snow and ice. The work below had made me so warm that I had no objection to being the middle man on the rope. The bitter morning cold had given way to warm sunshine which cheered us no end after the physical discomfort of the early hours.

By 11.45 a.m. we reached the rock band and here Drexel again went first. The following hours were the toughest of the day. None of us had a stance safe enough to be confident of holding a fall. We couldn't hammer in any ice pegs because black rock glimmered under an inch or two of snow and ice. Delicately balanced, with the utmost care Drexel nicked out slowly and steadily one step after the other in the thin icy crust lying on the smooth slabs. We were aware of the necessity to tread warily and that any one of these steps breaking away would in all probability result in a fall. Our interest in the surroundings had disappeared. Tensed up, Welzenbach and I watched our friend at work. The face now fell away almost 600 metres at a phenomenally steep angle. Perched in the middle of this band of icy rock slabs we were obliged to be passive observers of Drexel's step-by-step progress, our nerves inevitably stretched to breaking point. It was evident to us that later in summer, with bare rocks probable, any attempt on the summit would be stopped here. To negotiate a vertical interval of about 20 metres by a right-hand traverse

232

of some 50 metres occupied nearly three hours.

To complicate matters even more during this traverse, our rope was somewhat too short. As the middle man I often had to follow in places virtually devoid of holds, straining my calf muscles in a supreme effort as I desperately clawed into the icy surface. During these periods any belaying on my part was completely out of the question and Welzenbach, as last man and in a slightly safer spot, just had to belay us both as well as possible. I had to devote my entire attention to remaining upright in extremely exposed positions with poor holds and practically no steps.

But even these minutes of utmost concentration passed by. We breathed a sigh of relief as Drexel completed an admirable lead by overcoming the last few metres of the slabs and reached the snow slopes of the summit flank at about 2. 30 p. m. He tracked a few steps in firm snow and was able to set up a sound belay. Willo and I soon followed. We took our first proper rest, ate a snack, and then proceeded with the last and easiest part of our task. Easy in that the technical difficulties had decreased, steps no longer needed cutting, and the snow had softened so that we could kick steps.

Once again it was my turn and after the snail's pace of the previous few hours I relished the prospect of gaining height minute by minute. Although our task was now relatively free from danger, it remained quite strenuous enough in view of our earlier exertions, and our hopes of getting to the top soon were not realized as quickly as we anticipated. The final 300 metres of the summit snow flank, still rising at a considerable angle, required $2\frac{1}{2}$ hours of tiring tracking.

At 5 p. m. we finally stood on the few bare rocks marking the summit. We shook hands and Welzenbach's eyes gleamed with joy at this hard-won victory. Yet again he had fulfilled one of his long cherished plans. I often saw Willo laughing, but I only witnessed such a happy and victorious radiance in his eyes after our finest triumph together, the direct ascent of the Lauterbrunnen Breithorn North Face, and here again after

233

our fight for the Nesthorn face. For an hour we relaxed in the sun facing the beautifully shaped Bietschhorn, appeasing our rumbling stomachs.

We commenced the descent (4) at 6 p. m. It took $4\frac{1}{2}$ hours and was awfully strenuous in soft, wet snow. On the glacier which had turned into a sodden morass during the day a small mishap befell me. Suddenly I sank to my waist in a deep puddle of freezing slushy water. Learning the lesson of this incident we subsequently concentrated our undivided attention on the route. By faint torchlight we luckily found the moraine on which the Oberaletsch hut is situated and in the knowledge of soon being inside this cosy building we happily scrambled up the slope to it.

The day had taken its toll on us (5) and our plan to start as early as 3 a. m. for the Aletschhorn no longer held any priority. We all slept till late in the morning. It was the last day of our holiday, so after descending via the Belalp to Brig we drove homewards in Welzenbach's car.

This was the last great route that I undertook with Welzenbach. Who could have imagined that it would be the last major success in his wonderful and bold climbing career?

Author's notes:

1. They climbed the short North-West Flank of the Dôme de Rochefort to the foot of its summit rocks, because the head of the Mont Mallet glacier rising to the depression between the Aiguille de Rochefort and Mont Mallet was barred by enormous bergschrunds that year. Strangely, the party did not bag the Dôme de Rochefort. Photographic documentation of the exact line taken was supplied by Erich Schulze in May 1979.

2. An influential association of élite mountaineers founded in France in 1919, but not restricted to French climbers.

3. The ice cliffs which in 1933 caused such time-consuming technical difficulties are nowadays, due to glacier movement, easily avoided to their right.

4. The party went down the west ridge, the ordinary route of ascent, to the Beich glacier.

5. They arrived back at 10.30 p.m., 20 hours after leaving the hut. Report in the Munich Academic Alpine Club Journal 1932/33.

Alfred Drexel leading on the Nesthorn North Face first ascent.

Last Alpine Climbs

ERICH SCHULZE, the only permanent member of Welzenbach's 1932 and 1933 parties, was unstinting in his praise of the man who had introduced him to the Western Alps and to big wall climbing: "Welzenbach whipped up our enthusiasm with his unquenchable spirit. He deserves all the credit for initiating our plans and realizing them. In the course of these climbs I recognized his mastery of mountaineering. His calmness and his caution matched by boldness and thoughtfulness, his presence of mind in all the situations we encountered on our climbs, his composure - all were unparalleled."

That year Welzenbach did return twice on fleeting visits to the Bernese Oberland. On 13th August - with Merkl, Schulze and Wieland - he attempted the North-West Face of the Ochs, the left wing extension of the Fiescherwand and even steeper than the main cliff, but his party was forced to retreat in deteriorating conditions below the summit headwall. Exactly one month later his plan to make the first ascent of the Mittaghorn North-West Face, now considered the easiest face climb on the Lauterbrunnen Wall, was foiled by weather bad enough for the undertaking to be abandoned at the bivouac site below it.

Shortly before sailing for India in mid April 1934 with the Nanga Parbat Expedition, Welzenbach spent the Easter weekend in the Berchtesgaden Alps, the scene of his first exploratory forays fifteen years before. On 31st March he ascended the Hoher Göll, on 1st April he traversed five peaks from the Schneibstein to the Kahlersberg, on 2nd April he climbed the Hocheck summit of the Watzmann. Finally on Sunday 8th April he managed a ski ascent of the Alpspitze above Garmisch-Partenkirchen in the Wetterstein, noting "Frozen snow on the run down".

Welzenbach's last logbook closes on Thursday 12th April 1934 with the entry: "Departure with the German Himalaya Expedition 1934. Separate logbook about this".

Above: Members of the 1934 Nanga Parbat expedition. Back row left, Wieland; third from left, Merkl; fifth from left, Welzenbach.
Below: Rakhiot face of Nanga Parbat.

Nanga Parbat Tragedy

A S A great alpinist Welzenbach was no exception in wanting to extend his climbing horizon beyond the Alps and to explore the virgin summits of the world's highest mountains. The peaks of the Himalaya, representing the total adventure, became his most cherished dream.

Obliged to withdraw from the 1928 Pamirs expedition due to illness and unavailable for Paul Bauer's 1929 Kangchenjunga expedition because of professional commitments, Welzenbach resolved to organize his own Himalayan expedition. His plans rapidly began to take shape during 1929. Sifting with characteristic thoroughness through Himalayan literature he soon concluded that the very highest mountains were not yet ripe for picking off and in any case demanded too long a leave of absence. Influenced by reading Mummery's letters and Collie's descriptions, Welzenbach chose Nanga Parbat, "a mountain offering realistic chance of success from among the 8000ers", as his objective.

Almost every evening Welzenbach perused books, maps, photographs and other documents. He corresponded extensively with leading climbers of several countries as well as with the British authorities in India and administrative bodies in Germany. (1) On 23rd January 1930 he presented a meticulous eight-point expedition plan (including 122 day time-table, budget, and team members) to the central committee of the German and Austrian Alpine Club who soon agreed to grant financial aid. On 12th March 1930 Welzenbach applied to his employers, the Munich City Council, for special leave and just six days later the British Consulate-General approved the expedition's entry to India and Kashmir. Arrangements were progressing smoothly until the German Foreign Office harshly decided to call off Welzenbach's expedition in favour of Professor G. O. Dyhrenfurth's 1930 International Himalaya Expedition (five of its eleven members were German) to Kangchenjunga on the dubious basis that only one Himalayan expedition from Germany was viable that year. Welzenbach reacted by planning even more thoroughly for 1931, but again he was cruelly thwarted. Paul Bauer, Welzenbach's companion on the first ascent of the Schönanger North Face and other Wetterstein routes in 1925 and a fellow member of the Munich Academic Alpine Club, had already started preparing his second expedition to Kangchenjunga for 1931 and objected to an additional Himalayan venture on the grounds that it would divide German forces. In the event the resulting dispute divided the leading German climbers of the day. Somewhat unreasonably, Bauer urged Welzenbach to renounce his aims so that all efforts could be concentrated on Kangchenjunga. In the light of existing Himalayan experience Welzenbach rated the chances of success on Kangchenjunga minimal (2) and refused to sacrifice his expedition. Mutual friends unsuccessfully proposed a joint undertaking. Again the German Foreign Office in Berlin decided it could only approve one Himalayan expedition for 1931 and, following a certain amount of skilful propaganda, Bauer's expedition was given priority. Even at this point Welzenbach was enthusiastically invited to join the Kangchenjunga party, but he felt too deeply hurt by the preceding wrangling to consider accepting. Severely embarrassed he had to cancel arrangements already finalized with numerous organisations and for the second successive year withdraw his application for a long absence from work.

Government approval of Welzenbach's Nanga Parbat Expedition was at last assured for 1932, but this third round of preparations began under the cloud of a growing economic crisis in Germany. Due to financial cuts the Munich City Council was now no longer able to dispense with Welzenbach's services for a lengthy period. Welzenbach's natural bitter disappointment surfaced in letters written during June 1931 to Fritz Wiessner, a leading German rock climber during the 1920s who had emigrated to the U.S.A.; "I have tried absolutely everything with all the relevant authorities... As things stand at present, I am simply left with no choice but to abandon my long cherished and very advanced plans." An excerpt from Welzenbach's letter of 20th June 1931 to Wiessner reveals how courageously he overcame his personal feelings and completely unselfishly volunteered to assist others in taking over his expedition: "I assure you that I have no objection whatsoever if you, Herron and Merkl want to attempt Nanga Parbat next year. I should be very happy to assist you by passing on the benefits of my preparation made to date...". Welzenbach's positive philosophy left no room for self-pity or envy, and it would be some consolation to see his groundwork bear fruit. On 13th August 1931 he officially notified the central committee of the German and Austrian Alpine Club of his own unavailability and added: "Meanwhile a new team has already been formed with my full approval and wants to pursue my plans (Wiessner, Simon, Herron, Merkl). The writer requests that the support intended for him be conferred upon the named group." Wiessner proposed Simon to lead the expedition but accepted Welzenbach's preference for Merkl (his recent companion on the epic ascent of the Grands Charmoz North Face) who also lived in Munich and could therefore be assisted more easily. Aschenbrenner, Bechtold, Hamberger, Kunigk and the reporter Elizabeth Knowlton completed the nine strong German-American Expedition. Significantly, no member of Bauer's 1929 and 1931 Kangchenjunga expeditions was invited.

Delayed at the outset by an enforced roundabout approach to the north side of Nanga Parbat due to the political situation, the 1932 expedition was further bedevilled by the inadequacy of its inexperienced and unreliable porters. Eventually Merkl, Bechtold and Wiessner reached the East Ridge of the mountain at almost 7000 metres just west of Rakhiot Peak, before the party was driven back by bad weather. The attempt had however succeeded in discovering the most practical route up the mountain by the Rakhiot glacier and the East Ridge, and Merkl was

240

convinced the summit would yield to the next assault. Sadly, it did not bode well that he still underestimated the scale of the difficulties in reckoning to have been "within five of six days of victory", and did not appreciate how his failure to keep support camps occupied had potentially endangered their retreat.

The 1934 Nanga Parbat Expedition was planned with wholehearted support from Hitler's government. It was seen by high ranking German officials as a convenient vehicle for already prevalent nationalistic propaganda - an attitude not shared but out of necessity tolerated by the climbers. Substantial financial backing from the sports organisations of the German State Railways, complemented by grants from the German and Austrian Alpine Club and the German Scientific Aid Council, enabled Merkl to mount a much larger and far better equipped expedition.

This time Willo Welzenbach was at long last able to take part. He was appointed deputy leader, responsible also for organising the climbers' food, was in charge of the main party during the journey, and acted as treasurer. Even so, it cannot have been easy for Welzenbach to forgo the leadership of an expedition that had essentially originated from his own plans, but he fully accepted Merkl's right to this role on the basis of the invaluable reconnaissance he had led to Nanga Parbat in 1932 and by virtue of having secured the necessary finance. Even if Welzenbach expressed no misgivings about his position, friends warned him against subordinating himself to Merkl's command, and his mother urged him: "Insist upon being climbing leader. Do not go otherwise." The events of the expedition were to underline the wisdom of this advice. Welzenbach did confide to his longstanding friend Hubert Rüsch that he was aware of Merkl's inability to lead the expedition efficiently in the field, but that the irresistible desire to fulfil his dream of attempting Nanga Parbat had overcome all scruples about joining the party. He reckoned on exerting his stronger personality to the benefit of the expedition. He failed to foresee how

241

inflexible and immovable Merkl would be in his behaviour and tactics.

The other climbers selected by Merkl were Aschenbrenner and Bechtold of the 1932 attempt, Bernard (doctor), Drexel (Welzenbach's companion on four north wall ascents in the Bernese Alps), Hieronimus, Müllritter, Schneider and Wieland. (3) A three man scientific contingent of Finsterwalder, Misch and Raechl completed the party that voyaged to Bombay and travelled on overland to Srinagar. Here the expedition was joined by its two British transport officers, Frier and Sangster. A Swiss businessman in Rawalpindi (Kuhn) and the German Consul (Kapp) were late additions to the party.

Some 35 Sherpa and Bhutia porters were enlisted in Darjeeling for the duration of the expedition and up to 600 local porters employed for the 175 kilometres long approach march from Srinagar which was begun on 2nd May. Most of the local men were paid off 17 days later upon reaching the snow-line at 3450 metres above the Fairy Meadow and on 25th May Base Camp (3967 metres) was established at the north foot of the mountain. Welzenbach's main impressions recorded during this approach march were of admiration for the "outstanding performance of the local porters in crossing snowbound passes with their feet shod merely in rags and home-woven straw sandals", of "deeply cut gorges where the track cut across slabby cliffs as steep as the rocks of the Wilder Kaiser" and of the so called Fairy Meadow, "a marvellous spot surrounded by tall fir-trees" with an awe-inspiring view of Nanga Parbat's North-East Face.

Although the badly crevassed Rakhiot glacier presented far greater route-finding difficulties than in 1932, and in spite of adverse weather conditions, good progress was made at first. Camp 1 (4468 metres) was established on 27th May and on 1st June the advance party (Aschenbrenner, Drexel, Schneider and Welzenbach) set up Camp 2 (5340 metres). Ill-health amongst several porters threatened logistical problems and Welzenbach's concern about lack of support was incorporated into his

242

Willo Welzenbach.

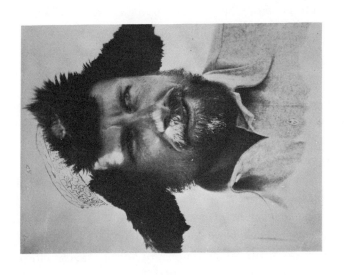

On Nanga Parbat, Willy Merkl.

report back to Camp 1: "... We are now sending all the porters down, except the cook and our orderlies, because we have
nothing left for them to eat. Those remaining here will be fed
in part out of our rations. Tomorrow we'll attempt to establish
Camp 3 with our orderlies. Then in the evening we'll send
them back to Camp 2. We are taking tents and blankets from
the men going down today, because we are glad of whatever
gear is up here. We hope that you have all that is necessary
at Camp 1, otherwise you'll have to send them onto Base Camp.
Now to the most important thing - If our advance is not to be
delayed, send up to us by tomorrow evening ... porters with
provisions, above all porter rations, one load of petrol, one
box of sahib food and if possible our personal rucksacks ...
Don't load them too heavily so that they can climb quickly..."
Privately in his diary (4) Welzenbach expressed stronger reservations about the organisation: "Load carrying problems
are gradually becoming insoluble. We came up to Camp 1 with
24 porters, but were supposed to continue with 16. Our porters
are working like Trojans but all the same some vital loads are
getting left behind. We are receiving no support from Base.
Apparently they don't properly appreciate our position".

Next day, with the use of short skis, a provisional site for
Camp 3 was found at 5770 metres seemingly above all serious
glacier problems and Welzenbach's confidence soared: "One
can now see virtually the entire planned line of ascent up to the
Silver Saddle. One can't imagine that the route will present
us with any serious difficulties." Instead trouble came from
the retained Balti porters who went on strike because their
tsampa rations (barley meal forming their staple diet on the
mountain) had not yet arrived.

In his report letter of 4th June from Camp 3 to Camp 2,
marked to be sent on down for Merkl's attention as well, Welzenbach first summarized his group's progress (far less
straightforward than anticipated) and the deteriorating state of
his porters: "... an attempt was made to push on upwards,
but we got stuck on the incredibly crevassed glacier. We tried

244

four different lines before finally starting back down to Camp 3 at 1 p. m. During the descent Peter (Aschenbrenner) set an enormous slab avalanche in motion... Our porters are exhausted. We are keeping the cook and his assistant here. We are sending the other 8 down to Camp 2 where they must have a rest day tomorrow. Please spare them any work and give them plenty to eat..." Welzenbach then emphasized his single-minded determination that nothing unnecessary should be allowed to check the expedition's advance and he reiterated his growing disquiet over the unsatisfactory deployment of its work-force. While he acknowledged: "Your note about the strike by the Baltis does of course explain the difficulties with supplies", his resolute reaction exemplified his commitment: "We do not contemplate descending or even waiting because of the difficulties with supplies. Whatever happens we shall try to reach Camp 4. All the same we are living in hope that now and again some loads will be sent up. In my opinion all our resources should be employed to attain our ultimate objective and it is a great pity if any days are wasted due to organisational difficulties. Consequently I suggest that without exception all the Darjeeling men should be used for keeping supply lines open and that we should make do with the Baltis at B. C. and at the lower camps. Can't the Darjeeling men be claimed back from our scientists and the Baltis put at their disposal? They are excellent for valley tasks and for load carrying lower down. The Darjeeling men are really too good for menial jobs as servants in the valley now that the conquest of Nanga is at stake. I am not making these suggestions for the sake of criticism but entirely in the interests of our cause. Just when the assault should be gaining impetus, it is unacceptable to see it coming to a standstill because we in the lead do not have enough porters and food..."

On 5th June, in response to simultaneous letters from Merkl and Bechtold with conflicting instructions, Welzenbach noted: "We are being urgently advised to retreat as reinforcements can't be guaranteed. We assess the situation more optimistic-

245

ally and decide to proceed at all events, as long as we still have something to eat ... It is aggravating to witness fine days being wasted because of organisational dilemmas holding up the assault." Accordingly Camp 4 was established on 8th June at 6185 metres.

A traumatic blow soon overshadowed the expedition. Drexel, Welzenbach's closest friend in the party, fell ill at Camp 3 and descended exhausted to Camp 2 where he collapsed completely the next morning. Despite heroic efforts by Wieland and several porters to rush up oxygen equipment overnight during a blizzard he had already succumbed to pulmonary oedema late in the evening of 8th June. The "shattering news" reached the advance party at Camp 4 and immediately the entire expedition descended to Base Camp, stretchering the body down for burial. Hieronimus wrote that Drexel's death upset Welzenbach more than anyone else and that "when he got down to Base Camp he was absolutely despondent, his condition causing the expedition doctor, Bernard, grave concern."

On 10th June Welzenbach wrote briefly to his parents from Base Camp: "Spirits are at a low ebb ... This is a sad start to our undertaking." A detailed letter followed on 12th June: "Yesterday Drexel was buried ... When the long awaited porter rations arrive, we shall recommence the assault. It is no secret that there has been a remarkable organizational mistake regarding the supply of porter rations, for even without Balbo's (Drexel's nickname) tragic death our first assault would have come to a standstill due to inadequate reinforcements and supplies. Now Uli Wieland had prepared a very-well devised new plan ... according to which the summit would be reached by the end of the month ... The attack will advance in two teams spaced two days apart. I shall again be in the advance party ... Please do not worry about me. Balbo's death, which was after all caused by desperately unfortunate circumstances, must not let you fear that something similar could happen to me."

Unfortunately the tsampa did not materialize for another ten thoroughly frustrating days of beautiful weather. During this

246

crucial and largely avoidable delay at Base Camp the mounting dissension and mental pressures, later so carefully and hypocritically concealed in Bechtold's official expedition report and in his expedition book (5), reared its ugly head. In this context it is relevant to point out that Bechtold and Merkl had been great friends ever since their childhood and schooldays together. However, such considerations do not justify the heroic characterization of Merkl, described by Bechtold as a "born leader of men", and the distortion of his actions during the expedition. In addition, it seems that Bechtold wielded considerable influence over Merkl, and Welzenbach branded Bechtold as an evil power in the running of the expedition. Such condemnation may well indicate an additional personal motive behind Bechtold's general glorification of the expedition and its leadership which - though it appealed to attitudes prevalent in certain circles in Nazi Germany - did a disservice to mountaineering history.

Already on 12th June, in an extra note home marked "confidential", Welzenbach reported a "deplorable clash" between Merkl and Schneider. Schneider had faulted Merkl for "irreverent behaviour" in ordering publicity photographs of Drexel's body being transported down the mountain and of the actual burial. In Welzenbach's view "he merely said what most of us were thinking." This open disapproval infuriated Merkl to such an extent that he wanted to "banish Schneider from the expedition" because "he considered that all criticism undermined his authority." Such irrational impetuosity caused an indignant Welzenbach to denounce Merkl's moral character: "Merkl is increasingly trying to act like a dictator who tolerates no comments. He really seems to believe that a stern and uncompromising attitude serves to establish his authority and to suppress the inferiority complex which he obviously feels as an upstart ... In Balbo we lost an effective mainstay in the battle against Willy's delusions of grandeur and persecution mania..." In conclusion Welzenbach declared Merkl to be "emotionally unworthy of his position as leader" (6), adding:

"I am assuming a cautious attitude for the time being, but I fear that we will have a row sooner or later. At all events we have drifted further and further apart mentally during the course of the expedition." (7)

Welzenbach's growing agitation at hanging around Base Camp and wasting precious time waiting for the porter supplies is very apparent in his letter to his parents dated 16th June: "... Our chances are steadily diminishing. Time flies and we can't move because there's nothing for the porters to eat at the higher camps." An added anecdote shows that Welzenbach had retained his sense of humour: "A few days ago I tripped over a tent's guy line in the dark and banged my nose on the end of a food box. The box broke into pieces, but my nose didn't fare too badly. On taking the plaster off today, I saw that it's become even more hooked than before. Will no doubt right itself..." To keep in training, on 19th June five of the party started early for Jiliper Peak (5200 metres). A long snow ridge led to the top and Welzenbach recorded: "Müllritter and I, who were a fair way ahead, waited for Bechtold and Merkl below the summit so that we might reach it together. Hieronimus had given up lower down." During these trying days even Welzenbach admitted feeling listless and dispirited for a while, distressed by the loss of Drexel and depressed at the increasing prospect of overall failure. However, time soon rekindled his fighting spirit. Both he and the harassed Merkl no doubt now wryly recalled the expedition's instructions from von Tschammer und Osten, their patron and Hitler's Minister of Sport: "The conquest of the peak is expected for the glory of Germany."

Eventually on 22nd June the long-awaited tsampa and other provisions arrived. Just before setting off on the second assault, Welzenbach finished a long letter home, making no secret of his restless impatience after two weeks of allegedly unnecessary inactivity and elaborating on the organizational inadequacies as well as the irrational behaviour of the expedition's leadership: "Now at last the renewed assault on Nanga

248

Left: Nanga Parbat from the Fairy Meadow.   Right: Welzenbach training on Jiliper Peak for the Nanga Parbat attempt.

Parbat should begin ... The attack should proceed in two groups - first group: Merkl, Welzenbach, Schneider, Aschenbrenner, Bechtold, Müllritter. Second group: Wieland, Bernard, Kuhn, Sangster. The departure of the entire first group was originally fixed for today. However, Merkl and Bechtold can't drag themselves away from Base Camp and won't follow us until tomorrow. Thus our advance will of course be delayed yet again. I believe that Merkl has still neither realized what is at stake nor that the success of the whole undertaking ultimately depends on taking very active measures. Otherwise we shall return home without reaching the summit and it is inevitable that Merkl will be called upon to account for what was achieved with the 175,000 or 200,000 Reichmarks (the undertaking will cost that much). For the present letter-writing at Base Camp appears to be more important to him than the advance towards the summit. He likes it here in the role of pasha which he will probably have to give up when it is either do or die higher up... You will be wondering why I'm telling you all this. Well, because I don't want to entrust it to my diary. You never know whose hands diaries will fall into. For example, Merkl seized Balbo's diary immediately. On the other hand, these matters really do seem important enough to be recorded in case there is a dispute one day as to why the expedition did not turn out as would perhaps have been desirable. Balbo was buried on the 11th. On the 12th or 13th the expedition should have started again immediately, irrespective of whether the tsampa was there or not. Then we would now perhaps be making our summit bid. We would have had sufficient other provisions to be able to manage without the tsampa if necessary. This way we just let precious time slip by. The past four days even brought cloudless weather which we did not utilize. Till mid July the weather ought to be reliable; after that it becomes unstable. But will we make it by then? Hardly with the tactics employed so far! The expedition is also too large and cumbersome. In it there are several camp-followers who are only a burden on the advance because they require porters, food and tents. These men are no use to the expedition but all the same want to go to the summit. You can't hope to take a party of ten to twelve up an 8000 metre peak. The result is that nobody gets to the top. But all preaching is of no avail here. Willy always knows best. In addition he is awfully capricious in his decisions; today he says one thing, tomorrow another and he tolerates no advice ... I am pinning all my hopes on Schneider and Aschenbrenner who with their driving enthusiasm will perhaps help us yet to achieve success." Apart from severely censuring Merkl's shortcomings, this letter illustrates that Welzenbach - had he been given the position of leader - would have avoided the critical errors that culminated in tragedy. Merkl's unsound tactics and lack of judgement had already initiated the circumstances that were to lead to the demise of three climbers and six Sherpa porters.

In successive days the advance party ascended to Camp 4 which was re-occupied on 25th June. At Camp 3 Welzenbach noted: "One feels a lot better for getting away from Base Camp at last and seeing some progress, albeit slow, being made." On the 26th and 29th Aschenbrenner, Schneider, Welzenbach, Müllritter and the porters battled upwards against fierce winds and dumped loads for Camp 5 (6690 metres) sited below the North-East flank of Rakhiot Peak. Even though their porters had to descend to Camp 3 for further loads on the 27th, it might be judged a little extravagant in view of the time already lost that six of the party including Welzenbach spent the day climbing the South Chongra Peak (6448 metres). The ascent certainly boosted Welzenbach's confidence: "I am in top form and tracked the whole way from Camp 4 to the summit." Resting on the 28th he wrote his last long letter home: "We are now all gathered here. Tomorrow we intend to commence the actual assault. We are all of the opinion (and we have finally converted Merkl to our way of thinking) that pushing camp sites slowly up the mountain is senseless and that the attack must be forced through to the summit. We hope to get by with three to four small camps between here and the summit. By this method the out-

251

come could well be decided within a week. I am in very good physical shape. In my view three to four members at the most will reach the top. Aschenbrenner and Schneider seem to have the best chances. I hope I'm also among the few that reach our goal..." On the 30th he added: "I will possibly have no further opportunity to send you news for some time, but you will be kept adequately informed by the Press and Radio. " The same evening Welzenbach noted a few problems in his diary: "Bernard reported that Kuhn is suffering from a bad bout of mountain sickness and has been sent down to Base Camp... Bechtold complained of severe stomach pains and can't eat anything. There is a risk he'll have to descend... It is now high time to step up our summit bid as we are already very low on fuel. "

Welzenbach's diary entries describe the first four days in July: "Sunday, 1 July. Schneider, Aschenbrenner, Merkl and I set off for Camp 5 (with 9 porters) ... The ascent was very strenuous. One already feels the marked effect of breathing in air with less than half the normal amount of oxygen. During the afternoon the onset of an icy gale drove us into the tents and our sleeping bags. ... We slept fairly well. I'm absolutely parched with an awful thirst. In the morning pulse rate 80, breathing normal. "

"Monday 2 July. The gale that had blown throughout the night persisted during the morning too... In the afternoon Schneider, Aschenbrenner and I attacked the ice slope up to the Rakhiot Peak and prepared it with ice pegs and fixed rope for the porters. Towards evening we abandoned our task due to the cold and the wind. During the afternoon Wieland, Müllritter and Bechtold had come up from Camp 4 to Camp 5. There are now 7 sahibs and 16 porters here. A fierce storm develops in the evening and continues all night... "

"Tuesday 3 July. In the morning Müllritter descends to Camp 4 feeling unwell. The weather is bad for most of the day. All the same Merkl, Wieland, Bechtold and I complete fixing the steep slope up to the Rakhiot Peak with ice pegs and some

200 metres of rope to make it passable for our porters. Towards evening we get news from Bernard at Camp 4 that he and Müllritter are alone there and that the two Englishmen (transport officers Sangster and Frier) have descended to Base Camp as they are not trying for the summit. Good weather looks likely tomorrow."

"Wednesday 4 July. It is calm and fine. Departure for Camp 6, to be placed in the saddle between Rakhiot Peak and Nanga East Peak at about 7000 metres." This is the last surviving extract from Welzenbach's expedition diary, dispatched as carbon copy pages with his final brief letter home on 4th July from Camp 5: "Dearest Parents, Enclose a few pages of my diary which I'm sending down with a messenger. It is too strenuous to write more. At this altitude one has very little energy. I'm well. Love. Yours Willo."

Of Welzenbach's efforts on Rakhiot Peak Bechtold wrote: "The indefatigable Willo should have taken a well-deserved day off with Aschenbrenner and Schneider. But he couldn't bear staying in his tent. Wherever there was a job to do, he always insisted on lending a hand. He was the first to leave camp and trudge towards the steep face. He was breathing heavily and was troubled by a rasping cough. But his reserves of energy were truly inexhaustible. On this occasion I was amazed at his indifference to the cold. While some of my fingers got frostbitten in the cutting north wind, despite my woollen gloves, he continued to work with bare hands."

On 4th July fine weather blessed the start of the summit assault proper. With six climbers and 17 porters it was far too cumbersome an attack (unnecessarily so), susceptible to certain failure in the event of problems, and above all placing an impossible burden on the expedition's logistics by leaving no substantial support below. But Merkl's ultimate dream centred on most of his leading climbers making the first ever ascent of an 8000 metre peak in a virtual pilgrimage. It was a misplaced concept fraught with unforeseen dangers and already soberly criticized for its tactical naivety by Welzenbach who realized its futility but did not envisage its tragic potential in his letter home of 22nd June.

That day everyone coped well with the thoroughly prepared route up to the shoulder of Rakhiot Peak and across its exposed West Face - a severe test upon their porters' abilities despite the placing of fixed ropes - to Camp 6 at 6955 metres, sited in the first depression on the long snow ridge running westwards to the Silver Saddle. That evening spirits were high and the mood optimistic. The technical difficulties of the Rakhiot Peak had been overcome and snow conditions had improved immensely during the preceding settled weather. The party believed it just needed to keep going resolutely upwards to succeed. They remained unaware that the daily denser and slowly rising clouds down below were heralding the imminent approach of the monsoon, and that snow storms already developing at Camp 4 would prevent Müllritter and Bernard from stocking intermediate camps as planned.

Next day, 5th July, with Welzenbach and Wieland tracking ahead throughout, the party crossed the tower called the Moor's Head, descended into the saddle beyond and proceeded upwards again to establish Camp 7 at 7050 metres on the billowy snow crest which became known as the Whipped Cream Roll. Stormy winds and severe cold tested everyone's endurance. That night was a thoroughly miserable one for all. Both Welzenbach and Wieland complained of breathing difficulties, and Merkl grew irritated at the continuous disturbances. Towards midnight and despite 27 degrees of frost, Welzenbach, unable to sleep, lit a candle and wrote up his diary. In the morning Bechtold volunteered to escort two sick porters down. In two days the assault party's porter support had dwindled from seventeen to eleven men. Consequently provisions and equipment were of necessity cut to the bare minimum.

The scene was set for what was expected to be the final two-day push to the summit and back. Shortly after 7 a.m. on 6th July (8) Welzenbach led off upwards. He was soon overtaken by Aschenbrenner and Schneider who - clearly in top form -

spearheaded the route up to the Silver Saddle (7451 metres), cutting a staircase of steps for the porters. In just $3\frac{1}{4}$ hours they reached the saddle. Here they waited for the others until Welzenbach appeared at 12.30 p.m. with two porters. While Schneider plodded on up the plateau towards the Forepeak (7910 metres) in the hope of finding a more advanced and sheltered camp site for the summit day, before continuing Aschenbrenner discussed plans with Welzenbach who stayed behind to wait for the rest of the party. Still going well and feeling fresh, Aschenbrenner and Schneider soon reached almost 7750 metres (four original source reference estimates (9) for their high point vary between 7600 and 7900 metres) at the foot of the Forepeak and found a suitable prospective site where they again waited. Soon after 2 p.m. Merkl and Wieland at last emerged onto the Silver Saddle with the main body of porters and prepared to pitch camp there. Schneider went back in a vain attempt to persuade the tired party to advance further and after sitting it out for another $1\frac{1}{2}$ hours Aschenbrenner too descended. Thus Camp 8 was finally established just above the Silver Saddle at 7480 metres.

Despite a rising gale the party was still absolutely convinced that victory for all must be theirs the following day. Never in the history of Himalayan mountaineering, nor again till 1950, had an expedition got so near to the summit of an 8000 metre peak. Indeed, controversial speculation later centred on whether Aschenbrenner and Schneider - but for two long waits totalling 4 hours for the others to catch up - could not have reached the summit of Nanga Parbat that afternoon. They believed they were 4 to 5 hours from the highest point and that they could have safely completed the ascent, but they also believed it was only right they should go to the top as a team of five and they were certain that this aim would be achieved within 24 hours. The defamatory suggestion (10) that Merkl objected to Aschenbrenner and Schneider going on ahead to the summit and so grabbing the glory has been emphatically refuted by Schneider. Today it is known that, in view of the effects of climbing at high altitude and the nature of the terrain, they were greatly underestimating the task ahead of them - yet in 1953 when Hermann Buhl made the first ascent of the mountain in a phenominal solo climb, he started from a camp 150 metres lower than the 1934 expedition's Camp 7, had to track the entire route and already felt "at the limit of (his) capabilities" ascending towards the Forepeak - at which point, by contrast, Aschenbrenner and Schneider "felt no trace of fatigue."

It was soon to become evident that the expedition had thrown away its great chance. Overnight the onset of a terrible monsoon storm turned a tantalizingly near triumph into a desperate struggle for survival. On the 7th the party sat out the worsening blizzard, unable to get the stoves working to prepare food or drink. Gale-swept spindrift penetrated the tents and got into their sleeping bags, as they hung on in the hope of some improvement in the weather. Most likely, an immediate retreat could have been effected that morning, but their decision to wait was influenced by their limited experiences during the 1932 expedition when no storm lasted long, added to which they had five day's rations left. While unjust contemporary criticism from outside Germany implied that Merkl and Welzenbach in particular saw themselves as indestructable after surviving three days and nights trapped in a storm on the Grands Charmoz in 1931, and may even have relished overcoming peril for its own sake, they certainly did not recognize the danger of prolonged exposure to the elements at this altitude and the rapid rate of physical deterioration in such circumstances. In fairness to them relatively little was known about these subjects at the time. The second night was even more frightful and, worse still, the tents were sustaining serious damage.

On the morning of 8th July the party unanimously decided to withdraw to Camp 4 and, sure of getting there that evening, they fatefully left behind most of the tents and equipment in order to travel light and in anticipation of their next assault. Outwardly everyone had seemed in good condition according to Aschenbrenner and Schneider (11), but the descent was soon to prove how weakened they all were. The altitude had already

256

affected Merkl's judgement so much that he left others to take all the decisions. It was at the suggestion of Welzenbach and Wieland that Aschenbrenner and Schneider started tracking down with three porters and everyone else was supposed to follow close behind. Below the Silver Saddle they were battered by the full fury of the elements as they groped their way down the slope. Then came exhausting trail-breaking in deep fresh snow along the treacherously corniced snow ridge with visibility less than 10 metres. Quite high up Nima Dorje slipped and though his fall was held his pack was swept away. As a result the five men were left with just one sleeping bag between them, making it imperative to reach Camp 5, the highest site remaining properly equipped. Upon reaching easier ground just above the half buried abandoned tent at Camp 7 Aschenbrenner and Schneider unroped and continued ahead after exhorting the porters to keep right behind. They later defended this dubious decision to proceed independently, allegedly taken in the joint interest of speed and to save the porters' strength-sapping route-finding detours. Notwithstanding their instructions these three weary porters immediately lost contact and sheltered at Camp 7. Aschenbrenner and Schneider passed Camp 6 which was virtually submerged in snow, battled on over Rakhiot Peak and descended the fixed ropes to a deserted Camp 5 where they ate and rested before wading on in a final effort through waist-deep snow down to Camp 4 by early evening. Here they were welcomed by Bechtold, Müllritter and Bernard who had been repulsed by the awful conditions in an earlier attempt to re-supply Camp 6. Aschenbrenner and Schneider still confidently "expected everyone else to arrive at any moment", rather surprisingly so - after all no one had caught them up during their long stop at Camp 5, and no one did arrive that night. Strictly speaking, they should have at least kept in contact with their porters throughout, and later accusations that they hurried down prematurely and even irresponsibly were not entirely unfounded. On the other hand, they could hardly have anticipated the troubles afflicting the main party. In blizzard conditions at high altitude weakened climbers understandably tend to act according to impulse without always deliberating logically or lengthily over their actions. Afterwards it was certainly a despicable injustice when, following arguments and acrimony among the survivors and contemporary German climbers, a so-called "Court of Honour" was maliciously convened by Hitler's Minister of Sport, Von Tschammer und Osten, to accuse Aschenbrenner and Schneider, the Austrian members of the expedition, of having abandoned their German comrades to save their own lives. During these proceedings the presiding leading Munich mountaineers, doubtlessly under heavy political pressure, declared them to be "without honour".

Meanwhile up on the Silver Saddle the plight of the main party (three climbers and eight porters) had worsened dramatically in the unrelenting storm. After only two hours of painfully slow descent and still on the traverse from the Silver Saddle to the so-called Whipped Cream Roll Ridge, they decided to bivouac at about 7250 metres despite totally inadequate equipment. Later the surviving porters reported that it was Merkl and Wieland who were unable to continue that day. Nonetheless, it seems almost unbelievable that three mountaineers of the calibre of Merkl, Welzenbach and Wieland were unable to force their way down to the tent at Camp 7 during a whole day. This can only indicate how rapidly deterioration set in at this altitude and how little strength they suddenly had left. The terrible ordeal of this bivouac in the open drained their last reserves. One porter died that night, Merkl's right hand and both Wieland's hands got frostbitten. The party had just two sleeping bags for its eight porters, and one for the climbers which was shared by Merkl and Wieland. Selflessly, as Kitar later related, "Welzenbach slept on the snow without a sleeping bag... Next morning Welzenbach was still the strongest of the sahibs. To facilitate the route down to Camp 7 he rammed his axe into the snow and attached a rope by which we porters descended." Belaying the porters and his two climbing companions down this ice slope took its physical toll on Welzenbach and he had reached the very limits of his endurance as he struggled down to Camp 7 with Merkl on the 9th. Wieland collapsed and died in the snow just 30 metres above the tent. Three porters who felt ill had remained at the bivouac above.

Merkl and Welzenbach now felt physically unable to continue, but due to lack of space they suggested the four porters present go down to Camp 6 immediately. However, due to the blizzard, these four had to bivouac in a scooped-out snow hole that night, but next morning caught up with the three porters left behind by Aschenbrenner and Schneider. Three of these seven men died of exhaustion in the still raging storm during the descent from Rakhiot Peak to Camp 5 and the four severely frostbitten survivors staggered into Camp 4 in the late afternoon of the 10th. During the following day brave attempts by the climbers at Camp 4 to mount a rescue operation foundered in the now bottomless snow. They were powerless to help in such impossible conditions and were repeatedly repulsed below Rakhiot Peak.

On 10th July Merkl and Welzenbach stayed put at Camp 7, deciding they were too weak to get down without assistance. They had neither food nor fuel. They now believed that their sole hope of salvation depended upon help from below, probably encouraged by glimpses of people moving at Camp 4, and did not realize that the ever deeper snow made the route up over Rakhiot Peak impassable to those at Camp 4. Welzenbach knew that he was a spent force and a sick man stricken with pneumonia. Of the three porters who had sat out two days at the bivouac above, Angtsering and Gay-Lay came down to Camp 7 on the 11th - Dakshi having died the previous night. The tent was full of snow and Angtsering cleared it out at Merkl's request. Merkl and Welzenbach were sleeping just on rubber ground sheets. A clear indication of Welzenbach's suffering comes from Angtsering's later account at Base Camp describing him as "writhing with pain on the snow" when he and Gay-Lay arrived and "writhing with severe pain in the tent" the next day. (12) On the 12th, as there was nothing to eat, Angtsering

259

suggested they should try to go down as quickly as possible, but over-optimistically Merkl still favoured waiting, confident that the men who could now be seen heading upwards from Camp 4 towards Camp 5 would arrive with supplies. However it was not to be and meanwhile their strength and lives were rapidly ebbing away.

During the night from Thursday 12th to Friday 13th Willo Welzenbach died in the tent at Camp 7. He became the fourth European victim of Nanga Parbat after Mummery, Drexel and Wieland. Here almost within reach of his highest and greatest objective he was struck down by what he at least would have believed to be the hands of fate that determine the individual's destiny.

On the 13th (13) Merkl, hobbling with the aid of two ixe axes, and the two porters struggled down to the saddle where they dug out an ice cave for the night. Next day Angtsering battled courageously on alone over Rakhiot Peak and arrived totally exhausted at Camp 4. In a long-drawn-out last desperate effort, probably on 15th and 16th July, Merkl and Gay-Lay dragged themselves up to the Moor's Head. Here the 1938 German Expedition came upon their bodies. In the pocket of Merkl's jacket they found Welzenbach's last letter, a pathetic plea for help written on 10th July 1934 at Camp 7. In full it read: "Camp 7, 10 July. To the Sahibs between C. 6 and C. 4, particularly Dr. Sahib. We have been lying here since yesterday after losing Uli during the descent. Are both sick. An attempt to push on down to 6 failed due to general weakness. I, Willo, have probably got bronchitis, angina and influenza. Bara Sahib (= Merkl) is in a generally exhausted state with frostbitten feet and hands. We have both had nothing warm to eat and practically nothing to drink for 6 days. Please help us soon here in C. 7. Willo and Willy."

The tragic outcome of the expedition inspired controversial debate for many years. In his valedictory address as retiring president of the Alpine Club on 10th December 1934, J.J. Withers touched perceptively upon its failing: "It is difficult -

perhaps presumptuous - to comment at the present moment on the causes of this, the greatest catastrophe that has so far occurred in the Himalaya - an accident surpassed in magnitude generally by but one, the loss of eleven lives in one day on Mont Blanc in 1870. But it will occur to all that the leader threw away the one great advantage conferred by having a large party at his disposal. The all-important lines of communication were neglected. No fewer than 16 Europeans and porters were located at the highest camp, VIII, leaving the three standing camps immediately below entirely empty. When the great storm broke over the highest camp and retreat became inevitable, the great, unwieldy party, deteriorating rapidly, found all camps above Camp IV swept away or submerged. Had these been occupied and held, if only for 24 hours, retreat without casualties should have been comparatively simple (14) ... Willy Merkl, like Dr. Welzenbach, had survived with impunity many tempests and much exposure in the Alps. He and his brave companions forgot, I fear, the difference between an Alpine storm at 10 or 12,000 feet and a Himalayan blizzard at 24,000. "

Welzenbach himself had pointed out in his letter home of 22nd June that far too many climbers were attempting to reach the summit together. A much safer and far more sensible procedure would have been to advance with four climbers above Camp 6 and to set up just two men at Camp 8 for a first summit attempt. Such an assault would not have stretched the expedition's support resources beyond breaking point.

An often overlooked yet major contributing factor to the disaster lay in the slow rate of progress up the mountain, seriously underrated until the storm broke. As the aftermath of Drexel's death resulting in the descent to Base Camp of all the party and the shortage of porter supplies, 17 invaluable days were lost (Camp 4 abandoned 8th June, re-occupied 25th June) and a ten day spell of fine weather went wasted - to a large extent unnecessarily so. Without this crucial delay the summit assault could have been completed well before the arrival of the monsoon. As it was, although the route presented no

261

exceptional technical difficulties, its considerable length involved an enormous expenditure of energy at high altitude prior to the final summit attack. Surprised by a terrible storm (15), exhausted climbers at the limits of their endurance lacked the ability to retreat efficiently. The appalling disaster had no parallel in mountaineering history - not just because of the number of victims, but because of its protracted agony with lingering deaths from exposure, exhaustion, cold, illness and starvation.

Welzenbach's expedition diary and letters home confirm his tremendous contribution to the expedition effort. Of greater significance, they reveal his burning resentment at the avoidable delays and with the inadequate leadership. They illustrate that his appreciation of the necessary strategy would have prevented the dreadful tragedy and this accentuates the ultimate irony of his death as a victim of Merkl's misguided tactics.

Death evokes diverse sentiments and prejudicial editor Colonel E. L. Strutt's cryptic note in the Alpine Journal (16) was a less than magnanimous tribute albeit tempered with recognition of his exploits: "Technically Dr. Welzenbach was among the most skilful climbers of post-war activities. His feats, remarkable both on rock and snow, are recorded in many instances in this Journal. Great as were his powers and successes, the same remark may be applied to his methods as to another long departed and still greater mountaineer (17): '... the virtue of prudence was conspicuous chiefly from its absence...' As the most daring of climbers and best of comrades, the name of Welzenbach will be remembered in Alpine history."

A far more generous and appropriate assessment was forthcoming from the eminent French climber Lucien Devies in the December 1934 issue of the French Alpine Club publication Alpinisme: "He was an exceptionally talented climber, unreservedly the complete mountaineer... Undoubtedly with Willo Welzenbach's death the greatest and most important mountaineer of the post-war period has passed on."

262

In belated recognition of Willo Welzenbach's unstinting efforts on Nanga Parbat and as a small tribute to his memory, there is now on the Rupal Face of the mountain a "Welzenbach Icefield" and a "Welzenbach Couloir". Memorial plaques have been erected on the rocks below the Meiler hut in the Wetterstein and by the track near the Schwaiger hut in the Glockner region. (18) In Munich a road bears his name, while on the South Ridge of the Aiguille Noire de Peuterey the third tower became known as the Pointe Welzenbach at the suggestion of the French even within his lifetime.

Author's notes:

1. Heinz Tillmann, for many years a close friend of Welzenbach and of his parents, made available to the author a vast and fascinating file of Welzenbach's mammoth pre-expedition correspondence, including letters to and from Capt. George Ingle Finch (member of 1922 Everest expedition), Brigadier-Gen. Charles Bruce (part-time member of Mummery's 1895 Nanga Parbat expedition, leader of 1922 and 1924 Everest expeditions), Major Kenneth Mason (Superintendent for the Survey of India and founder member of the Himalayan Club in 1927), Sydney Spencer (Hon. Sec. of Alpine Club), Dr. Ernest Neve (Hon. Sec. of Himalayan Club in Srinagar), Col. E.L. Strutt (Alpine Journal editor 1927-37), H.J. Todd (Political Agent in Gilgit).

2. Ironically, in 1935 Bauer was to openly maintain that Nanga Parbat offered better prospects of victory than Kangchenjunga.

3. Commenting on the expedition's composition, Col. E. L. Strutt conceded: "It would be difficult to find a more formidable attacking force, to which is added, we understand, a contingent of the 1933 Everest porters." (Alpine Journal Vol. 46 p. 210).

4. With each letter to his parents Welzenbach enclosed carbon copies of his latest entries in his expedition diary.

5. Bechtold, F. (translated Tyndale, H.E.G.): "Nanga Parbat Adventure" (published John Murray, 1935). Its review in the Alpine Journal praised Bechtold for "his loyalty to comrades" in writing "a great but terrible story - unsurpassed since Scott's immortal diary."

6. Merkl's exceptional physical endurance and capabilities remain undisputed - They were to be exemplified in the final effort to retreat from the mountain. In the Alps he had been a popular and valued companion with many friends, Welzenbach included. It was his moral qualities that were shown up as inadequate for

263

the testing task of leading this expedition.

7. Welzenbach's criticisms were written privately and not for publication. They are now revealed in this book for their contribution to an explanation of the expedition's failure and to correct historical misconceptions arising from contemporary misrepresentation of personal roles.

8. Times quoted for 6th July are mostly based upon Aschenbrenner's diary. Times given by Schneider in his account, by Bechtold in his official report and in the book "Nanga Parbat" (Elek Books 1954) often do not tally and seem inconsistent with the facts. There are also discrepancies between these accounts.

9. Altitude estimates: Aschenbrenner, 7710m. Bechtold, 7600m. Schneider 7850m. and 7900m. (the latter figure based upon a height of 7950m. for the Forepeak which is actually only 7910m.).

10. Repeated by G.O. Dyhrenfurth in the November 1970 issue of Alpinismus magazine.

11. A later witnessed statement taken down from the porter Kitar on 27th October 1934 (and confirmed by Kikuli) asserted however among other things that Wieland "was very ill" during the night of 7th to 8th July.

12. In reply to a later letter from Welzenbach's father requesting more complete details of the events, Emil Kuhn explained that this was the only information in Angtsering's Base Camp account that had been excluded from the porters' published statements, "probably on purpose to spare your respected wife further anguish."

13. Welzenbach's body was left lying in the tent. This camp site was not reached again until 1953 and needless to say no trace of it remained.

14. Bechtold later argued that such an interpretation was invalid because the party failed to descend even to Camp 7 due to Merkl and Wieland being incapable of continuing and was rapidly exhausted by the terrible bivouac in the open (Himalayan Journal Vol. VII p. 35). His naive counterclaim overlooked the assistance that a support team close at hand could have given to a smaller assault party.

15. The bad weather rising from below caught the party completely unawares. For several days a blizzard raged on the lower slopes of Nanga Parbat below 6500 metres while the assault team continued oblivious of its threat under a mainly clear sky, albeit windy.

16. Alpine Journal, Vol. 47 No. 250 p. 156.

17. A.F. Mummery who died on Nanga Parbat in 1895. And "greater", hardly.

18. There are also plaques on Nanga Parbat on the Moor's Head and near Base Camp in joint memory of Merkl, Welzenbach and Wieland.

Plaque at Nanga Parbat base camp.

Appendix

Among the important research material and relevant observations pertaining to its analysis that the author intended to include in this book we have already referred to the compilation of a list of Welzenbach's mountaineering achievements in the Alps in a Publisher's Note. This subject represents but one of five appendices planned by the author. The unpublished but extant material for these appendices consists of the following.

1. **List of Welzenbach's climbs.** Six foolscap pages containing lists in date order 1919-1934 with three columns for comments under separate headings/observations. Numerous observations jotted down.

2. **Biographical notes about Welzenbach's companions.** Quarto page of 40 names divided into three columns under the headings: regular, fairly frequent, casual. No trace of any written up notes on this subject.

3. **Catalogue of Welzenbach's logbooks and diaries.** No trace of any notes on this subject.

4. **Bibliography.** A complete and extensive bibliography was to be included by the author. A draft script amounts to three quarto pages listing some 48 books, and excludes journals and magazines for which there is another page of notes referring to relevant journal headings. Elsewhere several pages of journal references consulted, amounting to over 150 entries, have been traced.

5. A list of principal German and Austrian persons consulted either by interview or correspondence who contributed importantly on matters relating to the objective assessment of Welzenbach's achievements and putting these achievements into their proper perspective vis à vis the state of knowledge and attitudes in mountaineering in the 1930s versus the 1980s. One quarto sheet of names without notes which the author clearly intended to add. These names, now including some interviewees who have died since last seen by the author in May, 1979 are:

Eugen Allwein	Gerhart Klamert	Erwin Schneider
Paul Bauer	Hans Reimer	Erich Schulze
Anderl Heckmair	Eugen Röckl	Maria Schwembauer
Walter Hofmeier	Hubert Rüsch	Ernst v. Siemens
	Heinz Tillmann	

Note extracted from Author's handwritten MSS which is headed "to conclude Nanga Parbat chapter" but was not presented with typescript for the book, reads:

Nanga Parbat was finally conquered by the 1953 German-Austrian expedition. Hermann Buhl's phenomenal solo climb to the summit ranked as the most outstanding Himalayan feat achieved at that date.

This expedition was organised by Karl Herrligkoffer, Willy Merkl's step-brother. Though aged only 17 at the time of his idolized step-brother's death, over the years Herrligkoffer had felt a growing compulsion to take up the challenge which had already cost the lives of 31 men. His desire, as he expressed it, "to set the seal of victory upon the heroic efforts of his dead comrades and to fulfil a sacred trust" motivated the preparation of his Willy Merkl Memorial Expedition.

As in 1934 dissensions on the mountain regarding leadership and tactics marred the expedition and resulted in lengthy recriminations afterwards.

RGC, June 1980

Index